Charlotte Du Cann

was born in London in 1956. She w[...] the *Independent* and wrote many outspoken articles on consumer culture for glossy magazines. Her previous books include *Vogue's Modern Style* (Century) and *Offal and the New Brutalism* (Heinemann). She now cooks and dances and lives out of a suitcase.

[Mark] Watson

[was] born in London in 1962. After studying languages, he worked as a psychic healer and gave workshops on self-transformation. He now sings and performs and keeps moving.

He also took the photographs for this book.

CHARLOTTE DU CANN & MARK WATSON

REALITY IS THE BUG THAT BIT ME IN THE GALAPAGOS

TRIPS IN THE AMERICAS

Flamingo
An Imprint of HarperCollins*Publishers*

f l a m i n g o	The term 'Original' signifies publication direct into paperback with no preceding British hardback edition.
ORIGINAL	The Flamingo Original series publishes fine writing at an affordable price at the point of first publication.

Flamingo
An Imprint of HarperCollins*Publishers*
77–85 Fulham Palace Road,
Hammersmith, London W6 8JB

First published in Great Britain by Flamingo 1994
9 8 7 6 5 4 3 2 1

Copyright © Charlotte Du Cann and Mark Watson 1994

The Authors assert the moral right to
be identified as the authors of this work

A catalogue record for this book
is available from the British Library

ISBN 0 00 654716 8

Set in Apollo

Printed in Great Britain by
HarperCollinsManufacturing Glasgow

FOR OUR PARENTS

JOSEPHINE & RICHARD WATSON

MARLEY & RICHARD DU CANN

CONTENTS

ACKNOWLEDGEMENTS

For their generosity and hospitality:

Andy Harris and Susan Ward Davies in London; Jo Owen and Phillippe Jordan in New York; Alberto and his family in Mexico; Bob and Tricia Newill in Aldeburgh, England; Aphrodite Georgiadou in Athens; Concha Mendoza in Antigua, Guatemala; Pedro and all staff at the Residencial Londres, Santiago, Chile; Ursula, Esther and Siegfried Apel in Puerto Varas, Chile; Doña Maria in Vicuña, Chile; Rosa and all staff at the Posada del Maple, Quito; Liliana Laserna in Bogotá; Enrique and Immaculada and all staff at the Hostería de la Candelaría, Bogotá; Noeleen McElroy in Dundalk, Ireland; Raymond McDonagh and Roy Holmes in Dublin; Seamus Moran and Bob Melzmof and Aileen Blitz in New York.

With special thanks for their love and support, Jane Travers and Andrew McElroy.

INTRODUCTION

When I first met Mark I was a fashion editor and a would-be storyteller. I wove elaborate parables out of blue frocks and found poetry in French lapels and I was spinning a pretty tale out of a relationship I was having at the time. O, you know the kind of slum paperback stuff we all churn out: Everything Will Be Fine. I Am In Love. Tomorrow Will Be Better. I Believe In My Work. That kind of number, when really all I wanted to do was tell a good story. But as they say, how can you sing a song when you ain't got the words?

Anyway, one night my girlfriend and I cooked a dinner party. It was one of those fashionable Italian suppers we used to like to make with lots of raw ham and mozzarella and broad beans and a complicated seafood risotto and bottles of cold white wine and almondy biscuits.

'I've asked Mark,' she said. 'You'll like him, he's witchy like you.'

Halfway through the meal, probably as I was handing out that troublesome risotto, I looked down the table and saw Mark sitting at the end. He smiled at me that big open-hearted beautiful trickster smile of his, and I grinned back and I said to myself, 'That man is going to be my friend.'

And so it was. I can't remember what we talked about that night. I remember that he and his boyfriend Francisco and my flatmate Andy and I all got riotously drunk on the fashionable white wine and Mark gave me his card. It read: THE TAROT: Mark Anthony Watson.

On a brilliant spring morning three weeks later, he read my cards (You'll leave your job, he said, you'll leave this relationship, he said, you'll leave this country, he said) and we went for lunch at a little café round the corner. I'd never eaten lunch before at twelve o'clock or without wine: it was a new experience. Mark spoke Spanish with the waitress and as we left said, 'Here, I'm feeling full of energy today, have some.'

He placed his palm facing but not touching mine and sent a bolt of energy ZAP! WHAM! through me. It was like someone turning an old key in a rusted lock. On my way back to catch a bus, I sang all the way along the canal, and felt the new sun warm my face.

I had found my new language teacher.

We became friends very quickly, and as soon as Mark had shown me the tarot as a new kind of vocabulary, I longed for every occult lexicon on the shelf, every ancient and modern healing practice. I'd always liked the idea of using stories to heal. I never thought they were written just to entertain, relieve boredom or pass on moral instruction. Novels that revolved around bourgeois manners and society always bored me rigid. Even when I was an English student I could never see the point of Jane Austen. I liked stories that were real, stories that were magical, stories that when retold showed us how we might transform ourselves, using our native powers of imagination.

Most of this kind of fiction is stuck either on the anthropologist's shelf (see under Tribal Wisdom), or on the psychologist's shelf (see under Classical Mythology) but I didn't want to end up scribbling some academic footnotes. I knew that no song and no story has any transformative power unless you put yourself into it, name its territory and walk its land, and then bring back its riches.

Mind you, at the beginning, before we began this book, I was borrowing from everyone's library: astrology, numerology, shaman rituals, power animals, crystals, chakras, James Hillman and the whole archetypal crew. I'd go down to the market near where I lived in London and pick up another mystic North American paperback, and haul it back with the mozzarella and beef tomatoes and completely forget the bread. That summer I lay every day in the bath with some stones from beaches I'd been to and a slosh of lavender water and some whacked-out music and drift off altogether elsewhere. After I'd beamed back I'd write it all up and ring Mark.

'I have to read to you what happened today, sweetheart. It's really weird.' (Everything was weird then, it was practically my favourite word.) And then we'd meet, o anywhere: Victoria Station was a favourite meeting place because Mark was working at a lot of festivals then outside the city. And I'd recite my inner travelogues, over cups of indifferent British Rail coffee, on the telephone until three in the morning, in empty Indian restaurants eating late lunches. Out of synch, out of time. (You're right, Mark was very patient but you have to know that he did star in practically all of the meditations, as did his mother Bridget.)

In the evening I would sometimes go round to his flat with a bottle of wine and he, Francisco and I would read each other's hands and cards, throw the I Ching, have healing sessions and seances and channel. Mark gave me a past-life regression in which, much to my chagrin, I did not metamorphose into some ancient Egyptian goddess or famous poet, and once we dressed up as the major arcana of the tarot and took pictures of ourselves. It was like being a kid again, running wild in a sweet shop. I hadn't had so much fun in years.

I left my job, I left my relationship, we went to Mexico and we took magic mushrooms. My friends began to look at me askance. 'O, for God's sake!' cried Andy as he discovered me, posed corpse-like with meaningful pebbles in the candlelit bathroom. My neighbour Lucinda, staring one day at my travelling bag, just shook her head. Jung she could cope with, a rethink about Joni Mitchell she could cope with. 'But, Charlotte, English folk songs? What the hell is happening to you?'

'I am finding my new point of departure,' I replied pompously. But in truth I did not know.

One night I sat next to a jewellery collector from Hanover who told me he once put a Celtic brooch in for auction but when it came to the sale he had to buy it back for ten times the price. 'It had this power,' he explained. 'So I could not sell it. I think now we have reached the end of decoration, of curlicues, of style. It is time to unearth the things of deeper meaning. Time to be archaeologists, not historians.'

I tried to do some digging in my old culture. I went to see an installation by the sculptor Joseph Beuys, as recommended by the perplexed Lucinda: it was called The End of the Twentieth Century. I walked about the sleeping basalt blocks in the empty gallery and watched Beuys' sad shaman face loom out of the television. The dignity of the people lies in their sovereignty, he prophesied. In the future, everyman will be king. It was time, I thought, to quit being a grateful subject.

Out of the blue I asked Mark to write a book with me. OK, he said. 'Let's write it in Mexico,' I said. OK, he said. And that was it.

Or rather that was how it began. Before we started I had to finish a book of prose so I went to Greece for six weeks. Every day I wrote up my meditations and every night I dreamt of Mark. Back in England he was having a lousy time: moving house, splitting up with Francisco, overworking at the festivals. I missed him like a twin. I used to phone him from the vegetable shop in the village, amongst the soap and the piles of lemons and the giant ladies' knickers and in spite of all the trauma, I could hear the excitement in his voice about the future. It felt like a big holiday was going to happen.

'I love you,' he'd yell down the crackly line. ZAP! WHAM! like a bolt of blue.

But holiday it was not when I returned. After we'd curled up on each other's beds and read out each other's poems and notebooks, we realized something had changed. The fun had stopped. It was time to work. My meditations stopped, the dreaming ended, my journalism began to dry up and Troy, my book, proved impossible to sell.

'It's not about answers, it's about messages,' sang Mark's answering machine.

Yeah, well, this was a hard one.

I realized that all the game playing of the last year was really a kind of preparation for the real thing, like a baby will play around with sounds until he learns to talk. When I got back I saw that this exploring with Mark, which had been a relief from my old life, was not the sidetrack but the main line. Old London life, the bright lights, big city life, the dancing, the drugs, the shiny magazine work, the crammed address book and the ever-ringing phone, were all coming to an end. Moreover our friendship had shifted, into something far deeper and more dangerous than the sweet playmates of the previous summer. I had drifted away from many of my former friends, Andy had left the flat, and I saw more of Mark's friends and family and we became closer. And as we became closer we were forced to look at the dark and difficult sides of each other. And not run away. Which is not easy, even when you love someone.

But there was always the fiercer love for freedom, this desire that was really strong in both of us and that somehow we knew we were each other's liberators and to achieve liberty we had not only to remember our creativity and spontaneity but that we had to wrest each other from the stories we had locked ourselves into. I knew I had to lead him out of a door and onto a stage, and he had to teach me to let go of an old house in an old city.

If I had known how hard this next stage was going to be, I probably would have run a thousand miles: losing all my work, selling everything I owned including the flat I lived in, my mother being diagnosed with cancer, Mark having to go into hospital . . . Tell me about the escape route!

But somehow we hung on and somehow we let go.

'I do my work and I leave,' Mark likes to say. And leaving is sometimes the hardest bit of the work.

'Well,' said Nick the night club owner, 'you were here for the beginning and you are here for the end.' The Café de Paris, nightclub of a decade, was closing.

'It's over for you,' said my friend Karen, who's from Brooklyn and knows everything about the scene. She says it's over for New York too where the fierce talk is about a group called Deee-lite who sing about love and attitude and doing the right thing.

I am standing at the top of the stairs and trying to recall the past. I remember, I remember. What exactly do I remember? Well, not very much: getting out of my head and dancing mostly, and sometimes getting a quote and sometimes losing my heart, and saying hello to a lot of people who had nothing much to say except smile back. But I won't remember it badly: it was fun and that was fine, it's just that now it is over, dead and gone.

Tonight is retro night: no one is talking about the future. There are model girls passing by with crystal laughter and beautiful young men dancing with themselves, and a cabaret from Harlem. I suppose this is a good enough way to say goodbye: goodbye to words like serious and important and major and grown-up, goodbye to my fashionable vocabulary, goodbye to Sancerre at lunchtime, goodbye to black, goodbye to my fast life, all that double kissing.

As the Greek poet, Cavafy, once wrote:

> As one prepared long since, courageously,
> Say farewell to her, to Alexandria who is leaving.
> Above all do not be tricked, never say it was
> All a dream, and that your hearing was deceived.

I fight the narrow and straight battle to the exit.

'Once you go, you know there is no re-admission,' warned the doorman.

'Yes,' I said. 'I do.'

Hey ho . . . time to hit the road.

1
~~~

MEXICO

HEY MEXICO!

~~~

Hey Mexico, my new found land! Mexico where I flew out of the schoolroom and the office into something else, where the houses are pink and clocks don't exist and every time you ask the way, you receive a different answer. Mexico, where nobody knew me and nobody I knew knew Mexico.

Except for Mark of course who used to live here and had come out three weeks earlier and now has come to meet me. So I am arrived at the airport at midnight in this unknown land and I'm asking where are we going? And Mark says, 'I had a vision of us sitting on a weather vane and you were pointing east and I was pointing north.'

You see, it was upside down from the beginning. I mean, what can you do with that kind of direction?

Mexico City, the biggest city in the world, whacks you out with its pollution and altitude. It's high up on a plateau which is straightway strange coming from Europe where all the cities are either in the valley or ports of exit, and straightway you have to walk at a different pace. You can't run in Latin America, it's either too high or too hot, and rushing about to fit life into a plan is a waste of energy. If you do you just go against the flow. Which is something my confrère doesn't like to do.

'We don't need to inform ourselves about anything, Charlie,' he says as the taxi dodged and swerved through the dangerous traffic. 'If we are clear and open whatever we need will come. We're not going to fill ourselves up with other people's opinions and facts, otherwise we won't leave any space for our own experience.'

Now Mark when he goes abroad is not like other people: he's not interested in what kind of sunglasses you're wearing, or eating chilli con carne, or going to museums, being a foreigner. He likes to live in a place exactly as if he were at home only with free time, and he likes to sit in cafés and talk to people (you have to know here that he is completely fluent in about 57 different languages – the first word he taught me in Spanish by the way was *flojera* which is a kind of legitimate laziness, it still is my favourite). So when we were in Mexico City this is what we did: we rode on crowded buses, watched soap operas on our hotel TV, ate a lot of Mexican breakfast in old-fashioned cafés, took photographs of ourselves in the post office, the ballroom of the Spanish colonial club and the cake shop surrounded by enormous yellow fiesta cakes and we walked with everyone in Chapultec Park on Sunday, past the balloon sellers and the candyfloss carts and the women who sell mangoes dipped in red chilli and cut like pagodas. The acrobats performing the Aztec calendar whirled upside down, and there was this big storm with colossal rain and lightning: it was strange and magical and felt dangerous and something in this, in the circus faces of the people in their bright clothes, in the way they stood calmly while we ran, disturbed me, excited me in my heart and my guts where I least expected it would.

But I still kept on thinking, there is something wrong here: we should be DOING something. So we're in the Zocalo, the main square, and I remember I AM A TOURIST. And I'm stopped outside some main culture, the Cathedral.

'You go into that church, if you want.'

'Aren't you going to come with me?' I asked (hey, Mark, aren't you a tourist too?).

'No,' he says. 'I'd rather wait in a café.'

Like I told you, Mark is no fan of complicity.

Now I go to churches and cathedrals, and temples, whatever, wherever: Bombay, Madrid, Venice, Kyoto, Washington DC. I like a sacred spot which is weird because I'm not even religious. But when I go to a new city that's what I do: go to the zoo, go to the market, go to the main place of worship and that's how I get my bearings, know where I am. So here I am standing on this crooked floor of the Mexico City cathedral not knowing where I am, smelling the familiar musty smell of Catholicism, peering into the familiar side chapels, the plaster saints with doll's frocks on, the electric candles and the woman messing around with the flowers in a devout manner and I'm trying to find it a beautiful experience. But I can't: it just feels like a big powerful gaudy edifice controlling the souls. But not this one. Uh-huh.

There's this guy poring over some guidebook and trying to be impressed with a murky painting of a saint and I'm thinking even if every surface was covered with Raphael and Rubens this place would still give me the *definitivamente* creeps. So I leave.

'How was it?' Mark asked.

'It was fine.' I lied. Which is how I got to miss another coffee.

Oaxaca! Fabulous Indian markets, those chillis on a string and tin mirrors and brightly woven cloth and skeleton sweets! The pinks, the turquoises, the aquagreens, the lemon yellows! The place for the I-was-there-and-bought-this-one-off-bit-of-folkloric-for-only-a-dollar-proof-of-a-holiday-well-spent trophies and presents that fulfil the same function (o yes, Mark and Charlotte went to Mexico, you know, and bought this naif-painted animal especially for me so now I feel that I've been there too).

Forget it. *Nada*, amigo. We didn't buy a thing.

At first I felt mean (hey Charlotte, where are the presents . . . because you've always got to pay at some point for having a nice time abroad, haven't you?). Then I felt I was missing an opportunity of a lifetime (hey Charlotte, you could really do with another fifteen candlesticks and another Third World blanket for your overcrowded flat or is this the Museum of Mankind?). And then I felt guilty. What are you doing here, Charlotte? I mean you're not even going to the beach and getting a suntan!

Actually we did go to some ruins but, looking back on it, all I can remember about them is that Mark felt ill with the altitude and I liked the colour of the watermelon juice in the café. And we took some great photographs (mostly of ourselves and a tree).

We took *great* photographs in Oaxaca, although I had a problem with these too in the beginning. Ten years in the styling business makes you jumpy around cameras.

'Wait, Mark. I've got to readjust my hair . . . Not my legs, they're awful . . . Move it to the left, there's a car in the way.'

Mark doesn't take a blind bit of notice of this quality control. He just snaps the shutter.

'Your hair is fine,' he says. 'How's mine? Shut up about your bloody legs . . . I love your legs . . . The car is there, we're living in a city aren't we?' And so on.

And then there was the roof episode. OK, Mark decides to take a panoramic picture (or rather twenty) of the sunset from the roof of our hotel. He's standing and snapping the hills in sequence and I'm going crazy.

'Mark, you can't just take them like that with all that twentieth-century stuff in the middle!'

These hills are like great antediluvian beasts sloping towards the city and the light is the colour of sapphires and there is the whole of the ugliness of the world in front of the lens, washing lines, telegraph poles, television aerials, great blocks of grubby concrete.

'You can't edit out what's there!' he yells, pirouetting slowly in the dissolving dusk. 'You can't edit out the truth.'

'Look, I'm Libra rising, I like beauty . . . Is that a problem?'

SNAP SNAP goes the camera oblivious of my squeamishness.

'What are you afraid of? What are you pretending isn't there? Television? I want to take the whole picture.' SNAP SNAP SNAP.

I went downstairs and slept, at least I thought I slept, and I dreamt that Mark's mother came into the room and told me that her kingdom had been disinherited and that Mark had to reclaim it. I woke up in a sweat as the sounds of the Mexican night came pouring in through the window.

'Bridget was here,' I said.

'Really?' said Mark, as if I'd just asked him where the nail scissors were.

'I think I just had a hallucination.' Actually this wasn't such a big deal because I'd been trying out mescal and Coke as a happening cocktail during the roof shoot.

'So tell me about it,' he said. So I did. That's what he's like, very breezy, very so what, uncomplicitous, when it comes to extraordinary experiences. But when it comes to little things, like editing out some ugly pylons, things you'd do without thinking, he gets on the stage and makes a philosophical speech about it.

'Precisely,' he says. 'Without thinking.'

Well, thinking didn't get me anywhere in Veracruz. Even Einstein's brain would have had a problem going anywhere fast in that heat. Veracruz, hot and sticky, hot-under-the-collar sea city, where the myna birds mock and caw in the sweaty palm trees and the marimba bands play in the square all night long. Veracruz is a real port – seedy, sexy and dangerous. You walk around half terrified someone is going to poke you with a knife and half hoping they're going to poke you with something more interesting. We had a lot of nightmares in Veracruz and one night a woman offered Mark a young boy for sale. O yes, something was definitely stirring very far from the reasoning head.

Sex came up between Mark and me. Well, it had to at some point, I guess. There are some things you can't edit out. All he said was that he was going to look for this guy he liked earlier, and that was it, WHAM! Up went the curtains.

'Well, that's my holiday ruined,' I said in my best high-tragic manner, and exited into the hotel room.

I tried to escape into my book (*Jung and the Tarot* . . . it wasn't the best of comfort zones) but my cosy little Mark-and-me travel bubble was bursting all over the show. Here I was in some no-postcard town with nothing to do, where it was too hot even for sunbathing, in a hotel where the swimming pool was underneath the car park and had pigeons flying about and my book was making no sense and now my best friend was deserting me for someone else. Hey, you on the tightrope, there goes your safety net! I mean, how could he? Leave me here, standing on one leg, *wobbling*?

Of course it was an ugly attack of sexual jealousy but I was still seeing myself as a far-too-nice girl to admit that to a growling female self at this stage, so I solaced myself with the prettier abandonment theory. Circa aged 2½.

Well, this is what happens when you stop thinking with your head – all the beasts come out to play. But something else happens too. You start looking at the world outside the mental compartments you forced it into, outside of the itineraries, the schedules, and the look-at-my-marvellous-library. In Mexico I learnt that freedom isn't a concept, an idea, a seventeenth-century poem by Marvell or a political slogan. Freedom is taking the whole goddamn picture and letting your best friend be himself.

We are travelling on a bus, down from the plateaux of Oaxaca towards the Caribbean coast of Veracruz, through the desert cactus forest, and up into the wet highland of Chiapas (the cold sharpness of pines at the breakfast stop) and the mist thick as wool at the mountain passes, and down again through the warm afternoon rain into the jungle valleys, and the fields of fireflies at dusk, through the coffee plantations and the banana trees and the waving maize and the volcanoes and the women washing amongst the boulders and a shoeshine boy polishing my shoes at the bus-stop and a dwarf singing at our departure and all the time feeling this huge distance between these unnamed towns coloured blue and green with their curly cathedrals and their mathematical trees and these boys running past my window shouting *cacahuates! tamales!* swinging buckets of ice and cola and women with baskets of warm chicken and tortillas wrapped in banana leaves and trays of little glasses filled with custard and I am not saying anything, I am not pointing at anything, not naming, just looking and watching the sky for vultures and sometimes sleeping against his shoulder, curled up like a cat, rocked by the bus, moving silently, slowly through this enormous changing land.

Changing.

Changing.

We are travelling on a bus.

And one day we arrive at Palenque, the site of an ancient Mayan city and a dusty town and stay in a pink hotel with a tropical garden. The owner is a woman who looks after many sick animals and she rules serenely over her house like a firm, benevolent empress. One morning we meet a man with the yellow eyes of a snake at the bottom of a waterfall in the forest outside the ruins. He swims naked in the waterhole and sells us magic so that we may see things beyond our normal sight.

We take the magic in the garden of the Empress. We sit by the green swimming pool. We wait. We swim. I laugh. That duck cannot quack, I say. Mark laughs. Nothing is happening, he says. But we cannot stop laughing.

I forgot who I was, where I was, when I was. I forgot myself and saw Mayan figures performing rituals on the ceiling and Mark with burning antlers on his head. Was the other world just a dream and why was I on the toilet again? It's about letting go, laughed Mark. Where's the key to the suitcase, I need to know the time? Time to go out, I laughed and pointed to the shimmering outside world. What is my name, for God's sake?

Mark was a thirsty jaguar, a raging volcano, a golden eagle. I flew on his back into the night and then spiralled into earth. I *was* the Earth – dry, poisoned, barren. Where was the water? And as I paced the room, like a caged cat in the late jungle night, I felt my life would never be the same again. How could I fit back into those little boxes when I had seen this timeless, mythic land inside of me and all those wild animals? And how come we had known all these things?

So you can imagine after that it seemed like a letdown, this ordinary reality, serious and quiet, as the way back often is. And this is how it started in a cold apricot-coloured room in San Cristóbal de las Casas, me in tears and Mark (really) trying to find the keys to his suitcase, and then in a grand suite in Morelia where Mark got so sick with overload he had to shut the curtains on the mountains and I watched videos.

'I don't think it's about West, do you?' he said.

'I don't think it's about rainy cities, boys at bus stations with callipers, or losing my sense of humour,' I said and, remembering the weather vane, added: 'I think it's definitely about East.'

Which is how we ended our journey at the spa town of Ixtapan de la Sal. You see, though I had laughed about these crazy directions before, whenever we went widdershins around Mexico, that is against the sun, something went wrong: the buses that were being hijacked forced us to go to Veracruz, not directly to San Cristóbal and the more we went west the sicker Mark had become. So here we were in the perfect location for recuperation: a fifties style hotel with swimming pool and rainbow-coloured chairs, and a watery theme park where Mark and I lay like silent porpoises in the warm sulphurous waters of the spring, and had our feet massaged in the morning.

'You are both healthy,' pronounced the reflexologist. 'But you (meaning Mark) have something a bit wrong with your eyes, and you (meaning me) have something wrong with your throat. It is not serious.'

'But I've got 20/20 vision!' exclaimed Mark as we walked off to breakfast.

'Maybe she was being symbolic,' I said.

But Mark wasn't listening. He was in a serious temper. We sat at a market stall and ordered our food. A rich American woman pulled up in a large car and ordered a shopping bag from the window, shouting at her chauffeur, and a small dog was run over by a lorry: it howled and howled in the boiling sun and no one went to its rescue. I stared hard into the Madonna lilies on the *fonda* table, and tried to ignore the horrible scene.

'Don't even think of going into a victim trip,' growled Mark, and carried on eating his eggs and beans as fiercely as possible.

'I wouldn't dare,' I replied, trying not to smile at the extremity of the bad mood.

'Good!' he said, washing his plate with a tortilla, and burst into laughter.

Hey Mexico! Where I met Mark and Mark met me, where the houses are pink and clocks don't exist and every time you ask the way, you receive a different answer.

ADIOS MEXICO

~~~

Adios in Spanish means hello as well as goodbye.

Today is 20 June 1991.

I am flying to Mexico for the sixth time in as many years.

As I relax into my KLM seat, my eyes vaguely turned towards the television screen showing a green map with a pointer and a readout informing us of how high we are, the cruising speed and the remaining flight time, I realize this is the first time in weeks I have really breathed, really relaxed. The first sensations of relief give way to an unease which I feel in my body but cannot pinpoint. I am aware of the slight throbbing under my arm – it is still only a month since my biopsy and three weeks since the doctors said my health was fine after all those months of tests and stress. I know my real healing has had to do with giving up my psychic work and moving, moving into new landscapes. The words to a spontaneous poem called 'Shaman Trail' I spoke direct onto tape in my friend Nigel's recording studio almost a year ago, spring to mind.

There is only change; there is only moving . . .

A strange fatigue invades me and I wonder what the hell I am doing on a plane to Mexico. No one will be there to meet me. 'When your spirit wants to make deep contact with you, you have to be alone,' I had said to many people.

'Do you think I ought to be staying in England and thinking about getting a place with Greg?' I said to my mother in the car on the way to High Wycombe just the day before.

My mother had paused before giving me the answer I knew she would give.

'It would be so easy for me to say yes to that question, Mark.

But we both know that would be the wrong answer.'

It made me sad to leave my lover of four months behind, but we lived in different worlds: he with his desire to settle in England and get some kind of security, his own private battles and his spliffs; me with the knowledge that my time in London was now very much at an end and the urge to live in a bigger reality. We had never even discussed the possibility of living together. I was always leaving. He was always staying . . .

Only from where I am sitting in the plane just now, reality does not look so enormous. What if Charlotte and I don't hit it off after all? We are both so intense. God, how will we stand each other? How will I stand her? Will Blanche come out? Will the sale of Charlotte's flat go through? Will I be able to write? What are we going to live on? God, I am so tired. Some shaman!

Charlotte left this morning for New York . . . we shall meet in Mexico in three weeks. It's her thirty-fifth birthday today. I wonder how she is. The image of my mother hugging her in the empty Westbourne Park Road flat as they cried together, comes to me time and time again. Charlotte's family seemed to refuse to acknowledge her departure altogether.

What does lie behind the pasty magnolia walls of English indifference? The nursery rooms of childhood perhaps, where mouths were hushed and feelings denied . . .

But to me, at a leaving party given for Charlotte by an old friend, her father whispered, 'Look after her and let us know your address as soon as you settle for a while somewhere. Her mother worries, you know . . .'

As the stewardesses walk up and down the aisles serving drinks and salted cashews, the anger I felt both at Charlotte's family for not saying these things to her, and at Charlotte for her self-pity (which I saw as a subtle attempt to spoil my peace and fun in the face of my family's abundant support) rises up in me again.

We'll do what we want to do anyway. If our parents encourage us, all well and good. If not, so what? It is time to leave useless old legacies and power games behind. We are adults.

'Don't forget, Mark,' my friend Joasia had said to me in the airport, 'if things don't work out well, you can always come back. You won't have to feel any shame . . .'

My mother looked at Joasia with relief in her face.

'I didn't dare say that,' she said. 'He would have thought I was being controlling.'

I remained silent and smiled faintly. I was unsure of my feelings.

It is with practically no joy, and a certain numbness, that I arrive in Mexico City. The exhaustion I feel seems greater than that of all the past months put together. Am I really OK or did the doctors make a mistake? I don't even know where I shall stay. I take a cab to a tall modern hotel near the Alameda in the old colonial part of the city which is my favourite. The driver recommends the place — he is evidently on commission — and I could really care less about where I am right now. In the lift up to my room, I realise the cab driver meant 25,000 pesos when he said *veinticinco*, not $25. I paid him three times as much as I ought plus a two dollar tip. I swear about it to the boy carrying my bags. I feel lonely. I shall give my oldest friend in Mexico, Alberto, a ring, when I've settled into bed, and announce my arrival.

I am led to an enormous suite for a very reasonable price, high high up in the tall hotel. But as I enter everything looks so grey. Grubby. Almost dirty. Still, there's the strip of paper, trademark of all decent Latin American hotels, advising the visitor that the toilet has been sanitized for your convenience and protection. And the corridors seemed bright enough. It's just this room, or rather rooms, with their outlook onto the Alameda and a view of the Latin American Tower, that feel so dismal.

I remove the disinfecting sign and sit on the toilet, still reeling from the plane journey. As I look into the pan afterwards, the familiar bright red blood of a burst haemorrhoid greets me. I do not know how this affects others, but on the infrequent occasions where I suffer a haemorrhoid, the sight of the blood always makes me feel weak, as if I'm losing some of my life force. In the mirror I look as grey as the suite itself. The exhaustion increases. I take a bath and, somewhat refreshed, I put on my Giorgio Armani birthday suit. It is past midnight by this time. I go out for something to eat.

'Be careful,' says the boy at the reception. 'It's dangerous around here at night.'

Passing by shadowy taco stands and a dark space where a building had crumbled in the 1985 earthquake, I arrive at the local Denny's fast-food joint, which is like Maxim's compared to McDonald's. As I enter, I hear a low wolf-whistle. Seated at a table with a soft drink is a most unattractive woman of about forty with frizzy dyed-red hair, coarse mestizo features and a squat round body. She whistles again as I look at her, and I laugh, not knowing what else to do. Opposite her at the same table is a thin effeminate boy with a sly smile. They are engaged in conversation. I sit at a table on the other side and order Aztec soup and a mineral water.

'Hey! You invite me to join you?'

I regretted my assent even before I nodded it and kicked myself for lacking the courage to say no.

'You look like a film star,' said the woman as she sat down, her face assuming grotesque proportions under the muddy yellow lighting. Her smile revealed teeth with gold rims.

I smiled tightly and did not speak.

'Where are you staying?'

'Nearby,' I replied, in no way willing to divulge my precise whereabouts.

'It's just that they mugged me, this gang of thieves, about half an hour ago, right outside in the street, and they took all my money and hit me so hard on the head (points to a non-existent bruise), I passed out. I feel so dizzy and I ache terribly. I have to stay in a hotel tonight. I was supposed to be going to Tijuana, but the people I was going with never turned up. I can't afford the hotel bill, oh, how my head aches. I need to get to Tijuana as soon as possible. I'm scared to go out into the street now, can I come and stay with you in your hotel room tonight? I'll give you a good time.'

'My girlfriend would not like that. She's waiting for me there now,' I lied.

The waitress brings my Aztec soup.

I stole a glance across at the boy she had been talking to and the sly smile was still there as he observed us from his table. Unease crept around my bones like a hungry cat. What if (like in the stories I had heard) they were part of a gang working together? What if they followed me and found out where I was staying? No, the hotel staff would surely never let them in. My head started to swim and my guts began to bloat. I felt uncomfortable and pissed-off.

'Your girlfriend is older than you,' said the woman. 'She is thirty-five and you are twenty-nine.'

'That's right,' I said, trying not to appear astonished at the uncanny accuracy of this information, and despairing of ever again attaining any semblance of normality, as reality slipped further and further from under my feet.

'I know things,' continued the woman. 'I'm from Veracruz. My family think I am a prostitute and my father hates me. But he put his fingers into my intestines when I was a little girl. I earn money any way I can to feed my children. But I'm not a prostitute. Do you think that's a nice thing to do, abuse your own child? Oh, my head hurts. I have no money. They took it all away from me in the street.'

'So many people suffer abuse,' I said, attempting some kind of two-way communication to stop this tiring monologue, whilst I planned a thousand getaways. 'My own mother was sexually abused as a child.'

'Ah, but me, I have really suffered,' the woman went on whilst I finished my practically freezing soup. 'Look at me. How old do you think I am? I am forty-two years old. A lot of people think I look younger. Do you think I look younger? (I was glad she did not wait for my reply. I did not want to lie again.) What do you think about that, being beaten up in the street and robbed?'

'You know, I really haven't been well myself lately. I had a minor operation a month ago. I'm OK now, but I'm really tired. I just got into Mexico tonight, long journey . . .' I petered out. By this time I was really bored with the sob story and the lack of response.

'My life is terrible. I just suffer. I must get to Tijuana. My head aches so.' Still no sign of any bruise or swelling.

The moment I finished my *sopa azteca*, I stood up abruptly, handed this creepy night-owl ten dollars, said goodbye and went to pay my bill. As I stood at the counter behind three or four other people waiting a very Mexican amount of time to be served, I glanced nervously over at the woman, who had remained at the table with her back to me. The boy with the sly smile had left. I half expected that she would follow me or nod to a group of men waiting outside in the street, so they could put a sinister plan into action with me as the target. But she just sat there, staring out of the window into the darkness. She did not look around. She talked to no one and no one approached her.

After what seemed an age I paid and left the restaurant. I hurried back to the hotel lonely and disturbed. From my room I tried to ring Alberto — he always goes to bed late. All the phone lines were down in the town where he lives. I called reception and told them to allow no one up to my room.

And I fell into bed, images of grey hotel rooms, toilet seats spattered with bright-red blood, and grimacing mestizo women with frizzy red hair stirring cauldrons of tortilla and maize soup on KLM planes, rising in my mind as I drift off to sleep.

I awake the next morning around seven-thirty, rested and clear of head. As I walk through the Alameda, further calmed by the gentle sunlight filtering through the green trees, I forget for a moment that this is perhaps the world's most polluted city, and enjoy the sight of men in suits reading newspapers whilst shoeshine boys work vigorously on their feet, and students with their heads buried deep in books or chatting quietly to each other. The remnants of a light mist slowly disappear as morning advances in the Alameda. The woman from last night already seems like a ghost.

I breakfast in the house of the blue tiles, a beautiful colonial building in the heart of the city, where the waitresses have wings like angels. There are peacocks painted on the walls and the light shines yellow through the tinted glass roof. I rejoice in the scrambled eggs with ham, the *cafe con leche* and the hot chilli salsa, uncaring of the latter's reputation as a haemorrhoid irritant. I smile at a beautiful young black woman sitting alone at another table. I am sure she is from the United States. She disappears suddenly and I think she has left, but five minutes later she reappears, her lipstick slightly brighter, her hair, which had been pulled back, now loose. She comes over and introduces herself to me with a smile of white, even teeth. She speaks in Spanish. I invite her to sit down. Silvia is a psychotherapist from Veracruz (yes, I love that café where the waiters wander around with ever full kettles of hot coffee and you bang your spoon on your glass to get their attention) completing further studies here in the capital. As we talk I notice she has a glass eye. It does not detract from her beauty.

Silvia's soft voice, the yellow light and the swish of the angel-wing waitresses gliding past with glasses of orange and papaya juice merge into the very soul of me, dissolving all vestiges of last night's disturbance and sadness. At least now when I think of Veracruz I won't see a grimacing mouth with gold-rimmed teeth. I tell Silvia I am going to Oaxaca when my friend arrives. 'If you ever have any problems with your health or anything, go to my sister and her husband. They have a clinic near Oaxaca. Just say you are a friend of mine. No problem. If you're in Veracruz, you must both come and see me.'

I thank Silvia, pay, and leave, my spirits bright in the noise and bustle of the Mexico City morning. I book a midday flight to Puerto Escondido on the Pacific coast, return to the grey room to pack and call Alberto. The line gets straight through.

> When we arrive without history
> Who are we?

We watch our faces change
In everyone we see.

And the language we speak
Does it surprise the tongue
As it trips out
And we discover

These are not the words
The normal little self would choose

And how much do we lose
As we let fall
The burdens of the selves gone by . . .

I will stay for a week in a German hotel in the seaside town of surfers called Hidden Port. The hot June rains will pour and pour down in the afternoons and I will keep the air-conditioning on in my room. Large black and brown iguanas will bask in the sun on the hotel garden walls after their breakfast of flowers, and the bright green young ones will waddle awkwardly but rapidly away, melting into the grass as I try to catch them.

I will sleep a lot. In my room. By the swimming pool. By the sea. Sardines in massive shoals will light up the water like silver glitter on the turning of the waves, and seagulls and pelicans will feast on the bounty.

I will call Charlotte in New York from a credit-card phone-booth at the end of a sandy street next to the beach, early one Sunday morning. Afterwards I will walk back down the empty street past seafront hotels, art and craft shops, restaurants with plastic bags full of water hanging in the doorways to deter the flies and a sign which says 'Real State Agents'. And I will be pleased it is so early and that no one is about.

I will spend the day with the Mexican son-in-law of the German hotel owner and play him the tape of Nigel, Blanche and me under the name Love Fund in the hotel restaurant under the great straw *palapa* as the rains fall heavily, and the tape of my mother singing Irish ballads; and we will eat lunch of delicious red snapper, and laugh, until a North American couple, she an English teacher, he a corporate executive come to release his stress, turn up and say 'can we put some of our music on?' and the worst of seventies schmaltz will hit our ears at a very high volume, but we will say nothing, simply look despairingly at each other because I have had my music on and this man has been working soooo hard and He is here for His relaxation. And I will hate the way they treat the staff and underneath the 'we always come here . . . we lerve the people' and the fatherly handing over of the tip to the fourteen-year-old waitress, a local girl, will be the patronizing 'aren't these little natives so sweet, so cute, so servile, but we know who's in charge here, right? MY HOLIDAY COMES FIRST!'

My Sunday Mexican friend who will have to leave early the next morning for his work at the enormous tourist development project of the seven bays further down the Oaxaca coast, will show me where the ocelot and the alligator and the lemurs are kept in small cages in hidden parts of the hotel, and we will eat pizza together by the sea in the stormy evening. I will wear my black silk trousers and best black shoes, and goodness knows why in such weather. I will be drenched by the time we get back. Oh but it will feel wonderful to abandon myself to the tropical rains, to let go to the moment, to let go, to let go, to be alive, to be free!

At night the lighthouse flashes on and off, throwing shadows onto the wall of my room as it hits the stained-glass windows like a slow stroboscope. The frogs are singing. I think of Greg, my family, I wonder whether Blanche will come. But most of all I know my life will be very different now, I can't go back, despite Joasia's comforting words in the airport just those few days ago. Comfort is not what I seek, not just now, but to let myself dream, then live out those dreams. I can feel her here though, my tall Polish friend with the laughter of sunshine. In fact, she recommended me the place . . . Was she here in this room?

I write my diary on the balcony early each morning, looking out upon the tabachin tree with its bright abundant red-orange flowers and then the sea beyond. One morning I visit a nearby beach where a musician with one eye clouded and unseeing lives, in a corrugated tin and straw hut. As I approach, a mongrel comes up to me and gently nuzzles my bare legs, then turns and runs over to a worker descending the hill and snarls viciously.

'Dogs always know when a person has been cruel to a dog,' says the man, and then prepares me a breakfast of chicken and marrow soup with tortillas . . . I think it wiser not to question the sanitation. The soup is good. The man with the blind eye tells me of a German girl he fell in love with but who had to return home, of how broken-hearted he feels, but he has his music. And lots of people visit him on the beach. I leave before the sun becomes too hot.

Then one morning I feel I need to move on from this hilly hidden port of iguanas and surfers . . .

I will return in three weeks with Charlotte and rent a white bungalow a little out of town where armies of ants march up and down the walls in the evening armed with bits of leaves and we will lie lazily in hammocks seeking shade by day and by night watching translucent geckos (kissers, the Mexicans call them because of the loud sound they make) creep upon moths at least twice their size and devour them effortlessly. And we will drink enormous glasses of sangria in the after-sunset glow before a dinner of seafood and rice, then saunter lazily back along the beach. Or take a bus. We will dance and perform sort-of cartwheels by the sea-shore and get bitten by greedy horseflies attracted to the sweat on our legs. Charlotte will call a psychic in New York from the credit-card phone-booth and the woman will tell her the work has been done. And from the same phone Charlotte will discover that the sale of her flat has indeed been completed. Then when it all becomes just too hot and lazy we will leave the hidden port and go to Oaxaca.

*   *   *

Meanwhile, arriving alone in Mexico City again, I get angry at a porter who grabs my bags, puts them in the taxi then demands a tip; I refuse, he gets angry, the taxi pulls off, me swearing, him trying to open the door. 'I'm normally a generous tipper, I just get fed up with people constantly asking me for money,' I growl, a warning to the driver as well as an airing of my grievances.

I take a bus to the town of thermal baths I visited with Charlotte the previous April. As we climb through the twisting piny roads to the high cold city of Toluca, the summer rains continue and fork lightning prods the mountainsides. In a village bus station an adolescent plays distractedly with himself through his trousers as he talks to his friend, and on the descent to the warmer mineral town a row of bright clothes hangs on barbed wire in the rain to dry. I book into the same hotel as last year, its grounds bursting with bougainvillaea and the same silent, good-looking Indian gardener tending them gently.

It is in this place of musty rooms with red carpets that the sadness of leaving my life and my lover in England becomes most acute. In the thermal baths of hot, opaque mineral water the colour of rust, I let myself be massaged. And a man I do not like the look of at all at first gives me the best reflexology I have ever had. Occasionally I feel my glands. They are unswollen for the first time in months . . .

Grieve, let go, let the spa revive you. Let the body and the spirit adjust to the new. Do not run away or try to fill the hours with so-called meaningful activity, they will only be hours lost . . . do nothing.

I visit the spa each morning. I give a bent old beggar woman in the street some change and she says 'May God go with you'. Sometimes I call Alberto and we just laugh down the phone, and one day I go to the bus station all painted blue, even the floor, and make my way to the Central Mexican town, the place of rocks, where I first arrived all those years ago and where friends still treat me like a member of the family . . .

Adios in Spanish means hello as well as goodbye.
I have said adios Mexico many times.
And each time I have arrived and departed a different person.

OAXACA NOTES

~~~

1. *Un Ratito*

The light glows soft and green at nine in the morning through the trees in Oaxaca's main square. It is neither sharp nor blurred. It is a light I can lose myself in if I gaze into it, at nothing in particular for a while. *Un ratito* – an indefinable lapse of Latin American time, which takes me from this place of tourists, this café where the clash of languages is like the colours on an Indian woman's skirt, to somewhere quite else . . .

2. *Waiting for a Free Urinal in the Café del Jardin or The Weighty Gift of Macho Heritage*

Fat little boy no more than four standing next to his father at the urinal. 'Papa, give me some money. I want to buy Mama a present.'
   Fat father: '*Ay si*, and why so?'
   Fat boy: 'Because she has behaved herself very well today.'
   Fat father: 'Ahh.'

3. *Soldiers*

I am walking along the wall of the army barracks in Oaxaca. Thirty or forty yards from me, by the entrance, stand two armed guards, seventeen or eighteen years old. As I approach, my eyes squinting in the fierce midday sun, one of the soldiers extracts from his pocket a small shiny metal object. Why on earth would he be wanting to load his gun now in this quiet street, I thought, alarmed. I hope he's not a mad, gringo-hater with sunstroke.

As I pass the guards I ask the time in my best Mexican accent. The other soldier tells me it is a quarter to twelve. The one cutting his nails lazily with a pair of steel clippers does not look up.

4. *For the Corn-on-the-Cob Seller*

The little Mexican boy is ten years old. He sells corn-on-the-cob by the main square at night. He looks up at me, soft brown eyes, says, 'Hola, gringo', his face alight with the sweetness of ten years and a sadness of centuries.

'Are you selling well tonight?' I ask him.

'Si,' is his reply.

His head barely reaches the handlebars of his yellow cart. You can hardly see him among the tall cheeky late-teenage boys, whistling at the girls and honking their horns as they pass in big cars; among the big white tourists – I am one – with loud voices and awkward gait; and the songs and balloons and startling Indian cloth. But there he is with his 'Hola, gringo' – a term I always correct when directed at me: 'I am not a gringo,' I always say. But to these soft brown eyes, with the sweetness of ten years and a sadness of centuries, proudly guarding their yellow cart with its corn-on-the-cob by the side of the main square at night.

I do not say this.

I smile.

And hope he's selling well.

5. *The Party's Over*

It is the last evening of the traditional nine-day Guelagetza festival held yearly in Oaxaca, with its folk-dancing on the mountains and the town full of hallucinogenic sweets and women with dizzying costumes.

Charlotte and I dress up and go out to eat.

In a concrete square near the Zocalo, by the cathedral, a group called Canto Nuevo sing of love, liberty and Latin-American unity to a large audience. The lead singer is a dark, mestizo woman of about forty with a soft, melodious voice and a gentle, almost expressionless face, which seems to gaze at some indeterminate point on a private horizon. In the background, parents, with their fists together, thump the base of enormous oblong balloons, which then fly through the air against the clear night sky, to be caught, or maybe missed, by the excited hands of children, reaching out. Everywhere, people are eating street food: corn-on-the-cob, *tamales*, even hot-dogs.

I am happy and hungry, listening to the sound of *kenas*, drums, guitars and these calm, beseeching voices. My sockless feet feel around the soft leather of the *huaraches* (a type of woven sandal) I have bought from the market just this morning, and Charlotte looks radiant in her new bright yellow skirt, full and long, and loose T-shirt, tied in the middle with one of my father's leather belts.

As the harmonies of the beautiful Pablo Neruda poem set-to-music rise, I lift my eyes to the second floor of the hotel opposite. The windows of the middle room are open and give on to a balcony. The lights are on and bright. A man, perhaps in his mid forties, walks across the visible area, totally naked. Charlotte and I exchange glances. Sex oozes almost palpably from the room and makes an incongruous marriage with the soft harmonies of the folk group. The partner of the man is not in sight. But I am sure he is not alone. The middle-aged figure walks back and forth in his room, uncaring of, or maybe even enjoying the fact that at least some of the concert audience will now belong to him. I feel myself more and more drawn to watch this display, this distraction from the music.

But the clear, high voice of the female singer sends the occasional shiver down my spine.

A younger man, perhaps in his early twenties, crosses the room opposite and sits on the bed.

The audience claps enthusiastically after a moving rendition of 'Yo Te Nombro Libertad' ('I Name You Freedom') by a Uruguayan poet.

In the hotel the men are dressing. Neither looks out of the window. Has the man paid the boy for his services? What an assumption. How do I know they are not lovers? But I am sure they are not. It is evident the younger man is preparing to leave. There appears to be a discussion and the man, standing, raises his hand as if to strike the boy, who is still seated on the bed. My stomach sinks. The window clears and for some minutes nothing is seen.

The oblong balloons fly as high as the cathedral. The female singer is having a rest whilst her four male counterparts play an instrumental. She smiles at the children around her and her shy, impassive face is transformed into one of beauty, peace, stability.

The boy reappears at the window of the hotel room; he has on a black leather jacket. About two minutes later, he emerges from the entrance of the hotel, and disappears into the Oaxaca night, away from the concert, away from the festivities. The man, now fully dressed, makes an appearance on his balcony, his stage, and claps along with the audience. Who is he? Is he drunk? Is it not dangerous to so shamelessly put on such a show before the Mexican public, not to mention inappropriate?

The man on the balcony sways to the music. He surely must be drunk, so unconcerned about his visibility.

I am glad to have enjoyed the music. The hotel scene leaves rather a bitter taste in my mouth, a grotesque feeling, that smacks of emptiness, violence, lonely desperation, unlove. Is it a potential nemesis I see here also? Is this why I have witnessed it? The scene would have been blocked from my view had I been slightly shorter or four or five feet away in any direction. I look around. No one else seems to pay any attention to the man on the balcony.

The folk group bring their show to a close with a Peruvian instrumental, the 'Dance of the Corn', a dedication to Nature, the

Land, and the right time for things. The audience respond wholeheartedly, me included. I do not look up at the balcony again.

6. *From a Café in Oaxaca, overlooking the Square, 8.30 a.m.*

In between the green the naked eye what does it see? Lifted up the gaze, out of, beyond itself, there's the shelf you could have been left (up)on, someone will come, someone will come. Through the blue the clear clear blue you know it's not true – you won't deceive the eye the passers-by can see it so can I. Having fun was once a party once a silly frock – destiny and the clock took care of that – it's time to pull the hat back from the brow . . . and don't keep asking how!

7. *Afternoon Truth*

Charlotte and I are reading the Dakini cards for one another one afternoon in the Café del Jardin.

I remember my old controlling unfree friend who said to us in that hotel in Mexico City before he left to return to his commitments, 'Now you two make sure you don't waste your time reading cards when you could be doing things, seeing things . . .'

'We have all the time we need to see what we need to see and do what we need to do,' I smiled.

'The things you say can be quite disturbing sometimes,' Charlotte says to me.

'I wonder if Blanche will come out,' I say.

'Truth does not sin,' proclaims the slim angular-faced woman of about fifty, as she marches past the café, dressed in a mini-skirt and brandishing a newspaper angrily. She looks more European than Mexican and is certainly untypical of most of Oaxaca's inhabitants. 'But it makes you uncomfortable, very uncomfortable.'

There is a card in the Dakini pack called Maya – How She Spins. The image is of an old lady wearing a shawl and working a spinning wheel in the sky.

'Tell your own stories,' I tell Charlotte. 'Don't let others do the spinning for you. Remember and honour your grandmothers.'

An enormous old Indian woman, dressed in multiple layers of cloth, a shawl wrapped round her head and a face of a million wrinkles, lurches forward from the shadows of the café's arches and asks us for alms. Magic has not died in Mexico.

8. *Tom and Shirley*

We met Tom and Shirley one afternoon quite early in a bar in Oaxaca's main square. I thought they were English. Tom was plump and wore a striped summer jacket and white trousers and reminded me of Peter Ustinov as Hercule Poirot. Shirley was tall and slim and refined. They made a most elegant couple. They came, in fact, from New Orleans. They were in their late fifties or early sixties. They were not married. Just good friends.

Tom was affable and patient and carried a laconic grin. He was a chef. Shirley was a rich widow with a wicked wit.

'He's the only one who'll put up with me, to travel with,' she said.

They both loved their gin.

They appeared not to have a care in the world, Tom and Shirley. They remembered Oaxaca from way back when there were no tourists. The waitress in the bar remembered them and gave them both a huge hug, a smile replacing her previously serious face.

Tom was leaving tomorrow, but Shirley would stay on. Alone.

Tomorrow we would see Shirley with her gin downstairs outside at a table whilst we lunched upstairs outside. She would not see us. She would stare out at the square. And sip her gin. And is this a mirror for us? No, thanks.

9. *From an Exhibition, Little Boxes of Nostalgia*

'Nostalgia is an alternative to oblivion.'

10. *It's not what you do it's the way that you do it, or Beggarwoman*

An old lady begs then blesses those that give and nearly everybody does because of her grace and her silver hair that never ends . . .

11. *Balloons*

Balloons, balloons, bright I Love You balloons, a brass band belts out bom bom bom tunes, while the full moon lights up the ribbons woven into the plaits of her native dark hair, candies and corn-on-the-cob sweeten the square.

A simpleton grins and rattles a tin, frightens the children, thrusts out his chin, and some people give and others say no, then grinning and rattling he melts into the crowd, young foreigners laugh, the kids resume play, policewomen aplenty patrol, grey or blue uniformed, armed, and proudly displayed on T-shirts of tourists jumps out: 'I ate grasshoppers here in this town'.

A man arrives with the eyes of a gentle cat, and a broad-rimmed sun-hat, and when he takes it off it leaves two marks upon his forehead, like a bull, its horns removed . . . He smiles, green-eyed, like you . . .

And the brass band belts out bom bom bom tunes and oh those balloons, those I Love You balloons . . .

A small boy sings at tables loudly and incredibly in tune, then leaves with a pocketful of pesos, and people are throwing plates backwards at the cathedral wall after their *buñuelos*, and wishing on a star; in a flash like the smashed plate the moment dissolves, irretrievable as the secrets held by these deep, dark-eyed women

selling their wares – incense sticks, hamburgers, slides for the hair and those grasshoppers fried with chilli and lime, herbs for amoebas and ordinary time disappears into shadows and colours on this bright full-moon night, disappears
disappears
and with it the brass band and balloon sellers
until
a market at midnight springs up from nowhere, there on the pavement outside the café, with hammocks and headbands and handwoven baskets, letter-openers, bottle-openers, rugs, belts and bracelets. Some leave their places for a look. Some buy.

At a table, two young, suspicious men, who speak in whispers to each other, approach a visitor and smile rotten-toothedly – 'amigo' – they reek of alcohol. The visitor gets up to leave, the two young men get angry; 'you are spitting at our friendship,' they spit. But they do not follow him. Instead, they sit and whisper to each other . . .
And that is how you know it's time to go
And leave the balloons, bright I Love You balloons, behind with the candies
and corn on the cob
and the sudden market
and the café . . .

CHIAPAS

~~~

I knew in the bumpy flight from the city of Oaxaca to the city of Tuxtla Gutierrez, the plane full of Italians, who, when we suddenly dropped several hundred metres in the sky, all shrieked with laughter, making me feel much lighter about the alarming sensation that my guts seemed to have been delayed somewhat in the descent . . .

I knew as we left the warm, sultry climes of Tuxtla and ascended into the misty Chiapas mountains, passing Indian women with bright pink shawls, and blue boxes hanging on trees to ward off the killer bees . . .

I knew as we got out of the taxi in that cold, high town of folklore and closed doors, and said goodbye to the Spanish couple we'd shared the hour-and-a-half trip with, and lugged our bags in the twilight along the cobbled streets to the same hotel we had stayed in the year before, which had a new name and was under different management . . .

That we would not stay in San Cristóbal De Las Casas.

Lion in San Cristóbal

Outside El Bazár café in San Cristóbal de las Casas, I saw a man with a lion cub on a lead surrounded by impressed onlookers; a fairly docile lion cub on a lead. It frightened the child leaning up against the car who wanted to play with it, and whose leg it joyfully (and firmly) grabbed hold of and attempted to bite, but there was no danger of that because its teeth were not yet grown and all its claws had been removed already, so it could not do the lion thing and rip him apart, and never would be able to. Though the child was not to know that . . .

A man standing next to me said, 'Do you like lion?' I said, 'Yes,' without thinking, and he said, 'Well, buy one then, it costs $700 and it's OK if you have a garden.'

'No, thanks,' I said, and added dumbly, 'six months in quarantine in England is not much of a life for a lion.'

All its claws had been removed and it padded and patted and reached out undangerously to the passers-by, and as I turned and walked away into the chill San Cristóbal evening, I wondered would they remove its teeth when they grew, or operate to keep its muscles weak, like parrots who have their wings cut.

O these undangerous animals!

Snake in San Cristóbal

I am walking across the square where speakers crackle with old pop music and the *mariposas de noche*, the giant death moths, swarm about the rainy-sour lamps.

Today we went to the forest to look at a house. It was pouring with rain, and I felt sad and defeated looking around its neglected rooms. We walked to the waterfall along a muddy path and the trees that were covered in cacti dripped in the silence and a little black snake slithered in front of my shoes, quite unexpectedly. I've never seen a snake before: not a wild one. A childhood friend of mine kept snakes in a tank and fed them goldfish and white mice but even when I dared put the python round my neck, I never felt that primal jolt of fear as when I saw the spiralling of this small dangerous snake among the leaves.

I go into a bar to wait for Mark. I order a tequila and start to write my notebook. 'What are you doing?' says a harsh voice. It breaks open my safe musing.

I look into the pockmarked face of the town astrologer. He is a Scorpio.

'This is the place they call the Frozen City. This is *el fin del mundo*, the end of the world,' he says. He is quite drunk and leers at me with his yellow eyes.

'I am the freest man you will ever meet,' he says.

'If you are so free,' I say, 'how come you can't leave?'

'No one leaves,' he tells me. 'Once you come, you cannot go.'

'Well, I am leaving tomorrow for Guatemala,' I tell him.

And I laugh.

SHARP GREEN ORANGES

Leaving behind
sharp green oranges
whose juice does bite the tongue
like limes
and the English woman
high up in the hills
who wants to laugh
but no one understands
least of all the man
she married
'no sense of humour'
she said
'and once the passion's gone
and the kids are come
then what?
I open up a business
maybe two
I must amuse myself
I can't go home'

this city of the traveller's saint
is pretty but it's very cold
the meat I ate that first night
was so tough and the sweet
seemed ages old
and all life seems to happen
behind doors
whose very closedness
locks the stranger out
and in the hotel room
at night and in the early morn
fireworks crack open
musty sleep
and everpresent church bells
which ring on
long after the ring is rung
remind me of the
cold and damp and dark
and not to stay too long
lest I
should find myself
unable to leave

the cafés with the
barefoot hippies
hanging out
and wasn't that the sixties?
too many flowers
too little power
and paintings of
the pretty city
and pretty houses
and pretty women
all done up nicely
with smiles

and lots of colours –
those ones were not
done by a native
by the way but by
a very white
very rich
European
bless her.

the fairy kings and queens
come here
gaze in adoration
at each other
and a pretty young boy
from Germany
mopes and sighs
(God I know that one from
long ago and far away)
dissatisfied by his lover

the native women
blue-shawled in the street
rough tied blanket skirts that scratch
and nothing underneath
offer each and everyone
a sample of their craft
'pulseras, compráme'
and the answer nearly always no
the questions almost always the same
whence do they come?
where do they go?
How do they live on a diet of no?

the mists wrap round this haunted town
this pretty town of bells
and traveller's saint

smiles when they come are few
hearty laughs
I heard none
and we shall not stay long
in this cold place
high in the hills
where the English woman
with the successful business
awaits the occasional passing
compatriot
to awaken her
sleeping sense of humour

and the oranges are green and sharp
and the mists whisper gloom and never

CROSSING BORDERS 1:
MEXICO TO GUATEMALA

~~~

'I think we're really on our way to Guatemala,' I said gingerly to Charlotte over coffee and cake in San Cristóbal de las Casas.

'I think we might be,' she responded.

I didn't think I thought that was such a big deal. I had spent so much time in Mexico and had never been to either the States or any other Latin American country. It was time for a change.

We dismissed the idea of staying in the wooden *cabaña* of an English acquaintance we made in San Cristóbal. It lay off the main road some twenty kilometres outside the town in the forest where jaguars once roamed and where now the stream foamed with detergent. It was peaceful and quiet.

'But sometimes you can hear lorries turn over as they come round the corner too fast; the sound of the crash echoes throughout the woods. Once we had the pickings of a fruit and vegetable lorry that went over. We ate for days on that,' said our acquaintance.

But as we sat under the roof in the pouring rain watching the mud paths turn to sludge, both Charlotte and I knew this was not the place to make headway with the book. The idea of being so isolated filled me with dread (neither of us drive), and Charlotte hates the cold, especially the damp mountain variety that lodges stubbornly in the bones like an unwelcome tenant and refuses to leave.

I bought a dreadful guide book to Guatemala at an extortionate price – books are so expensive in Latin America. It made the country sound like a commercial garden of Eden. *Guatemala Alive* had no intention of acknowledging the dead.

I began to accustom myself to the idea of leaving the land whose idioms I spoke so fluently. I felt safe in Mexico. I loved the food, the people. Though in Chiapas I was actually enjoying neither.

The Mexico–Guatemala border is only about six hours from San Cristóbal, but it would take us six days to cross it.

We said goodbye to the lady of the *cabaña*, who had gone from baking wholemeal bread and delivering it around town by bicycle to running a great vegetarian restaurant, and who treated the native women who worked for her like her own family. And we booked into the most depressing, run-down hotel, where the dirty magnolia paint was peeling from the walls. It was raining. Our room was next to the rubbish bins, the shower was freezing cold.

Do we have to give ourselves such a bad time about leaving a place?

The following morning I had a sudden panic about malaria in Guatemala (I had ceased to worry about such things in Mexico years ago) and visited a clinic where a young doctor read out to me from an enormous book all the possible and highly unpleasant side-effects of taking malaria tablets: liver damage, palpitations, nausea, LOSS OF HAIR! And charged me twelve dollars for the privilege. I bought a couple of packets anyway and wondered what was going on with me that I had become so neurotic.

We left San Cristóbal. Two hours away by bus, sunnier, warmer and lower down, is Comitán, where we stopped for two days. The food did not improve. We got our ten-dollar visas for Guatemala from the consulate which resembled a prefab. The British have to pay because of an on-going contention about Belize (ex-British Honduras and Guatemala's next-door neighbour), which Guatemala lays claims to. I would read several articles over the following weeks in Antigua about this issue, and I was always left wondering if anybody had asked the citizens of Belize what they wanted.

We took a walk to the main square in Comitán, where two men were rolling enormous logs, which often crashed into the litter bins and the seats, but sometimes made it half-way down the path. I had no idea what their purpose was and little inclination to ask. We met a young Scottish student, whom Charlotte said I frightened the life out of as I boomed out the story of how we left England, him seated on a bench and me holding forth in the fierce midday sun. I thought I was just being friendly.

I visited the house of Dr Belisario Dominguez, a native of Comitán, who became a politician and died during the Mexican Revolution. I walked through rooms filled with surgical instruments, photographs, newspaper cuttings from the time and letters of gratitude from the people of all classes and creeds whom he had treated. I sat in the sunny, well-kept courtyard with its deep pink bougainvillaea and wrote a poem.

Our hotel room was next to a very loud discotheque. Charlotte slept on blankets in the shower that night.

The journey from Comitán to the Guatemalan border is fairly short – about two and a half hours – and the scenery is stunning . . . lush green hills of all shades, parcels of arable land that stand almost vertical, thick-trunked palm trees with abundant fronds shooting joyously from their heads like wild green hair.

We did that journey. But we did not get out at the border and cross over into Guatemala. We carried on down to Tapachula, another four or five hours away, and Mexico's southernmost town. At some point now we were definitely going to have to cross that border. There were no other towns to procrastinate in.

But just for the weekend we booked into a rather nice motel on a hill with a hot swimming pool, overlooking Tapachula. You could almost see the heat rising from this semi-tropical town as you perused its flat layout.

I watched a lot of cable TV and knew that Guatemala was not far away. I kept the air-conditioning on and still I sweated. Charlotte drank margaritas and irritated me with constant questions and annoying references to crossing the border. The food in the motel was very good, and for Sunday lunch a huge buffet was provided, flanked by hand-carved figures of pigs' heads made from pineapples.

Monday midday we left for Guatemala, land of eternal spring and a very bad reputation in the human rights field, overshadowed only by having El Salvador as its next-door neighbour. I remembered Josiane relating to me stories of bus journeys she had been on in Guatemala where men were hauled from the vehicles and searched. Things were supposed to be calmer now than when she visited in 1986. But I was quite scared. Why couldn't we have stayed in Oaxaca? When I feel scared it often comes out as anger. I was in a foul mood by the time we arrived at the border crossing.

'When you come to the point just before the crossing,' offered the Mexican woman in the bus from Tapachula, 'you will be approached by lots of boys on rickshaws. Be careful of your luggage.'

This was quite the understatement of the year. As we stepped off the bus, what seemed like hundreds of deft, coffee-coloured hands grabbed the handles of our bags.

'Hey mister, I take you to the border. Change,' cried a million voices.

I ordered *tranquilidad* to try and calm my scratchy nerves, and Charlotte and I took separate rickshaws to the immigration office. The calls for change continued as we alighted from what I would have enjoyed as an unusual form of transport had it not been so swelteringly hot.

A dizzying array of calculators appeared before our eyes – 'quetzales, pesos, dolares' – and I attempted to make my own mental calculations amidst the tumult of voices. This only added to my confusion, so we changed what Mexican pesos we had left into Guatemalan quetzales none the wiser as to whether the exchange rate was good or bad. We left our bags with a rickshaw boy – keep your eye on those, I said to Charlotte – and I went off to get the Mexican exit stamps. Only Charlotte had lost her tourist card. *Un momento*, said the clerk as she took Charlotte's passport into another office. She returned with a piece of paper and asked me to write a letter of request stating to the head official of Mexican emigration that Charlotte had lost her tourist card, how long she had been in Mexico and please would the honourable gentleman bestow upon her the kindness of allowing her to leave the country. We should be grateful in the utmost for such considerate attention and generosity and we most sincerely regret any inconvenience this show of negligence may have caused, yours faithfully and appreciatively . . .

They stamped our passports. We collected our bags. I sweated. As we made our way to another rickshaw, we passed a long line of huge articulated lorries. Underneath them the drivers had slung their hammocks and were dozing peacefully, oblivious to the heat and the noise, passport problems and moneychangers . . .

'I certainly don't envy him his job,' said Charlotte of the rickshaw boy, as he pedalled us effortlessly, almost painfully, over the bridge separating the two countries. He could have been no more than fifteen. Below us in the river there were tens of people crossing by foot, the water up to their waists, bicycles over their heads.

We arrived at the Guatemalan immigration point, where we were charged another ten dollars each. I questioned the girl stamping the passports and she became vague and birdlike and twittered something about border crossings or taxes, and I could not hear what she was saying and I was too hot to argue. She began to sing like a parrot as she typed our names onto the immigration sheet.

'I hate all this,' I growled at Charlotte, who was silent. Over the border, more voices called out 'change'. We bought some more money from a man who disappeared into a very dubious-looking room on the dusty street, which seemed more like a public toilet than a bureau de change. I remembered stories of travellers who had seen so-called money-changers disappear into rooms with their dollars, never to come out again. But our man came out with our quetzales.

'You told us eight quetzales and now you want ten. EIGHT,' snapped Charlotte as she handed the money to yet another rickshaw driver, this time a man who had brought us to our bus for Guatemala City. I thought her Spanish was remarkable in that moment. I was always complaining that she did not bother to learn the language, and threatening to cease being interpreter. Something had obviously gone in. I was beginning to feel exhausted.

On the bus, a bright blue Bluebird, I bought a fizzy banana drink and felt very annoyed. My hands remained clasped around the bag with my camera in.

'I hate Guatemala,' I said to Charlotte.

'Oh no!' she replied.

I really don't know why I did not apply my theories of remaining calm under all circumstances and visualizing everything going smoothly. Well, perhaps I do know. I was secretly enjoying the drama of being afraid and annoyed.

Guatemala felt immediately very different from Mexico. As the bus left the border town and we moved into the countryside, even the landscape changed. It became softer somehow, very green and fertile. I have never seen so many Pepsi-Cola signs in my life. And so few Coca-Cola ones. (The Coca-Cola Company, so the story goes, had to make a rapid exit from Guatemala when two cadavers were found in one of their vats.)

Pemex signs gave way to Shell signs. Guatemala is not an oil state and Mexico's autonomy already loomed large in comparison. As the driver raged alarmingly through the countryside, I became aware of how few other vehicles shared the road with us. Compared to Mexico, this was ghost country. We passed bridge after bridge that had been blown up. At times the bus would pick up people in apparently the emptiest of places, and when we passed by the police checks all the standing passengers would duck, then rise up again, laughing as in a game. Surely the police knew the bus was over-crowded. A strange eeriness moved about in the space between my skin and my blood. I did not relax throughout the entire trip.

'It's not Mexico,' I said to Charlotte.

'No, it's Guatemala,' she replied.

At about nine o'clock at night, the bus veered around a mountainside and Guatemala City lay before us. All of it. It was an amazing sight as we descended into the valley – the dim flickering of the lights that seemed sometimes on the verge of going out – I remembered the glow of millions of fireflies in the fields before we came into Tapachula just a few days before, when at one point I did not know whether they were insects or stars. Now, on this other, clear, star-filled evening, there was no doubt about the nature of the city's illuminations. The place seemed so small. I was not too happy about arriving in the dark. I was not too happy, full-stop.

The bus station we arrived at was dimly lit and full of shadows. We collected our bags and got straight into a taxi. The city was very quiet. The few street lights there were seemed to be operating at an extremely low voltage, lending to the streets an eerie, surreal glow. This, I thought, is the city where children are 'disappeared' by the authorities in the night. Where violent muggings and terrorist attacks occur. I shuddered. We drove down a street with one Chinese restaurant after another, all appeared empty, and came to a broad avenue with the same dim lighting. The silhouettes of the trees rose up at each side of us like frozen nightmares. Our hotel lay near the American embassy, surrounded by a high metal fence. Armed guards lurked in shadowy corners with machine guns, and as we waited for the intercom to be answered and the door to be opened, I had horrible visions of being mowed down on a whim. I consoled myself compulsively with the conviction that I was not destined to meet my end on the dark streets of a Central American city, just because the guards happened to be bored.

I felt very relieved to be inside the hotel railings.

'We're in Guatemala,' I said to Charlotte.

'Yes, and it's not Mexico,' she replied.

2
~~~

GUATEMALA AND
HONDURAS

EARTHQUAKE IN GUATEMALA

~~~

'These people have no culture,' said the Mexican dentist on the bus. We are crossing into Guatemala. She is hopping the line for the day to eat Pollo Campero which is a sort of Central American Kentucky Fried Chicken. We are hoping to find a house for a month or two; we are tired of travelling.

'I just want to find some peace,' announced Mark as the bus finally lurched into the historical earthquake zone of Antigua.

Antigua is an old town of broken-biscuit cathedrals amongst green hills and abundant orchards. Its houses are painted the colours of the rainbow: old rose and turquoise and sherbet yellow. It has a big shady square inside full of shoeshine boys and an arched fountain where the Mayan women wash their bright geometric clothes and men on haughty horses trot by, striking their hooves on the cobblestones. At the end of the long straight streets at evening, the mist wraps its arms round the volcanoes like a lover and the air smells of pine and woodsmoke.

It appears like paradise.

'I know you!' says a voice that looms out of the shadows. It belongs to a woman with a lot of missing teeth and a small smiling child who stand beside her. 'I saw you at Doña Luisa's today. Don't you remember?'

I don't know who Doña Luisa is. I have only been here for two days. But I don't want to offend her.

'O yes,' I reply. 'Do you know where I can find a house?'

'Let's walk,' she says.

They start off at a pace and I follow them through the dark

streets. My Spanish is terrible and mostly Italian but I do understand that she has to walk forty-seven miles a day to work because there is no bus and the rent man is going to kill her and her husband has gone off with another woman and her baby is dying and so is her mother and could I, dear rich gringa, buy some medicine for them, O here is the chemists!

It is a wonderful performance. I give her some quetzales.

'Where is this house?' I ask her.

'Meet me tomorrow,' she says. 'And when we find it, I will be your maid.'

I rush back to the hotel and tell Mark of my encounter with magic realism on the road in Guatemala.

'Her name can't be Olympia.'

'She said it was.'

'*Limpiar* is the verb to clean in Spanish, Charlie,' he says and roars with laughter.

The next day I knock on the door of a very grand house by mistake. It belongs to Ann-Marie who says she simply has to keep the back door closed because there is no trusting the maids these days with their fickle hearts. Ann-Marie's house is like a palace inside. Of course I could rent her apartment that comes with three servants and a butler. Did I want that? No, she didn't think so but she is very excited because she is going to rent the whole place soon but she might know of another house for me and she whisks me through lush courtyards past rooms full of dark museum furniture and surprised guests to telephone a friend (who isn't in) and tells me she is yes absolutely *thrilled* she is going to France soon she does this house swap, you see, and now shall winter in the *seizième* and I am from London well that is marvellous too she did a swap in London last year and stayed in Sloane Square and that was fabulous and here is the number of the friend who was not in and I simply must come round with *my* friend and see the house properly and if I wanted to learn Spanish her best friend has this terrific language school just round the corner . . .

I rush back to tell Mark of my encounter with Ann-Marie.

'Very Isabel Allende,' he remarks.

That afternoon I knock upon the door of another house, and a woman, small and dark with bright eyes, ushers me through a corridor of plants up some steps into a space of purest white with very little furniture and two enormous roof terraces that overlook the volcanoes and some ruined cloisters and the gardens of the town and I think, ah, this is home. I feel like a ship coming into harbour.

'Is it big?' asks Mark.

'It's HUGE!' I reply. 'There are two bedrooms and a big white studio and terraces.'

'What's the kitchen like?'

'Minimal,' I said. 'Very Zen.' (It was empty.)

'What is the shower like?'

'Oh, it's fine,' I lied (I could see that it was one of those terrifying Latin American electric showers).

'Is it quiet?'

'Oh, yes,' I said. 'It's like a monastery.'

So we move in.

The next morning we are awoken by church bells that sound like saucepans and schoolgirls drumming and blowing recorders ('When All the Saints', Beethoven's Ninth) and fiesta fireworks (which sound like bombs) and conductors shouting, 'Guate! Guate!' (we are on the bus route) and dogs barking in the ruins and evangelicals singing lustily and cockerels crowing rustily and the doorbell ringing and a baby crying and somewhere downstairs a parrot who is mimicking everything with gusto. It is only seven o'clock.

'Jesus,' said Mark. 'What on earth is going on?'

Oh Antigua, Guatemala, is one of the prettiest towns I have ever seen, with its palms and fallen masonry and its houses painted orange and green but there is a lot going on under the surface that is not so quiet or so quaint, beyond these colonial walls of tumbling bougainvillaea. In the hills where I imagine there is gunfire amongst the morning noises.

On the slopes of the volcanoes grows one of the world's loveliest kitchen gardens. Each day the *campesinos* pour into town with their giant bundles of produce aloft the bright-painted buses (the buses painted blue and yellow and pink), their fruit and potatoes tied up in cloth amongst the travellers' suitcases and knapsacks and spare parts and car tyres and sometimes coffins (O all life and death is there on the Latin American bus), their children tied up in woollen shawls and their little chickens tied together with string. Each morning I leave the Señora's house with my basket and follow the straight street to the market, passing by children carrying home loaves of bread and huge bunches of fiery gladioli like flags. I walk amongst the mounds of crimson and scarlet chillies and golden corn and green banana and broad beans and perfumed quince and sweet potato, tangerines and blackberries (it must be autumn), mint and coriander. It is crowded in this place but quiet: the Indian women cajole and whisper and laugh under a blue sky and cotton clouds and the warm air smells of lilies and violets and fresh earth. They do not shout like the market men with raw faces in my country so far away.

I am enticed.

I ask how to boil the strange herbs and cook the myriad squash (one is prickled like a pale hedgehog) and I brave my intuition with the meat corridor (no freezers here). I do not brave the split iguanas but I do try the roasted freshwater fish when it is offered me and I learn to haggle in my terrible Spanish that is mostly Italian and sometimes even Greek in moments of exasperation (no one minds – the market language is Mayan) for my new sky-blue saucepan and my terracotta bowls and my handful of cinnamon sticks and tiny garlics and when I come home laden with these green fragrant things, I feel a singing in my heart. I am the only stranger there. But the women do not make me feel uninvited.

Mark comes home from Doña Luisa's (which is an American-owned café) where he likes to go for breakfast and write poetry. Sometimes he comes back with stories of people he meets (today he met three Irish nuns in white who work in the poorest parts of Guatemala City and an Irish clown who performs in all the hillside villages). And sometimes he comes back with a volcanic look on his face.

'I am fed up with all this guilt and complicity. I am fed up with tourists in dirty T-shirts pretending to be poor and vendors expecting me to buy bloody striped waistcoats. I said I had one already today and do you know what the woman said?'

'No,' I replied, cutting the stems of some red roses.

'But you didn't buy it from me!'

'God!' I said.

'I am not responsible for buying the whole of Guatemala.'

'No,' I said.

'And I am very fed up with all the waitresses complaining about the rich foreigners when their own don't even give them as much as a smile or a tip, depressing films about atrocities in Latin America, those bloody dogs. I hate humanity. I'm going to do a painting.'

I said nothing. I am having a convenient flower-arranging crisis. I am pissed off. It was calm in the kitchen before and now it is full of noise.

'And you don't have to look like such a victim either. I've told you before, if you want a quiet life, don't stay with me. Are those tomatoes *washed*?' he went on glowering at my guacamole.

'Yes,' I said. 'Of course they are.'

'Good,' he said and walked off, closing his bedroom door.

Cholera is one of those other secret threats in Central America you fear will one day knock upon your locked door, like the shower which I am now convinced is going to kill me with a giant electric shock, in spite of the rubber mat the Señora has given me and other precautions. Mind you, soon after we move in the electricity is cut off for most of the day and night, so this becomes less of a possibility. At night the streets are in complete blackout and the only lights that flicker are from our coloured church candles and the stars and the lightning that shakes the sky. When we drive back from the city on Independence Day, the bus driver glances nervously into the hills as the festival runners loom out of the darkness, carrying torches of flame. It is not a peaceful experience.

One evening the lights do not go off at the appointed hour.

'Why did the electricity stay on yesterday?' I ask my Spanish teacher Sarah (I have started lessons each day to lessen my Italian tendencies).

'The President was in town,' she explains and teaches me a Guatemalan proverb: 'The poor feed the duck that the rich men eat.'

'The rich man has locked his heart and thrown away the key,' I reply, inventing my own. Sarah looks at me astonished when I say riches are not only in the dollar, that in Europe people die without their family and without their god, that in Japan you can travel for three hours on a train and not see one green field, and in New York never find a vegetable that tastes of anything except plastic.

'The woman is a parrot in a cage,' I declare when she tells me of the terrible machismo of Guatemalan men, 'but she keeps herself there.'

'You are not a *victima*,' she announces, and I rush home to tell Mark this *astounding* piece of news.

'How do you like my flowers?' asks the Señora as I climb the stairs. She is holding a beautiful display of bird-of-paradise flowers.

'They are wonderful,' I reply.

'They are yours,' she smiles. 'You thought they were dead and you threw them away.'

'La-aaaa!' sings Lorito the parrot in a high operatic voice. We laugh.

'It's a miracle,' I say accepting the spiky bunch of orange and purple and green.

'Gracias a Dios,' she says, and carries on watering the courtyard.

I have been in Antigua a month now, living in the white studio above the Señora's house, and so far I have avoided buying a stripy waistcoat. I walk resolutely through the square at dusk where the embroideries hang from the trees and go to meet Mark for supper. We have taken to eating noodles in a Japanese restaurant now there is no power to cook. The waitresses complain they have to walk for miles to their homes through the scary streets. We drink Chilean wine in the candlelight and a group of musicians in claret-coloured cloaks come and sing us the songs of the faraway Andes. I see Olympia bring in a beguiled, bewildered tourist in search of a free meal. She pretends not to see me. Outside on the corner of the street there is a young man, about seventeen, I would say. He sits hunched up on the pavement, taking great care to cover up his shoes. He is watching everyone go by in the darkening street and reporting their passage to his grandmother on an imaginary telephone.

Into the beautiful tinderbox town, the people come and go buying up the living culture their own countries abandoned long ago: taking with them postcards and embroideries, books on Mayan folklore and curly painted crocodiles. With their brightly woven backpacks, they pass into the danger zone and out again, Peace Corps people, Spanish course people, rich Americans, zealous Germans, doing Antigua and going off to the lovely lakes to the jungle ruins to the famous Indian market. Are we going there? No, we say, we are not. We are tired of travelling. We are staying here.

We meet a man with scared eyes who has lived too long in Nicaragua and another who was arrested in El Salvador and was saved only by his Guatemalan friend's quick wit and presence of mind, and another who nearly drowned on a Pacific beach in Mexico they call Zipolite, the Beach of Death, and another, a tall pale Swiss girl who was chased by earthquakes all through Central America and was almost swallowed too by the alien sea, only this was Costa Rica ('Don't you think that was some kind of message?' says Mark to all these stories). And here in the Japanese noodle house a pale Englishman who sits sadly over his beer on another table tells us how he wants to die but right now he is helping the Indians save their land in the South. But he does not look happy about it.

'It is all very well that we buy a tractor for the village,' he says of Western charity, 'but we forget to tell the villagers how they can afford the fuel.' He is suffering witness to what is called 'the rusting hulk of the twentieth century': the machine that does not work. Our progress and our efficiency of which we are so proud.

'GRANDMA!' cries the boy urgently outside. 'The gringoes are going past. They are all passing by!'

On the way back from a spa in the woods one day, we found some empty cardboard boxes in the dusty road. They have been dropped by parachute. 'This box contains good flies,' says the label. 'If you find it, open it.' The good flies mate with the bad flies that cause disease in cattle. In such a way are the harmful effects of the parasitic insects nullified.

The children practising their military marching in the schoolyard stop and wave to us, at the travellers stopping by.

Mark is teaching me how to wash clothes with a piece of round orange soap, the Latin American way. He stands at the big outdoor sink and rubs the clothes against the ribbed stone with the soap, a piece of lemon and a scrubbing brush, and he rinses everything in the running water. I like to hear the rhythm of the wet cold clothes against the stone and the running of the water and I like to watch his strong agile hands and the sunlight falling on his bronze hair, how he makes that space for himself for cleaning things in the courtyard where the birds are singing and the drying, flying clothes that smell of the wind, how he is completely absorbed in it all. He says when he washes his clothes, it lightens his spirit and makes him feel connected to the earth.

'O, I feel like that when I make the evening meal!' I say. And something like love excites my heart.

I remember another white space where I lived with candles, how one stormy night I started to draw a plan of a house. It was a house on three levels with four doors that faced north, south, east, west. I called it the house of the four winds. In it lived a tribe of people who came from the four corners of the earth. On the first level, they lived and worked together. On the second, they lived and slept with their lovers and their children. On the third, each person lived and thought for themselves, in a tower that looked upon the stars. I remember this house when I look at Mark washing with the orange soap, and when I cut up the vegetables I have bought in the market. I know I will live there someday.

But first I have to let go of another house before I can make room for this one: for this sunny kitchen, for this singing green courtyard. 'I am closing my consulting room and opening my theatre,' as Mark said to me one day. We have to close some doors in order to open others.

I am letting go of a dark house: the house I lived in as a child, the house I lived in as a citizen. As I sold my inherited furniture, my educated library, my modern machinery and my fashionable black wardrobe, I begin to release these possessions from within me, these things that bring with them the pretty surfaces and the ugly turmoils of the outside world.

I could tell you many tales of what I saw and heard in Guatemala. I could tell you about the city where the walls of the Immigration Office have 'Don't shoot our workers' daubed in red paint, where journalists are shot for saying what they find and children whose hearts are pierced in the night for being what they are ('They say Fidel Castro wants them for his army,' says Sarah of these disappearances) and how once I saw a woman rush into a bank and sob because her house had been robbed of everything and the bank clerk could only gaze on stupefied. Or I could tell you about the town where the houses are violet and blue and the barber waves 'good morning', and a boy walks along the road with twenty hats on his head and the truck goes past with twenty striped mattresses on its back and how once I saw some girls clinging to car bonnets in the Miss Antigua Contest dressed in sugar pink and lemon yellow and o, all those colours and fruits and embroideries! But it is not the outside that engages my attention here but something else, a little nearer heaven and a little closer to the earth.

The electricity cuts deepen, the water is cut off daily, a State of Emergency is called but still underneath us the Señora sings to her granddaughter in the smoky kitchen and she talks to Lorito and the washing flies out on the line and the chicken and ducks are fed with corn and a huge cake is baked for a spiritual retreat once a week and I hear her low calm voice as she measures her clients for clothes in a back room. There is a lot of hidden rage in this volcano town, in this land of always spring but there is no guerrilla war under this roof.

One afternoon I go to bed (my womb has been aching for a week) and I dream that Mark has to go underneath the hill. The reason is given in a poem: 'The caged bird sings for all the world When the King comes to his Kingdom, all the world listens.'

The next night at four o'clock, an earthquake shakes the house and throws us all out of bed. 'Come downstairs!' calls the Señora and we sit together in the sturdiest room of the house, wrapped in blankets and she starts to pray silently. Her eldest daughter tells us how once they spent a whole month living in the hills under sheets. There is another tremor.

'The earth is angry,' says Mark.

The Señora continues to pray.

WHITE WALLS

the time of all stones turned is come
in an unknown town
I face a blank white wall
and every lie I told myself
in my safe country far away
reflects right back to me
'Deal with us
deal with us
you made us and clothed us
and fed us
Now deal with us'

THE IRISH LULLABY

~~~

for Bridget Josephine Dargan, my mother

Toorah loorah loorah
Toorah loorah looraly
Toorah loorah loorah
Hush now, don't you cry . . .

I am painting a picture of colours and shapes as they come into my mind. I am alone in this place of white walls with the windows to the volcanoes and the pines in Antigua, Guatemala. Charlotte is at the market buying fresh salads and pulses to make her lentil soup, and a chicken to roast in the oven of the Señora downstairs before the electricity is cut off.

I am alone with my paints and my colours. A dog barks occasionally; the church bells clang dully like someone banging on a dustbin lid. And now and then I hear the Señora calling out in her gentle, firm voice to one of the girls who works for her, the ducks need feeding, let's check the chicken soup. You can see her joining her *muchachas* in the housework. There is a complete absence of the master–servant attitude so prevalent in Latin America. The Señora was from a servant's family herself.

'We must learn to dominate two things as human beings,' she said to me once. 'Our instincts and our complexes. Otherwise they will be our ruin.'

Each time I walked through the patio of the Señora to climb the steps to our big white space, I would rejoice in the abundant green plants and bright flowers, and in the parrot, Lorito, who had been cageless for twenty-four years of his life until a year ago when the

Señora had had him one built. He would sing and imitate all the noises in the house – the laugh of the Señora, the doorbell, the dog's bark, the cat's miaow – as he enjoyed the morning sunshine and his cage. He rarely left it, despite the door often being left open. The Señora had never clipped his wings either, even after he had attacked people he had taken a disliking to on several occasions, screeching down at them from his perch next to the picture of Jesus on the cross, and digging his claws into their hair. And she had not sold him to a rich American tourist who had offered her hundreds of dollars for him.

'Lorito brings a lot of joy to this house,' she said.

So it felt good to know that below our empty space, but for the beds and a table and chairs, was a firmness, a wholeness, a foundation. That things flourished. And I felt fed like a plant. And able to bloom.

I am painting a picture of bright colours and shapes. I am alone. I hear a distant, familiar sound. A melody. It starts to ring through me like a church bell through the mists.

> Toorah loorah loorah
> Toorah loorah looraly

The other sounds grow dim and disappear, the Señora's voice, the parrot . . . I am suddenly in another land far from these volcanoes and pines . . .

My mother is from the land of leprechauns and plaintive song. She is dark and small and bright and lost the accent of native country long ago in all but her songs. She does not regret it.

My mother inhabits a world far away from sentiment and is passionately indifferent to what most people think. She is neither here nor there but somewhere on the dark bright sea, singing a song from a sailing boat only she knows how to captain.

My mother has a beautiful voice. She can silence even the most rowdy crowds when she stands up to sing in an Irish club. She sang at my twenty-first birthday party and had several of my friends in tears. She always sings unaccompanied.

I paint a white teardrop onto my picture of shapes and bright colours . . .

Hush now, don't you cry . . .

My mother lost her own mother at the age of seven from tuberculosis. This seven-year-old girl was left to sleep in her mother's deathbed the night after the corpse was removed. Her brother died a year later of tuberculosis, aged nineteen.

My mother is the youngest in a family of six children from Port Laoise, Eire. Four remain. After her mother died, she immediately had the job of practically raising her older sister's children. They were very poor. My mother was a rebel at school and received daily knuckle bashings from the nuns for arriving late. She loved her two brothers. And they loved her.

At the age of eleven my mother left for England with her father. They found rooms in north London at a time when signs still hung outside houses saying: To Let – No Irish, No Jews, No Dogs. My grandfather found construction work. My mother shared the landlady's bedroom and her bed.

The landlady was a cruel woman, who forced an eleven-year-old Catholic girl to eat before communion, and on one occasion burned her legs with a hot poker. My mother would lie awake in bed at night and hear the woman as she masturbated.

Throughout all the verbal and physical abuse, my mother never told anyone. Not her father, a painfully shy man whose soul only revealed itself through the old tin whistle he played, nor her two brothers who came to live in England a little later. The landlady spoilt the three men rotten. My mother would spend what little pocket money she was given on chocolates for this bitter woman, hoping in her young heart to buy, if not some affection, then at least a let-up to the continual bullying. To no avail.

My mother left this place of torture and silence when she was sixteen and earning her own money as a receptionist. Her father remained there until he died four years later, none the wiser as to the landlady's treatment of his daughter. I never knew my grandfather.

My mother returned to the house for the last time aged twenty, after her father's funeral, to collect some insurance papers. As she reached to open the drawer where they were kept, the landlady's walking stick came crashing down, missing my mother's fingers by a hair's breadth. The next thing she is aware of is someone pulling her away and the landlady's face turning blue. The policeman who rented an upstairs room had heard crashing noises and struggling and had come down to see what was going on. My mother stammered out the bare bones of the story. The policeman said he was surprised this had not happened before, and my mother left the house.

In January 1991 my father's brother died of a brain haemorrhage. His family lived in north London. As we drove up to the funeral service in Southgate, my mother suddenly shivered.

'That's the road I lived in with the Bancroft woman,' she said.

I paint another white tear onto the paper.

Toorah loorah loorah

My mother has a beautiful voice and is good with words. At fifteen she wrote a poem about Ireland's green fields. The teacher told her she could not possibly have written it and wanted to know which book my mother had copied it from. My mother ripped the poem up and never wrote another. She sang to her father a song she was to enter a talent contest with.

'Ah, sure, Josephine, ye'll never get anywhere with a voice like that.' My mother first sang in public when she was in her thirties.

How much abuse can a child take? What happens when the 'nevers' and the 'can'ts' outweigh the 'it's possibles' and the 'yesses'?

I paint another white tear . . .

Hush now, don't you cry . . .

My mother has given me a voice to sing and a treasure chest full of keys. Gold ones to unlock the spirit.

'You like it up here,' said the Señora, 'because you are closer to the heavens.' She also told me she loved to hear me sing.

Silver ones to quicken the mind. I inherited my mother's ability to see through many situations and people with a clarity that is sometimes painful.

And bronze ones to keep me down to earth.

The platinum key I have is my very own. I have had to earn it by breaking away from the pain of my mother, dealing with my own years of bullying I suffered at school and the threats of what would happen to me if I told anyone. And learning that the gifts I have inherited I must take out into the world.

But on this sunny day in the land of Always Spring in this big white space with my painting and my solitude, I honour through my mother all the abused children, including myself, and I mourn the waste that the abuse brings about.

I paint more white tears, like pearls, onto my paper, and I let my own tears run down my face; for the seven-year-old girl who lost her mother and slept that night in her deathbed; for the youngster who was sent to run miles across the dark Irish fields at night in all weathers to fetch milk for her sister's family; for the six-year-old who was fondled by a neighbour who could have been her uncle; for the dark silent adolescent with bright green eyes who was beaten and treated cruelly by a vicious landlady – and who among friends was the life and soul of the party; for the twenty-year-old who dealt with all the arrangements for her father's funeral whilst the other members of her family fell to pieces; for my mother who could not share her pain and could not continue to be the life and soul of the party and submerged herself in a forgotten place during her thirties with the help of a vodka bottle.

Sometimes my mother appears in a purple robe in a world more her own than these rocky waves, these cold depths, where she rises up and shows us where to go. My mother comforts the dead spirits who have lost their way. She talks to them and they understand.

Lately I see my mother making it in to land, coming in to rest and anchoring her boat in a safe harbour.

Toorah loorah loorah
Toorah loorah looraly
Toorah loorah loorah
Hush now, don't you cry

Toorah loorah loorah
Toorah loorah looraly
Toorah loorah loorah
It's an Irish lullaby.

WHO BLAMES THE FERRYMAN?

~~~

A CHAPTER ABOUT JUSTICE

I was brought up under the shadow of Blind Justice. That severe blindfolded woman, holding the scales, standing aloft on the dome of the Old Bailey, the supreme court of the land. My father (born illegally in the Inns of Court) always said to me: 'Truth in the courts is not truth, it is truth *insofar as the evidence will allow.*'

I always thought, even at the impressionable age of ten, that this was a load of bollocks.

Nevertheless the law fascinated me. I spent my adolescence learning how to read my father's briefs (purple ribbon for defence, white for prosecution), cutting out his trials in the newspapers and arguing with his students. I thought barristers were like knights as I watched them perform in Court Number One or Two, defending murderers and fraudsters and pornographers as if they were the sweetest men in the land, jousting with each other, playing to the gallery and trying to outwit the judge. My favourite film was *The Winslow Boy* in which the fierce lawyer gives up a high position to defend an innocent boy because as he says: 'Doing justice is not difficult but doing right is very rare.'

I stopped going to trials the day I saw a judge, a Welsh non-conformist, sentence a crime of passion very harshly. He was disgusted that the defendant, an Indian man, had 'fornicated like a goat, Ladies and Gentlemen of the Jury,' over the kitchen table and when he had killed his mistress in a fit, had turned the kettle off. As any calm normal person would have done.

'That is prejudice,' I said to my father. 'That is not justice.'

I didn't go back to the courts of England until Mark and I were just about to leave. My father and my brother were appearing in the same case. It was a famous case at the time: the trial of the

Townsend Thoresen company for the sinking of the *Herald of Free Enterprise* off the coast of Holland. It was an unprecedented trial because there were nine defendants, ranging from the man who operated the doors of the ship right up to the owner of the shipping line. The case was to determine who was to carry the blame for the tragedy.

I came into court just as the Prosecution was presenting its evidence. The lawyer was doing a terrible job. The judge didn't like him and snapped at his heels like a terrier. This made the lawyer stumble and start even more clumsily. The defence were all smiling at this. Because there was no room for all the defendants in the dock, they sat in two rows in front of the judge with their lawyers who strutted around them like big crows. This seating arrangement was unprecedented too.

Each time a Prosecution witness came forward, the Defence was asked to question them. They passed the questioning along the rows, declaring their client's innocence at every turn, like pass the parcel. It reminded me of that old English nursery rhyme: 'For the want of a nail, a shoe was lost'. Who will the buck stop at? I wondered. The Captain or the Architect or the Man Who Fell Asleep? (Actually, it didn't stop at anybody because the case was eventually dismissed because the Prosecution was inadequately prepared.)

I thought this was quite the stupidest trial I had ever seen. I felt like Alice at the trial of the Jam Tarts. I wanted to knock over the courtroom and throw up the pack of cards into the air. Everyone is treating this like a game. The Lion fights the Unicorn for the Crown, Tweedledum and Tweedledee fight for the Rattle and the lawyers fight for the blame and point their fingers away from their clients. Just as long as someone is guilty: because justice in the courts is not justice, it is justice that is seen to be done. To someone else.

I went to drink sherry with the lawyers.

'I'm going home,' I said to my father.

He said nothing but threw up his eyes in despair.

Now the English judicial system is famous throughout history for its hypocrisy. I don't give a fig for history and I'm not going to battle on its terrain. History just gets you stuck in that 'What do you expect, wars will always happen, boys will be boys, it's only human nature, serves them right, off with their heads' kind of arguing, and I'm not going to waste my time there. I now think that justice is not best handled by people who hide behind powdered wigs and black cloaks and speak a language no ordinary person can understand, who pretend they are face-less upholders of an immaculate system, cogs in a machine. I also think that a courtroom where the truth is only the provable truth is a pretty limiting space in which to review our actions.

We spend our lives pretending such systems and such traditions work, that only what is proven is true. We spend our lives taking sides: with the innocent, against the guilty. 'They shouldn't do that, it ought not to be allowed, pointing our fingers at Them (He hit me! She's wrong! They did it to me!). Because, no matter the complexity of the Whole Truth and Nothing But, someone has to get the easy blame in the end: Mum or Dad, or School, or the System, or the Tories, or the Blacks, or the Middle Class, or the Critics, or the Stars, or My First Boyfriend. Someone has to be punished for the slights we have suffered. Someone else has to be guilty.

But in the time of the Big Dissolve, this neptunian decade which is washing away our old structures, these polarities, these sides of right and wrong are being replaced by another paradigm, and by another kind of justice.

'The turn of the scapegoats is come,' Mark once said in a workshop. 'Having weighed your sorrows on the outside, you'd better watch out as that karmic scapegoat turns on the mountain and prepares to butt you off.'

'No one comes into this world innocent,' said Caroline Myss in a lecture. We are all responsible.

Every defendant was responsible in the case of the ship that drowned. They all had a part to play in the tragedy. And so did the people who took the ferry and those of us who watched helpless from the beach. The sinking of the *Herald of Free Enterprise* was a parable about greed: because it was cheaper to keep the doors open, to have the men working longer hours, to cross the sea more quickly, to buy this ticket rather than that ticket, the ship sank. We put our greed before our welfare, and forgot how fickle was the sea. For the want of a battle, the land was lost and all for the want of a nail.

ASDAK

'If someone I loved was killed, I could imagine killing their murderer.'

We are in the coffee town of Tapachula on the border between Mexico and Guatemala. It is 98° Fahrenheit.

'Don't you think that is taking the law into your own hands?' I said. I am quite shocked and very hot and drinking a large margarita.

'The Law!' responded Mark in a derisory tone. 'When Neville was knocked over by those businessmen because they jumped the lights and he attacked the car, he went to the police and do you know what the Law said?'

'No?'

'The Law said nothing about the businessmen's negligence of human life, how they just drove off without a word, the Law said Neville could be done for criminal damage.'

'Well,' I said after a while, 'you can't just go round killing people and bashing things up.'

'No, precisely, you can't,' he said. 'Why don't you have another tequila?'

I am learning to leave my father's old courtroom behind in this cactus land and learning a new kind of spiky justice. Mexico is not a country of systems, it is a country of surprises and surprising and unprecedented things are being turned around as I play with the salt on the rim of my glass in the silence when I don't know what to say.

Mark was not brought up under the shadow of Blind Justice. His grandfather threw the book at the judge when he refused to go to war. While I was dutifully reading my father's briefs, he was setting building sites on fire and shoplifting and I am quite jealous of this miscreant youth. At the age of nineteen he played Asdak, the anarchic judge of Brecht's play *The Caucasian Chalk Circle*. Asdak judges cases brought before him according to the accused's story rather than by a system or a book. He is loud and difficult and unpredictable and does not wear a wig. I like that. I think the role must have suited my friend well.

My father's eyebrows shot up in alarm when Mark told him he had been thinking of studying the law. 'Thank Christ you didn't,' he said and after a silence added, 'There would have been all hell to pay.'

'And nobody can go around saying they are the chosen race; whether they are Serbian, or American, Jew, Muslim, black, heterosexual or gay or whatever because sooner or later another special sect, another chosen race is going to disagree with you. You invite your fate.'

'You are saying justice is a matter of karma, rather than right or wrong?'

'I'm talking about responsibility,' he said.

I drain my glass.

'Are you enjoying that?'

'It was a very good margarita,' I said.

'Very good, very good,' he scowled. 'Ten out of ten, well done. Do you have to judge everything?'

'I can say what I like!' I retorted. 'I liked the margarita, I think it's a good margarita. What's the difference?'

'The second is pretending it's objective, like it's a proven fact. Stop abdicating responsibility. If you like something, own it.'

Oh, for goodness sake, I think, it's only a bloody tequila and lemon juice.

THE JUDGEMENT OF WOMEN

When we arrive in Guatemala I go to learn Spanish with Sarah for two hours a day underneath the shade of a grapefruit tree. Sarah is an unusual woman: she is a pioneer women's liberator in a land where men have almost complete authority (or so it seems) and there is no faith in the rule of law. Sarah wears trousers and only allows her husband to visit her one night a week, 'For diversion,' she says. 'Men are like avocadoes,' she says when I complain of the worms I found in mine yesterday. This is a country of hidden pests and underground justice.

Sarah has a shop in the market selling sugar and flour and she collects stories from the women who come to buy from her. Some of the women are locked up in their houses and are only allowed out once a week to shop. Sarah tells me how the men beat their wives, work them like slaves and keep mistresses. But she also tells me of the hidden women's revenges: of the spells they put on men to subjugate and humiliate them, how they steal up on their unfaithful husbands in the night and pour kerosene on their dicks and set them alight, and how they bewitch each other. Only last week, she said, her angry mother-in-law sent her some cursed marrows for soup (Sarah threw them away). All Sarah's stories end rather surprisingly with the discovery of Jesus. One story was about a policeman who raped a man's wife and ruined his marriage. The woman always blamed the man for not protecting her. One night the man sees the policeman in another town and he shoots him dead.

'It's the justice of God,' I suggest.

'No,' she said. 'It's the justice of man.'

In the evenings I watch the Indian women in their rainbow tapestry clothes go by with huge loads on their backs and babies wrapped in turquoise and pink shawls, and the men who saunter past with their hands in their pockets.

'It's so easy to blame the men,' I think. 'But it's so hard to confess how much we condemn ourselves.'

I don't know much about the justice of man but I do know about the judgement of women.

I once reviewed an exhibition of the avant-garde photographer, Man Ray. In his magazine photographs women were trussed up, cut up, dismembered and disfigured – their every power taken away in the name of beauty, art, fashion and privilege. None of the models was smiling but they did not complain either.

I have heard many voices raised in protest against the dehumanizing effects of fashion and photography. How men treat women like objects, how they ridicule them. I have seen many fingers pointing the blame, yelling guilty, but I never heard the prosecution put themselves in the witness stand. I never heard women take responsibility for their restrictions: I never heard the voices ask these questions:

Who put these clothes on?
Who bought the magazines?
Who pushed their feet into crippling shoes?
Who played those fairytale roles?
Who sat for Man Ray and the others?
Who scorned the ugly and the badly dressed and the stupid?
Who cast the spells?
Who lacked respect for their own sex?
Who put the babies and the burdens on their back in return
    for comfort, a safe home and a part to play?

Not men.

THE QUEEN OF SWORDS AND THE THIEF

'Oh, there she is again, that Queen of Swords, crossed by our friend the Seven.'

I will not fully understand how to dismantle the inner courtroom until I reach the northern red deserts of Chile hundreds of miles away. There one night under a full moon in Scorpio while Mark and I are reading tarot cards, I will face my own trial.

I have had some money stolen today. It has never happened to me before. It comes as quite a shock and I feel disappointed and let down. I report the theft but I do not accuse anyone. 'It was my fault. I left the money around. Shit happens. I won't hate the thief. I'll forget this tomorrow,' my logical self will say.

But a voice inside is giving me a very hard time. She of the fierce dry crown will not let me let it go. It's a sign, she is saying. Better ask yourself what you did wrong. You were an idiot to trust people like that. Asking for trouble, giving away your money all the time, as if you were embarrassed to have it. Give, give, give. Where's the receiving? What do you expect back? A reward for all your generosity? Love? You won't get it, you know. Because it's only a control. It's only a safety zone. And leaving your door open like that. Where are your borders? Go to gaol. Do not pass Go and collect £200.

'And you can get out of that court,' says Mark looking at my mournful face. 'Stop asking yourself what you did wrong: wrong, right, wrong, right. It gets on my nerves. All that looking back and wondering what you have left undone, feeling guilty and punishing yourself.'

I stare at him and smile (I don't know who is the worse prosecutor, the Queen of the Air or him!), and the full moon arises from behind the hill, this moon of thieves and detectives. I can't believe I still find myself on trial with that stern judge waving her bloody sword and glaring at the thief with his eyes riveted in the past.

'Why don't you ask instead, What can I learn from this?'

I met a man last month who told me he had been robbed at knifepoint on a beach. He had been warned twice not to go further down the beach but he still went. The experience, he said, had left him feeling invaded. His response was to buy mountain locks and chicken wire for his backpack and to distrust the natives of every land, in fact to distrust everyone. I don't want to respond like this, nor do I want to ignore the message of the robbery (but I don't want to do it from that heartless bench, or that miserable dock).

I want to know what the thief was doing in my house?

Why did I invite him in?

Why did I let him invade me?

Mark once quoted an expression in Spanish that goes like this: 'Al ladrón se le olvidó la luna en la ventana.' It's hard to translate. Literally it means: 'The moon forgot herself to the thief in the window.' Roughly it means: 'The thief forgot the moon in the window.'

The moon witnessed the event. So maybe now in the absence of a court, the judge and the sword, the moon should ask the questions. The bright moon in the still coppery clouds.

Why do you not see me here? she asks my thief. What do you take away? What do you destroy? What little death do you now bring to your own door?

The turn of the scapegoats is come, as Mark once said. The vandals within and without.

He does not interpret the expression in the same way. He says it means that the thief cannot steal the moon, and furthermore that in forgetting she was there in the smallness of his thieving, he forgets also the value and provision of the earth, and the power of the planets.

'Maybe the theft happened just so you could get out of the courtroom and look at the moon,' he will say.

THE WOMAN IN PURPLE

On the last day of 1990, the night of the blue moon, I sat next to a soldier at dinner who told me how he learnt to stand his ground. He told me that when he was sixteen his mother bought him a Pekinese pup for his birthday. He was furious with her for buying such an unmanly dog but his mother took no notice.

'You will love her,' she said.

'And did you?' I asked.

The soldier smiled and said she was the bravest dog he had ever known. Her huge eyes quelled the fiercest dogs in the district.

'The Pekinese were guardians of the temple,' he explained. 'They warded off the invader because they had no fear. Unless they were attacked by brute force of course when they had no defence . . .'

There was once a fearless woman who used to guard the temples and preside over justice. She was respected not as an instrument of anger or retribution but as a keeper of a vision, a vision of a whole and sacred earth. We forget her sometimes, she who can speak truth to power. She who can remind us there is another kingdom where our hearts are weighed and found wanting on a pair of golden scales.

Perhaps if we left the courtroom and stopped judging ourselves for not being someone else, for not being good enough, for not being perfect, for being wrong, perhaps we might learn to respect ourselves for what we are.

Perhaps if we forgave ourselves instead of blaming others for our maiming and our lack, for our robbery and our rape, if we were then willing to let the need for brutish revenge go and that determination to be right, if we appealed to something higher in ourselves, then we might come to know her, the guardian of our wisdom and our beauty, standing behind us.

Beyond the justice of man, beyond the judicial system, beyond Court Number One, the Appeal Court and the House of Lords, stands a figure, a woman with a blindfold on. The woman who sees truth beyond the evidence that is put before her, and a moon that lights her way.

SWIMMING POOL, CENTRAL AMERICA

~~~

I am lying at the bottom of the swimming pool, behind the pink walls of a hotel where rich Guatemalans and North Americans meet at the weekends for barbecues. You find this place at the end of an avenue of eucalyptus trees leading out of town. I like to come in the week when there's no one here except a nameless man doing lengths, and let my mind float away. You've got to let out a lot of air so you can lie at the bottom of a swimming pool, to be still in all that blue. The trick is not to panic.

Karen came round yesterday. She said the boy on the corner who talks all the time has Tourette's syndrome which is why he mimics everyone going past and shouts obscenities. Karen is a psychologist from New York with big teeth and a big smile who says you can't control your death but you can control the quality of your life.

'But,' adds Mark, 'for that you have to be constantly aware of your death.'

'Yeah,' says Karen, 'but you know, sooner or later, you always get back to the little bullshit.'

Karen despairs of her job as a problem solver.

'I'm just stuck in an old useless paradigm,' she sighs and helps herself to my cholera-free guacamole.

So I told her about *The Dancing Healers*. It's a book I found last week in Dona Luisa's library amongst the airport thrillers and out-of-date guidebooks, about a psychologist from New York who goes to work on an Indian reservation in New Mexico. One day he meets a guy who says he's going to die on Tuesday.

'Don't be crazy,' says the modern-medicine-can-cure-anything-I-will-rescue-you doctor.

'I was always going to die on Tuesday,' replies the man and smiles. Then he meets an old priest who asks him if he knows how to dance.

'You must be able to dance if you are to heal people,' he says. 'I can teach you my steps but you will have to hear your own music.'

The bewildered doctor discovers in his encounter with native American Indians that the true healer is not there to fit his patients back into society but to help them recognize their dance. That the most healthy, most meaningful thing in life was not a person's function, status, nor even their family but their dance, the unique pattern they wove as they went through this changing world. And to do that he had to know his own.

'Maybe the boy on the corner is there to remind us of our madness,' said Mark.

'Maybe he's there to remind us about our grandmothers,' I added.

Mark wasn't so impressed with that interpretation. Mind you, he's not impressed with much these days. 'Don't even think about it,' he growled today as I opened my mouth to say good morning. I mean, what way is that to start the day, as if it weren't bad enough with the electricity strikes so you can't have a decent cup of coffee until 9.30?

'You've got the Hanged Man again, Charlie,' he said cheerily when we read the cards later (always in a better mood after breakfast).

Now the Hanged Man is a major arcana card in the tarot pack. It's of a man dancing an absurd jig, hanging upside down from a tree. His head is buried in the earth but out of it shines a sun. 'You will be in the Hanged Man's place until you have learned the lesson.' (Of course he gets great cards like the Magician and the Sun and it really pisses me off.)

'And what's that?' I asked grumpily.

'Waiting and sacrifice,' he said. 'You have to lose your self-respect in the world's eyes and give up your safe and comfortable position.'

'Look, I undergo major shame every time I speak Spanish,' I retorted.

This is true. Who can hold on to their self-esteem without words to protect them? I mean, I used to be an intelligent woman in England who could discuss quantum mechanics and Yojhi Yamamoto's unstructured tailoring, and now I can't even ask for tomatoes without feeling like an idiot.

'I think it's a bit deeper than that,' he said. 'I think it's about listening.'

'I will tell you something foolish,' said Karen and told us a story of some friends of hers in London who worked like slaves all year so they could take huge amounts of drugs in Goa or Colombia, somewhere lush and cheap and by the sea. 'Can you imagine *that*?' she said.

I am lying at the bottom of the hotel swimming pool (the waiters in white jackets are walking by with trays of glasses for a function, the swimmer ploughs up and down above me). And I am thinking: what would happen if those golden drug people stopped one day? What would happen if they said nirvana was not to be found in some chemical paradise but in some place they could not remember, perhaps had never known? Would they, like the Bolivian tin miner kept in his awful drudgery with the help of coca leaves, suddenly halt in the dark and remember sweet air above ground?

A friend of mine in London said to his child who ran wild amongst his luncheon party, asking questions: 'Either you watch television, or you go to bed.'

'I don't want to go to watch television,' she said.

'Then go to bed.'

'I don't want to go to sleep.'

'If you don't do what I say,' threatened the father, 'the Hoover Man will come and get you. The Policeman will take you away.'

'I'll watch television,' she said.

'Good girl,' he said. 'Now here's a lolly.'

Children know all about death; but they don't get to control the quality of their lives. That power we as adults have to learn to take for ourselves. It happens rarely because it is bordered by such ancient fears.

If I let go of the sweet things that sugared my whole life until now – the lollies, the drugs and television, telephone conversations, parties, deadlines, work, quartets on the radio, poetry in bed, those flavoured vodkas in tiny frozen glasses, island holidays, pretty carpets and polished bowls from markets all around the world, all that neurosis about being hip and fitting in, all that little bullshit – would I get to meet him too, the grim reaper with his skeleton smile? Or would I be free to run around and ask questions, just like an unquieted child?

If I let go of this geometry that held my former life together, will I find another pattern that will make sense of this one? Will I have the courage to dance my own dance when I do not even know the steps?

'Grandmother, grandmother!' yells the boy on the corner. 'All the gringas are whores!'

Grandmother, grandmother, whose nimble fingers once sewed a thousand patches to make my patchwork quilt, what secret map did you weave for me with your coloured threads?

Tell me, is this a madness we all had – to want to belong?

A child I once knew loved to dance. Loved to run wild amongst the apple trees and sea poppies and loved to hear stories told to her by women who could have been her grandmother about goblins and will-o'-the-wisps and brave men who went adventuring across the seas for their god and their dangerous queen. But she was afraid of the dark and afraid of drowning, and she was afraid of the man who would come in the night to cut off her beloved brother's thumbs.

So she behaved herself. She went to sleep for a hundred years. And in her dreaming she sought out other changelings who had been locked in turrets, and ice palaces and iron stoves by their wicked step-parents. She sought to rescue them but they turned away because they could not bear to see their own anguish.

What she did not realize was that, like the good doctor, she had to redeem herself, and it was not a charming prince but the man with scissorhands who could cut through her enchanted brambles and wake her up with a cold and perfect kiss. Only the raven man — he whose presence was kept a secret by her father, the lawyer, her grandmother, the chemist, and her great-grandfather, the engineer — could release her from the spell of happy-ever-after lotus land where death never comes, so life cannot either.

How can you help anyone if you have not healed yourself and your families' histories? How can you know true love and understanding until you have faced that which can destroy it?

I am lying at the bottom of the swimming pool and I do not fear death by drowning. I am lying in the dark and listening for a new music.

Some days I hear only the pigeons sing in their cages (ter-eu, ter-eu) and the schoolgirls drumming but today when I walked back along the dusty eucalyptus path, I heard Mark singing, his rich voice echoed in the whitewashed room, a song sung by Mercedes Sosa.

'Cambia, todo cambia.'

Everything changes.

HONDURAS: RAINTIME

~~~

. . . the boys and girls are sweet and sashaying down the street and
the air is hot and damp and the big rain slides and slips off the palm
leaves and rivers the road and spins those American cars and
everyone is waiting under the arches (I've never seen such a rain
before) and in the morning with the women selling yellow cherries
at the corners the warm velvety rain turns to steam and Mark is
lying sweating and all and writing (sort of) 'the jasmine sweetens
the streets' lying here under the fan at the hotel in La Ceiba where
we nearly didn't arrive when the plane nearly fell right out of the
sky in El Salvador but here we are here we are where the coffee
is thick as treacle and Raymond the coffee boy says he will fix us
a typical breakfast with plantains and white cheese and beans
tomorrow but now he is off dancing down by the beach 'I'm like
the wind, I don't know where I am going' he laughs and washes
the glasses with a huge amount of soap and says 'If the door isn't
open, I'll keep a drawer open for you' . . . o the boys and girls are
sweet and sashaying down the street and even the Independence
Day drummers have that Caribbean beat that reggae dance in the
marching and our hotel sign blinks red and blue through the
shutter and Mark is lying sweating and all and we are watching a
lot of cable TV on big comfortable mattresses with fine white sheets
and the daughter of a Hungarian footballer makes me a margarita
like a sorbet and we have lunch in a garden and eat conch soup and
the wind-chimes sing and the waiter gives us a fallen mango and
a taxi driver gives us a banana ('Is it twelve o'clock?' asks Mark
'More or less' he replies) and there are a lot of trees ceiba trees
banana trees palm trees all sweating (I'm surprised they stay
vertical) and the boys and girls are black and modern and wearing

short skirts and that feels good and there are no tourists and no folklorics and that feels good but the heat does not feel so good so we get on a plane a really small plane and go to the island of Roatan and stay in the Lost Paradise Hotel in a little wooden bungalow on stilts which is more expensive than La Ceiba but cooler and of course by the fabulous turquoise sea and more bendy palm trees and coconuts and broken conch shells all lying about in sandy gardens and myna birds and cockerels and white Adirondack chairs all alone on the jetty and suddenly I am beginning not to care as much as I did about the writing 'Well that makes a change' says Mark as he is coming out of another shower that day 'I mean who can write when they're sweating all the time and what am I going to do with this hair?' and I say 'I am not going to have another conversation about your hair isn't it time to eat?' . . . underneath the trees the girls are gliding past in starchy churchy frocks on giant bicycles and the boys are hanging about in the sleeping fishing boats and we are sitting in the hot slippery dark with the lanterns swinging and waiting 'What have you got to eat?' I ask the girl who is carrying the drinks 'Fish' she said 'What kind of fish?' I ask 'It's fish' She yawns 'You want rum and all?' so we are eating fish with Pepe the Mexican cultural attaché to Guatemala who has a very private joke going on between the world and him and he says that a country is not so much in its geography but in its language and when you speak it you can't help but take on the native attitude for example his family were very glad he came back from Germany when he did because he was beginning to bark at them like a dog so what about Guatemala I ask and his eyebrows shoot up in a very amused way and says all that servility was getting on his nerves all that don't be embarrassed when you say thank you, and all this *qué manda?* you know what instructions are you giving me 'I don't want to give anyone instructions, do you?' . . . oh no I just want to lie here in this hammock in the path of this sun with these aquarium fish nibbling my toes watching a big bird sail by that I think is an albatross 'It's the eagle of the sea' I say to Mark 'No it's not it's just an albatross and nothing more' he

FAREWELL CABARET, MAY 1991 – LONDON: 'IN MANY OF THE PICTURES WE LOOKED LIKE GHOSTS . . . WE HAD ALREADY STARTED TO LEAVE.'

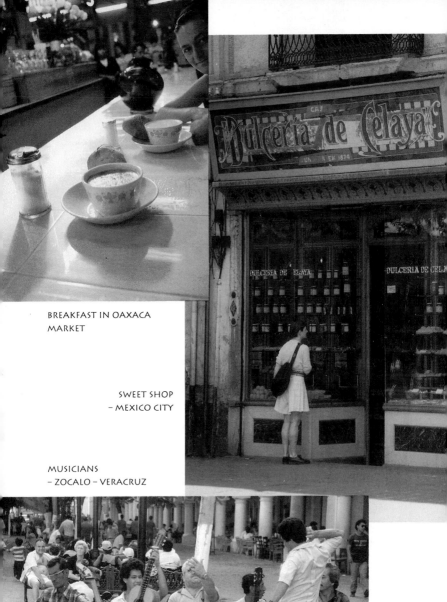

BREAKFAST IN OAXACA
MARKET

SWEET SHOP
– MEXICO CITY

MUSICIANS
– ZOCALO – VERACRUZ

ROOM WITH A VIEW – OAXACA

SINGING WITH LORITO
– GUATEMALA

WOMEN WASHING
– ANTIGUA – GUATEMALA

'O, AND ALL THOSE EMBROIDERIES!'

MONEY CHANGING
– AVENIDA AMAZONAS – QUITO

CLOUD-CAPPED VOLCANOES – GUATEMALA

ON A VERY SMALL PLANE TO THE
ISLAND OF ROATAN – HONDURAS

'IN THE EARTH AND THE RAIN
STANDS A TREE' – MEXICO

ANOTHER BREAKFAST – QUITO

HEY, HONDURAS,
I'VE ARRIVED!
– TEGUCIGALPA

LA SEÑORA CONCHA – ANTIGUA

ENGLAND V SLOVENIA,
AN AWAY MATCH

CROSSING BORDERS II – PASTO – COLOMBIA

JILL IN ECUADOR

CROSSING BORDERS III:
THE ONE-COACH TRAIN
THAT LOOKS LIKE IT'S
LOST THE REST OF ITSELF
– LA PAZ – BOLIVIA

'CHARLOTTE, WAKE UP!
LOOK AT THOSE ROCKS!'
– ALTIPLANO – BOLIVIA

'WELCOME TO CHILE –
DRUGS DESTROY MAN'
(ARE YOU SURE IT'S THE
DRUGS?)

LA VIDA BOHEMIA, WITH ANDREW – VALPARIASO – CHILE

says 'so shut up and stop naming things all the time' so I just let it be an albatross even though it's probably a frigate bird and let it fly away away with my old vocabularies and begin to speak with my body again lying on the wet white sand in the warm sea under this tree . . . I do not really want to be speaking English at Fosters' with three soldiers stationed in Belize on drug patrol 'We don't need to be there, we're a decoration' says one to me and goes on about John Major and the Fulham house prices 'Have another beer' I say and the other one tells Mark tales about scorpions in the jungle which is not a good scene with my friend with his malfunctioning hair in this climate so I say 'Let's go dancing' but we are going to a wedding first . . . no one knows who is getting married but there is a lot more beer there and giant suicidal land crabs which we try to avoid in the sandtrack now the electricity has gone and outside the swaying room on stilts an Icelandic girl with bright white hair is telling us she has given up drinking right now (she is seventeen) and that they are all drinking too early in Iceland these days at twelve or thirteen and that is terrible but Iceland is a good place only 250,000 people and hot springs and fishing but nothing much to do except for drinking really perhaps we could all go to her country and go drinking together well I say I don't really want to think about snow right now or writing or birds or Mark's hair because I am getting into the jeep and the jeep is wet with rain and there is an empty road ahead and banana trees waving and that feels good and I have got on my black dancing dress and I am going to dance in French Harbour until 3 a.m. and the rain can wake me up if it likes and I could tell you about the other places in Honduras but that's enough of Honduras now because I am not talking I'm flying and the stars are shining right down ah to the velvety sea the sea that rocks us slowly back to somewhere else before our languages separated us in our several geographies our bodies from our souls . . .

I WISH YOU WERE HERE BUT YOU ARE ANYWAY OR RAINY LAST NIGHT IN ANTIGUA, GUATEMALA WITH NO ELECTRICTY

For Bjorn

your footsteps left an echo
in this broken lonely room
I know you walk the earth
I know the moon I see
You witness also

And I am many houses
Many songs and many rooms
I must remember not to stay here
Not to linger long
Casting shadows on my heart
Which yearns to sing

I must remember all the gifts
You bring
That where the heart beats
To its natural time
Dances strong and loud its song

Something infinite is touched
And carried on ...

LEAVING ENGLAND PART TWO

~~~

We went back to England.

I went back for my mother's sixtieth birthday and to celebrate her recovery from cancer. I went back to go to the dentist and to sell this book and oh there were lots of reasons why I came back to England in October, in Fashion Week, with the falling leaves but mostly it was to realize that I had truly left. Once you go, you see, you can't come back. At least you can't come back to the same place.

I said I left England because it was full of ghosts. I felt hemmed in by my history, by my country's history, the dead past that everyone clung to like drowning men to timbers of a broken ship. Unwilling to leave, to let go of that life. But I did not know before that I had left my own ghost floundering there.

My old friends met me. They were not ghosts. They had not changed. Their lives had remained much the same: they went to the same places, drank the same drinks, the same walls held them in their coloured arms, the same company smiled at them across familiar tables as the Number Seven bus still turned the corner of Westbourne Park Road each day. 'And your sister, how is she?' asked the Indian man at my old corner store there. 'Still living in Hong Kong,' I said, as if nothing had happened in the last four months.

But ah, it had. I had changed. I had sat on different buses, and hurtled through different landscapes. I had drunk wine not grown under a European sun. I had met strangers each day (and they not always smiling), and no familiar wall held me each night. These things had altered me.

So it was my old ghost that met me here, the part of me that lingered on, not wishing to be disappeared completely.

It's a strange thing to battle with your own ghost, especially one you were quite fond of.

She put up a good fight.

As soon as I landed, the phone rang at Andy's house where I was staying. Hardly had I been in the door, had time to run a bath, and sit down to some scrambled eggs before that well-known edgy voice was on the other line.

'Hi, Charlotte, how are you heard you were back now this is the Features Department of the *Evening Standard* and we were wondering if you could write an editorial for us on supermodels. For tomorrow.'

Supermodels? Jeeeeeesus! Like I've been thinking a lot about Linda Evangelista in Guatemala.

'I've been away for four months,' I said. 'I'm not sure that I'm really into the flow any more.'

'That doesn't matter,' she said. 'It will give a better perspective.'

There was a pause. She had a point. I could write that article standing on my head there and then. Something like adrenaline grabbed my guts, and I had the taste of anticipation known to all the addicts and gamblers in the world. Ha, sweet temptation.

There was a pause, I hesitated. I was the only person who could possibly write it she said. The snake slithered into view. I held the shiny apple. Money in the bank and a nice headline. My scrambled eggs were getting cold. I took a deep breath.

'No, thank you,' I said. 'I've only just got back. Thanks for thinking of me.'

Twit! said my ghost.

'Remember,' said Mark in hot and sweaty Merida when we said goodbye, 'to leave gracefully. It's easy to be holier-than-thou.'

So I didn't preach to my old ghost, I went to meet her on her own home ground. I looked up at my old flat (it looked empty), I visited my cats (they looked fat). I told my father he was a bastard for not saying goodbye to me before.

'I didn't want you to go,' he said.

'Why didn't you just say that then?'

We smiled. I liked seeing my parents but I did not disturb any of the black clothes I had put in black rubbish bags in their garage.

Eventually I wrote some articles. I went to interview a woman who lived in a purple house. She did not want to discuss her paint schemes. She wanted to talk about Chile where she said you can watch the fishermen all day and not have to do anything. 'I find doing nothing very creative, don't you?' she said.

My old friends met me. Some of them shouted at me for changing. Some did not want to see me, some saw only the ghost of me, and others stared at me and I them, and we smiled sadly, as a gap yawned between us as wide as the Atlantic Ocean. Some of them were pregnant. My old girlfriend was pregnant and smoking and my sister was pregnant and not eating. I rose up in fury at this denial.

'Oh, they will survive,' they said. 'Babies are very strong, you know. They take everything from you.'

Tell me about living, I thought, tell me about giving, tell me we have a choice. My ghost told me to shut up and stop making a fuss.

I lived in Andy's basement room and watched the people go past the window in grey and black, moving through the mists, wrapped against the cold and damp. This is an enchanted land, I thought. This is a nursery land. And I don't believe in these stories of happy ever after and nicely behaved complicity, thank you for having me. Anymore.

I went to see a film: it was called *Meeting Venus*. My old friend railed in a Chinese restaurant afterwards that the love scene in the hotel was absurd. All that fumbling, he said, with the light off and the Giorgio Armani suit on. People are not like that. But I thought, O mirror, mirror on the wall, who is the fairest of them all, that is *exactly* how we are with our passion and our intimacy. And especially you, my celibate friend, who runs so far from the stickiness, the untidiness, the nakedness of love, so far that you shelter with a woman, and do not lie with the men you desire.

I went to see a film: it was called *Truly Madly Deeply*. It was full of ghosts. Real ones. But the most true, mad and deep thing in it was a poem by Pablo Neruda recited by the hero-ghost in clumsy Spanish, and the angry outburst by a Chilean exile in a London restaurant. And a man who said nothing but threw white birds unexpectedly into the air.

I went to see a film: it was called *Jacob's Ladder*, in which some Vietnam veterans were seeing visions of hell. In the end the old chiropractor, mender of bones and structures, tells the hero-in-limbo that angels and beasts are the same thing. Good and evil are the same. It all depends upon the seeing. We do have a choice.

My old friends met me and sometimes I didn't want them to.

'I am cooking some supper,' shouted Andy's flatmate from the stair, 'I've invited some people you like. Will you be in?'

'I don't know,' I said, resenting her control, liking her generosity.

You are very rude and ungrateful said my ghost. I was beginning to dislike this proprietorial, vain, know-it-all shade.

Get lost, I said. And turned on the answering machine.

I stared out of the window, and watched the big plane trees move in the wind. I thought. I could be angry. I could be clear. I could go into every reason why I disagreed with what I saw. I could be sorry for my spikiness, explain why I refused all these invitations. I could say why I shut my door.

My ghost was disappointed. Hey, Charlotte, relax, come out and play!

I am not here to relax, I said.

You are a real bore, she said. What happened that you got to be so dull and so unsociable?

I don't want to fight with you or anyone else.

Why not? she said.

I didn't reply. I just walked away. I left the city.

I went to see Andy's parents on the Sussex Downs and went walking with them in an ancient oak forest. I went to see Mark's family in High Wycombe and took magic mushrooms. I laughed and I laughed. When I sat down to supper with them in front of what looked like a fluorescent salad (Bridget has a wicked sense of humour) I couldn't eat a thing.

'This egg is unhappy!' I declared. 'It did not want to happen. This lettuce is not supposed to be there. It's from the wrong season. And what are these?'

'They are noodles, Charlotte,' said Bridget with a totally straight face.

'Noodles! Oh no!' screamed Mark and fell off his chair.

'Why aren't they in China?' I asked and howled with laughter until the tears ran down my face.

My old editor said to me (he was wise as he was vain), 'Never apologize, never explain.'

I try not to any more. I just try to walk away and do something else instead. I guess if you can stand by what you write in a newspaper, you can stand by how you are. Even if it makes you feel mean and misunderstood, and mostly alone. I think it is better than pretending to enjoy something when you don't or saying something you don't believe and being a party girl for the sake of your ego. For that is all a ghost is sometimes, a rootless ego in need of praising. Or just in need.

My ghost came back to me in Bolivia where I did not expect her. Andy brought her in a suitcase. She was very subtle up there in the Andes and played every emotional trick in the book. Andy doesn't love you as you are, he loves me she said, and pouted childishly. And so I was forced to let him go, my oldest friend, my last spar. The one who always met me and made me feel safe and sweet in a rock-a-bye land.

It's time to grow up, I told my ghost. Time to say goodbye.

Once you go you cannot come back, at least not to the same place. This decision requires vision and a certain ruthlessness. Because to live entirely in the present, that is never refuged in the past or afraid of the future, wrapped up in October mists, you have to let go of everything, and everyone. Like leaves from the falling trees.

*   *   *

I am a tree, bare and naked in another autumn, in another land. I am no shelter. No children hide in me, play games of conkers, steal apples, swing from my branches. No, not even that little English child in a yellow coat who loved me so, who brought me presents and hid them shyly at my roots. Ghosts flee from me now.

I am a tree. I transplanted myself. I drink a different rain, and my roots feed from a different earth, and my arms hold out and supplicate to different gods. England was my nursery garden.

But I left it. Long ago.

3

ECUADOR

QUITO: QUICKSILVER CITY 1
'I REMOVE'

~~~

Once upon a rainy night in Guatemala there was a Swedish man who came to dinner. I cooked him a cake, a pineapple upside-down cake. The man's name was Bjorn Blomstrand which means Bear Flowerbeach in English, and he made us laugh, the dancing bear: we laughed so much we jumped right out of our moods and the rain, and I in my laughter completely forgot that I put my cake the wrong way up and had not added any leavener so that it was an unrisen thing, and not upside down at all. We were talking about the writer Milan Kundera that night and so I christened the evening 'The Unbearable Heaviness of the Pineapple Downside-Up Cake'.

'It doesn't matter,' said Bjorn, 'because it still tastes as good.'

My salty soul loves the sea but sometimes I cannot stay just where I am comfortable, where I want to belong. Sometimes we have to be turned upside down and inside out, in order to see the world from a higher place, differently and more completely. My salty soul loves the sea: it loves to swim in pools, walk through the damp forest, sleep in the wild, the wet and hollow places. But my spirit also longs to be free, to live in the upper air, its true element, the cold bare mountain, amongst the dry pines and the snow, in the solitude and the silence. Oh, how my jealous soul clings to its familiar threatened ground and how I long to stay with it.

But I cannot see from this warm valley.

Quito is my first city of the south. Across the Equator, the great divide in the lands of all change, everything is the wrong way up. I am standing on my head, the salt comes out of the pepper pot and the moon smiles upside down. The sky is the colour of quicksilver, and the lights of the city flicker like a god's runway. In a high hotel room I think I am at sea: as the mists descend in waves, I hear a thin foghorn moaning and a man ringing a bell. The buildings blink like lighthouses to warn the hidden aeroplanes. I feel I am shipwrecked in my new geography but when I look up into the shattering light, into the morning, I think I have never seen such beautiful mountains. I want to go there. I want to go there.

But first I await the messenger, my mercurial god, who will help me turn this base metal into spun gold, who will show me the crack between the worlds: the gap in the sky.

I am being changed.

I am in a city of transformation. In my tower room, while Mark paints, I sit in bed, dizzy with this new altitude. I read a book called *Iron John*. I learn about metal from a poet-blacksmith called Robert Bly. I see how I was once a child of copper, a conductor of rage from my mother and my father (and all their unsung generations) and forgot how to defend my own kingdom. I see how I need the iron of the warrior and the gold of the king. And the magic of the Silver Woman, she who walks the skies, the woman of poetry, fishes, dancer, star and legend.

I am being changed: north to south, down to up, red to blue, closed to open, to let the Silver Woman in. At night in my sleeping, the Queen of Heaven comes to change the circuits, to tune me. I am a crystal radio. My head is full of electricity and my eyes burn in dark bruised sockets. I lay awake and I remembered this . . .

In that mushroom trip in England, I dived into the sacred well we visited you and I in Mexico. I found a night-blue stone there, cracked with stars, a lapis lazuli. I flew up to find you in the air. I flew through the crack of the two worlds, like a door it opened and I soared up through the blue sky, up into the purple layer where you reigned in that great temple. I carried the changeling stone in my mouth . . .

In Quito, mirror city, city of equilibrium, where nothing is too salt or too sweet, I am learning to balance upside down, guided by invisible strings. In a dream a magician comes out of a burned coffin in a dark house and teaches me to handstand on its rim without moving. In a reading of the tarot cards, Mark turns all my masculine cards on their hard heads (Judgement, Emperor, the Trickster my cleverness, the King of Swords my father, the Five of Swords my defeat, my weak coppery Knight, my old World).

In the Hotel Quito for breakfast, the Indian waitresses with gold glass beads and jewel-coloured skirts laugh like bells and pour abundant coffee in our never-finished cups. And they move their hands and pull the air as if tugging us like marionettes, up the spiral staircase, away into the garden.

In Quito, the holy alchemist's city, the city of I remove, I cut the old strings, the old webs that bind me and surrender my spirit to a higher player, like a puppet, like the acrobat who practises with a harness and a prayer before he knows how to fly without falling.

RED JAGUAR

~~~

'Well, that's great, Pat, but am I going to meet anyone?'

Pat the Palmist was reading my hand. We were all sitting in my empty flat and I was about to leave for Mexico via New York. The future was looking good according to her predictions but there was no love going on.

She stared into the runway of my palm. 'O yes,' she said. 'There is someone.' And she looked kind of faraway.

'He's not from England.'

'Yes,' she said.

Jesus, I thought, it sounds as though he's beaming in from Mars.

'Pat!' I said loudly, trying to bring her back to the reality plane. 'Where am I going to meet him?'

'There's an ancient monument,' she said. 'And a cave very high up.' And she started to draw indecipherable symbols on a piece of paper. 'You'll meet him by a sacred site. Like a temple.'

Fiesta

I am drinking a very large sangria in the Café Express and the men in pleated white shirts are greeting each other and throwing their hands up into the air. A man with a wooden leg clip-clops in a *carozza* past the open front door and a policeman is waving a lighted truncheon in the warm darkness and there is a society wedding at the church opposite and a young man in a morning suit, very handsome, leans up against the telephone kiosk and the little gardenia sellers are running in and out, in and out of the crowd with their trays and the hot damp air is filled with the smell of the waxy flowers and the traffic fumes and the sounds of the marimba bands playing in the square. I am in Merida, Mexico and watching the world go by.

I am staying in the Hotel Trinidad whose lazy corridors are filled with paintings and grey stripey cats and yellow basket chairs. In the mornings I sit by a swimming pool with drowned dragonflies and in the afternoons when the tropical rains fall I type in a room off the courtyard with a rusty fridge filled with bottles of dead water, which I share with two Cuban poets who smoke lung-wrenching cigarettes and are in Mexico for a conference on post-modernism.

'O you are a poet too!' they declared with delight, and talk to me about Ezra Pound and existentialism.

But by night I like to watch the world go by. I like to dress up and go out and celebrate. Something is opening up in me: something that felt so shut up and closed in the mountains of Guatemala, and now is coming alive in this flat fearless land, in this fiesta city. I walk past the plaza where the lovers sit in the white curved seats called *confidenciales*, and the families ride round in tricycles trailing coloured balloons in their wake, where everyone dances under the trees: young or old and the men in panama hats with bold Mayan faces, and the women in embroidered dresses with flowers in their shiny hair are walking together and laughing.

'It is time,' I write dramatically in my notebook, 'to embrace the masculine will and the penetrative force that is not rape or domination but a searching out and reactivating liberator of the earth's riches.'

Perhaps I'll meet the faraway man at a temple here, I wonder to myself.

'Are you a poet?' asked a young boy who sits down next to me. He was good-looking, about seventeen, with dreamy eyes. Quite drunk but I didn't care. I was in a good mood.

'Yes,' I said and smiled.

'So am I.'

Jesus, I thought, everyone in this city is a poet.

'Do you know there are three ages in ancient Mexico? The age of the Eagle, the age of the Jaguar and the age of the Snake.'

Well, I said, I had seen the eagle that descends from the sky to pick up the snake of the earth in the Mexican flag but no, I said, I didn't know anything about jaguars.

The Temple of the Magician

I climb aboard a bus where a man is blowing a trumpet and another is singing, and I go to meet Mark off the plane from Guatemala City. He is waving through the glass partition and smiling, wearing a new panama hat. And I am so happy to see him.

We go travelling together in the Yucatán, on swaying buses with the people who smell of warm earth sweetened by rain, through this flat land that is the colour of avocadoes, past the cactus fields and the jungle gardens and the houses with conical roofs of thatched palm leaves, past the ruins where the iguanas sleep. We swim in a sacred well in the turquoise water where the sunlight spirals like a spotlight and the roots of the trees above hang down like women's hair, and we stay in a blue hotel where old sepia photographs show how once there were giant phallic mushrooms surrounding the pyramids until prudish white explorers threw them away. We climb the steps of the magician's temple, and I get terrible vertigo for the first time in my life. But when I stand up at the top with my back leaning against the warm stone, and I see the swallows flitting in and out, in and out of the eyes of the temple and I survey the oceanic forest below me, I think, haven't I been here before? Don't I recognize this place from somewhere?

'Do you mind if I stay with you? I feel safer with other gringoes.'

'We are not gringoes,' I said.

He was a North American youth: a student brain chemist. He was pale and covered in mosquito repellent. His camera was broken. He said he hated every Mexican city he had been to because of the horrible poverty.

'Where are you from?' I asked.

'New York.'

'Well, the poverty in New York is far worse than in Merida.'

'But there are rich people there.'

'There are rich people in Mexico,' said Mark.

'It's not the same.'

'So why did you bother to come here?' I asked.

'I wanted to take photographs of the Indians in San Cristóbal de las Casas.'

'How would you like to be photographed like a practically extinct animal?' snarled Mark.

'No wonder your camera broke,' I added.

'It was for the weaving, really,' he explained. 'Because soon there won't be any left.'

We stared at him, at the man who would be a brain chemist.

'I can't think why,' I said.

We walked to the bus and three Mexican girls walked past and giggled.

'Why are they laughing at me?' he asked us. 'Why am I so funny? You know, I really get so paranoid here. People always seem to be laughing at me. It really makes me feel uncomfortable.'

'What do you think they feel like when you point your camera at them?' asked Mark.

Perhaps you should ask yourself that question when you laugh at Mexicans in your own country, I thought.

'I hope he wasn't the person Pat had in mind,' I whispered to Mark and we climbed on the bus.

'I don't think so,' he laughed.

On our way back to Merida we went to the site of Chichen Itzá, and we were so late the guard let us in free. We tramped across the wet grass and I took a picture of Mark standing on top of the High Priest's temple in the falling dusk, the temple where the snakes run down the steps and there is a red jaguar throne inside. He stood at the top and lifted his arms up: one to shield his eyes and the other to point right across the forest. I went inside the temple and stared into the eyes of the red jaguar, the jaguar with its emerald eyes and its teeth of flint, the red jaguar that is kept behind bars.

Meeting Marko

I have just arrived in Cuenca, Ecuador. It is November. I am changing hotels this morning because I have decided that life is too short to sit in a dark hotel room feeling lonely and locked up. I have made a decision that I do not want to be in splendid isolation for the rest of my life. I am opening the doors, I am making a space, I am inviting you into my house. I go and have breakfast in a coffee house and write up a story I heard in Quito about three travelling puppeteers in Argentina.

'Hello,' said a woman. 'Where are you from?'

'England,' I said and smiled. 'What do you do here?'

'I am a teacher,' she replied, 'but at night my husband and I make puppets. We are puppeteers.'

'O look!' I said. 'I am just writing about that in my notebook.'

Today is a magical day in a magical city. On my way back to the hotel I see a poster for an exhibition and a 'Ceremonial Event' with a strange space figure on it. 'It's a happening in Cuenca,' I think. 'How strange. I must go to that this evening.'

For lunch I go to a Mexican restaurant and write up about the temple of snakes I went to six weeks ago in the Yucatán.

'Hello,' says the restaurant owner. 'Where are you from?'

'England,' I say and smile.

He is from Mexico City and he tells me about the ancient Mayan music that is playing on the tape. It's from the Equinox Festival at Chichen Itzá.

'O look!' I say. 'I am just writing about that in my notebook.'

It is a magical day.

A man comes in. He is very tall and dark. He goes to sit by the window.

The students are talking at the next table, Americans. The man is trying to impress the girl with his great opinions about film. She is looking glazed and somewhere else.

'Yes,' he is saying, 'but *which* Bergman do you like best?'

I sigh and look over at the man by the window who is talking to the owner's wife in Spanish. 'Come and talk to me,' I think and continue to write about the temple.

'Would you like to come to my show?' says a voice.

Tall man. Green eyes. Great smile. It's the space-age invitation.

'I'd love to,' I say. 'I was coming to that anyway.'

'Are you from England?' he asks.

'Yes,' I say. 'Where are you from?'

'Slovenia.'

'*Where*?'

'Slovenia,' he says and laughs. 'I'm sorry, I don't normally attack people like this but I had to talk to you.'

'O I wanted you to,' I say and laugh too. 'Would you like some beer?'

His name is Marko. He left his books and his clothes in a street in a city in what was once Yugoslavia and went to Patagonia with his camera.

'I am travelling north,' he says.

'I am travelling south,' I say, 'to Tierra del Fuego. How appropriate that we meet on the equator.'

We talk for three hours: about deserts and Celts and violet wine and a place he knows in the Andes, very high up, which you can reach by horseback and see a condor fly each day into a cave. We talk about *Alice in Wonderland* and giving everything up in 1991, this back-to-front mirror year that he says is the year of the Devil.

'They call me the *sacerdote* here, the priest,' he says. 'But I am fed up of living like a monk. Pick a card.'

I pick the Queen of Hearts.

'Is that a good card?' I ask. 'The red Queen?'

He laughs and rumples my hair. 'See you tonight,' he says and walks away.

'What's yours?' I shout after him.

He turns and takes a card from his top pocket and waves it: it's the Joker.

Equinox

'O I know where I've seen this forest before,' I said excitedly to Mark. 'And that jaguar, and all the birds, and the temple and those twin snakes.'

We were sitting in Valladolid on our last night before returning to Merida, drinking a strong anise and honey drink called Xabentum. It is ten o'clock and there is a funfair on the other side of the square, full of sweetcorn stalls and tortilla stands and fairy lights that swing from the trees.

'Do you think our imaginations can become our reality?' I asked.

'What do you mean?' he said.

'I mean, if we explored our magical lands enough, the places we see in our meditations and in our dreams and when we are on mushrooms – do you think one day the worlds would just cross over, so there wouldn't be a gap or a glass bridge or anything? It would just be our everyday reality.'

'What reality?' said Mark and stared into me with his obsidian eyes.

'Are you Alice?' asks the gallery owner.

'No,' I reply. 'I'm Charlotte.'

I'm walking around Marko's exhibition waiting for the show to begin. His paintings are of strange gods and animals and tracks and symbols. I am thinking, haven't I seen these somewhere before?

'Shall we go?' says a voice behind me.

Tall man. Green eyes. Great smile.

'But your performance . . .' I say, pointing to the audience.

'If they really want to see it, they will stay,' he replies. 'I am full of electricity today. Let's go and celebrate our meeting. Life is a fiesta, *puta madre*.'

As we walk down the steps, I catch sight of the first painting of the exhibition, I hadn't noticed it before. It is called Equinox. It's of a red temple with two snakes that fly up into the air like birds.

'That's the temple at Chichen Itzá!' I exclaim.

'Yes,' he says. 'I drew it last week in that restaurant. I was sitting just where you were sitting at lunch.'

'It's a great temple, isn't it?'

'I don't know,' he says and looks into my eyes. 'I've never been to Mexico.'

THE ENCHANTED CITY
OF CUENCA

~~~

There is a magical hour in Cuenca: follow me. It is dusk in December and everyone is hurrying home, past the market streets and the swinging lamps that shine and spit in the falling day. The tinsel sellers and the Baby Jesus sellers whisper their bargains as you walk round every corner – Aguirre, Torres, Correro, the streets begin to melt. Women collecting jars of yoghurt, men stitching hats in the panama shops, the bright skirts hanging from the rafters. O all the colours and the smell of popcorn and roast pork from the corner stores, and everyone packing up boxes and babies on their backs, rushing past, a man with a squirrel on a lead, a couple sitting patiently in the back of a banana lorry, rushing past, down the steps, towards the buses (the river runs silently on a bed of stones through the emptying city) and a man sleeps oblivious in the emerald grass of the park, under a perfectly sculpted tree, disappeared in rum.

This is a noisy town. When I arrived one blue morning a week ago a cortège of motorcycles screamed past me and a riot of students ran and hid behind closing shutters, followed by a tank and tear gas. I went into the cathedral (its towers bright as lapis) to find peace but I did not find peace there. As the Indian women knelt devoutly in their childish skirts of pink and orange and whispered their prayers like bees, they held their babies close to them and a man roared like a trapped tiger: I believe in God, I believe in God, over and over again and recited a service in the absence of a priest.

I walk swiftly past the beggars under the arches. I am on a

mission. I am buying flowers for Gregory (black-blue pansies and cornflowers from the lovely flower market). We are leaving tomorrow. I am buying medicine for Mark (he has just arrived), I am buying myself a beer (I am writing a letter to Blanche in a strange hotel with a courtyard where the parrot will not talk and the Andean singers with long black hair have long silent breakfasts and invisible travelling salesmen knock at my door in the night). I am on a mission, walking past. It is good to keep moving in this city otherwise you might just get stuck.

'O you're escaping from reality,' said the Californian in the El Dorado café (the shutters are down, they are expecting another riot).

'No,' I said, 'we are not escaping.'

'And anyway,' snarled Mark (he was not feeling sociable), 'what is reality?'

'Reality,' said Lisa (whose real name is Phyllis and once Cally until she went to Colombia and discovered Cali was a drug capital. 'I just call her Cuenca,' said her quiet husband ruefully). 'Reality is the bug that bit me in the Galapagos. Look!' Lisa shows us her reality bite and says I have to have a massage with Alex in the El Dorado sauna. 'He had my legs in the air, I mean I am *totally* naked and he kisses me three times on the forehead. Have you ever had such a massage?'

No, we said, we hadn't.

'Anyway what's to do in Quito?' She was leaving tomorrow.

'Whatever you want or nothing at all,' replied Mark and suggested forcefully that perhaps travelling wasn't always seeking amusement on the outside.

'Oh,' drawled Lisa/Phyllis/Cally/Cuenca. 'My inner world is so rich I can't stand myself.'

We are rushing past and not standing still, living in a blue hotel now where the maids bring us roses and little chocolate biscuits and leave cards that say 'Good night' on our pillows. In the mornings I like to drink coffee and eat cheesecake in an Austrian coffeehaus, run by a fiery blonde Austrian woman (with her four blonde children), and in the evenings eat a plate of spicy chicken at the Polleria Colombiana, roasted on a spit with beetroot and pale maize. Sometimes we go dancing to African music in strangers' houses, taken by Gregory. We spend a lot of time with Gregory whom I met in an ice-cream parlour, in his dark Parisian attic with swinging ham and bottles of wine and rusty flowers and poetry books and strong marijuana and O this is all just too bohemian to be *believed*. Gregory takes us up into the cloud forest to a secret waterfall, and we climb through the mossy undergrowth, grabbing hold of roots and moist earth and walking with naked feet across slippery mossy stones and lying under a hot blue sky with the grass tickling bare white skin, and the smell of wild rose and eucalyptus leaves, and a rock lying on my belly connecting me to this sacred earth. Maybe no one came here before, except for god, and stood in this pure icy water. I feel I could stay here for ever, sitting on this ancient branch, standing in this well of stone, leaves and moss in my hair, damp skin smelling of rain.

Gregory takes photographs of us and reads French poets in the square one Sunday and we sing and listen to jazz and dance in his attic that is so French and so bohemian, and he plays the flute on the back of a pick-up truck and smiles so happily underneath his African hat, when we come back from a week in the south. We eat ice cream and we tease each other and he is so romantic, I don't think it is quite real, all this attic-style and buying the waitresses flowers. I think he is in another country, locked in another forest. Scared of invasion. I have a dream in which Mark and I are standing on a mountain in a different land and Gregory cannot join us, unless he dives deep into a scarlet lake, to be purple in between our white and our gold.

We go to Cajas with two Swiss brothers to four thousand metres where the air is as thin as a whistle and the eagles cry amongst the boulders and the lakes look like little pocket mirrors in a giant's overcoat. The still water reflects the earth and the sky. They say the Virgin Mary appeared in this bare valley. They say the ancient Inca gold is still buried in these silent mountains.

'The Ecuadorian Indians drink a lot and beat their wives,' one of the brothers tells me (what do you *do* in this place?).

'That sounds like Europe,' says Mark, and stares out of the jeep window.

'The European woman cannot love properly,' the other remarks. He has come to find a Latin woman with a soul and forgiveness in her eyes.

'Perhaps you should find your own,' I suggest, and stare out of the jeep window.

'They say the ancient gold is still buried here,' he continues. 'We can be archaeologists and just dig it up.'

Leave it as it is! I say, do not dig it up. Do not take it away, lock it up in a museum or a rich man's house where it does not belong. Leave the sacredness in its appointed place, like your heart and your soul within. Go find those first and see if you would love another man to rob them, in the name of art and history.

We eat trout by a river in silence, the rain falls. The wind moves the eucalyptus trees. The brothers are bored and go home to their safe mountain. Gregory does not surface. We are walking past and moving on. We do not stay in Cuenca. Suddenly on Christmas Eve, we change direction in the airport, say goodbye to Gregory, the attic and the rushing streets. We do not go to the beach. We are going somewhere else.

THE VALLEY OF THE SUN

~~~

Southern Ecuador

We descended into the sacred valley where everyone lives for a long, long time. The little bus ran down the green mountains into a warm dusk of singing frogs and sugarcane fields and flickering fireflies. We walked up a lane of dripping leaves and came to a house where Indian women were making a tea of flowers in the kitchen and carried babies on their hips. A black cat sat on my lap as we ate a late supper. Someone rocked in a hammock outside on the terrace and a small green parrot teased a russet dog. That night we were given a *cabaña* made of creaky bamboo with gaps big enough to see the moon, and we slept the sleep of tired children.

I am sitting naked in a little stone room in the darkness with the steam of eucalyptus branches rising and I can hear the sounds of breakfast being made: the cool yoghurt in earthenware bowls, the fried plantain and corn and sliced papaya and lime. We are taking San Pedro today, the holy cactus juice from the mountain. I stand on my balcony by the drying coffee beans watching the men working in the fields. There is an owl beckoning me in between the sunflowers, and a condor spiralling up into the cathedral of clouds, up up up. I see the tribe, the ancestors and the ancient city in the mountain, in the mountain shaped like a woman's body with a man's head. I fall into earth.

I fall into green.

The sun chases its shadow across the fields, a donkey laughs, the women walk back from the river. Mark roars: he grows enormous like a giant warrior, and then he throws his legs over a chair and laughs again like a king returned, the insects buzz around my head, the turkey cackle, the rain is falling, the women in the house are making loaves of bread and the babies are asleep under the papaya tree. Mark spits like a snake, I dance in a spiral. A woman gives me a massage and across the plains of Africa I chase the locusts away.

This world is made of glass.

The donkeys bring the stones back up the hill and the snake of fire is still on the hill, and I spit out the poison of that metal world as the poison of the cactus runs like fire through my body, and in the garden the sunflowers turn their heads and the invisible river chuckles over stones and the light shines on the stones between the cactus gate by our balcony and the owl is still winking in the garden between the shivering green corn and the hummingbirds still hover and the hornets go away and the bee pollinates the flowers and the bird brings back the egg, and the cows come down the hill to be milked and the horses gallop home up the lane and the moth circles the lamp and in the far far mountains that are the colour of amethyst now in this endless day I seek out I seek out and the sun falls down and Orion chases the sky and I let everything go to hear the whole valley singing and the moon turns upside down and smiles at me because the children sleep with the lions and tigers on this golden day . . .

GREGORY
~~~

Cuenca, December 1991

O Gregory, Gregory. You showed us cloud forests and waterfalls that no one else knew; you broke your shower when I telephoned you, you broke your chair; you broke these things. We came in a taxi to fetch you but you were not ready, you followed on later.

We sang among friends in your flat of the night with its candles and shadows; we sang harmonies from the top of our heads at the top of our voices in your flat at the top of the Paris Hotel. You sang the bass line. And sometimes you played on the saxophone; then no one could sing along.

I massaged you, feet first, then your back, you do not have to take off your shirt; and I talked of controlling mothers to an English girl, and of not taking responsibility for other people's madness. I talked. You let me talk. We spoke together another time of men, of women, of boundaries.

Charlotte and I left for a week to a breathing hilly place in the south, full of green and bamboo huts where people live long. You came to me there when I had drunk the juice of the cactus of the doorway and you wanted to make love with me. Charlotte dreamed of you and the red red sea. Why will you not show your passions? You would not cross the red sea yet.

We came in a yellow taxi and you were not ready. I cannot come to the sea, so I came with Charlotte to the flat of a friend full of light and something like home in the town of I remove; and I broke the lock of the door to the balcony. I was trying too hard to open the door. I opened it with the wrong key; it came open but the lock shattered; I had to replace it. There were times when I wanted to make love to you. I did not say this to you clearly. You did not push me away when I held you; you did not push me away.

You took us to parties and showed us your beautiful dance in the cool cool high small town of Cuenca; your cool dance full of strategy. Why will you not show your passions? Why did I not say that I wanted to lie with you and run my hands over your slim boy's body?

Everyone was cool and mellow at the parties; though didn't we all suck rather too desperately on the one joint of grass that was going around? You danced a beautiful dance.

You beat me at a game called Go and talked to me of Zen and T'ai Chi. And you would not come yet and you would not cross the red sea.

That day I stayed in bed and felt myself splitting. That splitting in the middle of me that is not happiness. I have been angry with you that you brought this out in me. We have to be clear, I said to Charlotte. I can be clear, she said to me. I do not wish to be cool. I know the desperation of being cool. I can be cool and cold as can be when I'm six feet under.

In the airport awaiting our plane to Quito, we asked you to the table. Please could your friend wait downstairs? We need to speak to you alone. I feel discomfort at what I must say. I need a joint, you said. Yesterday I felt spent and exhausted. It was linked to my friendship with you.

That day I saw you in the town of I remove we looked at each other. I was distracted by you and interrupted my plan to order mineral water and see if anything happened. You looked at me once or twice. I smiled. You did not smile. You did not respond. I went shortly upon my way.

When we met again in Cuenca you recognized me but I did not recognize you.

Long before we met, when I first arrived in this land, I painted a picture of a man in a hat dressed in blue and standing on the top of a rock inside an open door with the hand of fate ushering him through.

I took a picture of you on a rock dressed in blue with a hat on at the top of a waterfall in the Cloud Forest.

I do not think this is the end, this departure in the airport, you with tears inside, Charlotte and I clear, but a part of me wanting to make love to you. Why does vulnerability bring this out in me?

Yesterday, spent and low, I stayed in bed. I slept a fitful sleep in the afternoon and dreamed of an old lover, a Chinese dragon like you. I played something like father to him for one year and a half, and denied my own needs; he was a child wandering and without a home; he made his home within me. From the dream emerged all the old frustration and the anger I had felt at denying myself a lover who could equal the love I had to give, who could equal my passion, and whom I could allow to give back to me. I felt glad when this man disappeared from the dream. In my waking life I left him suddenly one morning when I knew I could give no more.

So I could not come to the sea with you, Gregory, though I knew you would be hurt; I must wait for you to come to me. You will come if you are meant to come. You said you thought we were like birds of the night. But I am no vampire. I drain myself when I give too much and now I must be centred. I must pay attention to my own needs.

I know there is passion in you, Gregory. I know the intensity and the depth of our rapid friendship moved your emotions just as it moved mine. I do not think this is the end. Will you cross the red sea?

GREGORY'S RETURN

So Gregory you came and then you left
You did not cross the red sea
At least not with me.
I'm glad I told you of the sex you brought up in me.
Yesterday a new friend Amy
Spoke of shame balls;

They hit you on a sudden
When you break taboos and speak of hidden things
And then are greeted by the stone face of denial
I had none of this —
I quit the shame
And keep the balls.

LETTERS TO MEN

~~~

Jane's Flat, Quito, Ecuador

26.12.1991

Dearest Bjorn,
At this precise moment I am sitting in the bed of a friend called
Jane whom I met in Quito several weeks ago, and who has kindly
lent Charlotte and me the use of her flat whilst she is galavanting
around the Galapagos with her mother, who is a Lady. Charlotte
is in the next room bleaching her moustache and shaving her legs.
More of Jane's friends, an English couple, are in the third bedroom
sleeping (I think). Jane has a huge flat. And a lot of friends.

We totally forgot about Christmas and thought yesterday was
the 24th until the taxi-driver corrected us on the way to get
something to eat. 'Why are all the shops shut?' I asked. 'They
always close on Christmas Day,' he said. In England, I'm sure
anybody would have thought I was mental, but there was no sign
of cynicism in his voice or face at all. Charlotte and I were quite
thrilled at having forgotten the anathema, but we still treated
ourselves last night to a wonderful meal in Quito's poshest hotel.
French nouvelle cuisine, five courses, including things like
langoustines and red snapper, and of course turkey in a fabulous
red wine sauce, rich and reduced . . . mmmh, a salad and two
delicious sorbets. And I devoured Charlotte's leftovers. Her
appetite isn't as vulgar as mine . . . I'm starving to think about it
and I only ate two hours ago. Anyway the whole lot came to $40
between us. Amazing.

Enough about food and money. What has been happening on the
inner as well as the outer? Not that I make much of a distinction
between the two these days. I have made some discoveries

*regarding my relationships with men. No wait, I'll come to that
later. OK. Right, we arrived in Ecuador on 12 November, spent
two weeks acclimatizing in Quito, I did lots of paintings and wrote
a few poems. Charlotte read and stayed in bed a lot then flew
south to Cuenca earlier than me. She has a habit of doing that.
Well, she was born three weeks early, I was born three weeks late,
so it's probably just old pre-natal patterning. We seem to get the
timing right between us most of the time though.*

*In Cuenca she met a Slovenian artist. 'Where?' I said.
'Slovenia. Ex-Yugoslavia. Don't mention the war,' she said. He is
very tall, apparently, and she assures me that the vibe was more
than platonic between them. No action as yet, though I'm sure
when they meet in Quito soon there will be. Ah, here she is, her
moustache freshly bleached, her legs as smooth as milk. She is now
about to pluck her eyebrows and says will I stop telling you about
her toilet and send you her love . . . and remind you that we are
keeping an eye out for your potter's shed.*

*I followed Charlotte on to Cuenca five days later, and we stayed
in a hotel called the Inca Real for about ten dollars a night each,
where the maids leave goodnight cards and chocolate biscuits on
your pillow every evening and turn the top sheet down all ready
for you to jump into bed. I did more paintings and wrote some
more poems, about friends mostly, and then . . .*

*We met a French boy/man called Gregory (same name as my
last lover in England). He plays saxophone and dances beautifully
and we all became friends very quickly . . .*

*Then Charlotte and I went to a sacred valley for six days . . .
Did you go when you were out here? We stayed in a bamboo hut
in a place called Mother Earth, ate healthy, home-grown food,
relaxed and enjoyed the amazing countryside. We also drank the
juice of a cactus called San Pedro and tripped out for twenty hours
during which time I performed a psychic operation on Charlotte to
remove an old emotional block . . . Yes, another one. And
Charlotte helped me to free myself of my very old wasp phobia
and all it represented. After that I was more than content to allow*

the wasps' nest above my bed to continue its existence,
maintaining unprecedented calm when, upon opening my eyes each
morning, it was the first thing to greet me. I even started talking
to the little buzzers.

Oh, and under the influence of the cactus, we could hear people's
thoughts and see through their bodies. Charlotte's just said 'So
what's new about that?'

When it came to dinner that evening, no one, but no one wanted
to sit next to us. I kept talking about my theory that everyone has
suffered some kind of abuse, and people did not want to know.
Then a surprisingly self-effacing Deutscher Mann came and sat at
our table because there was no room left anywhere else, and
fiddled ridiculously mit the bowl of salad. Through my San Pedro
eyes he was completely red from his upper chest to the top of his
head. It was really like being alive was a very embarrassing
experience for him.

'Oh, for God's sake, stop fiddling with it and just dump it on
your plate,' said Charlotte crossly. What a dummkopf. *That'll*
teach the Germans for being so Alles in Ordnung . . . *I giggled*
when I remembered that they lost the war.

We returned to Cuenca fresh and excited and really looking
forward to seeing Gregory. We had a great few days and we were
supposed to go and spend Xmas with him by the sea, but the day
before I felt exhausted and drained and realized I had not been at
all centred or creative in myself, distracting myself with the
beautiful, elusive Gregory.

So here we are. When are you coming to see us? We plan to go
to Bolivia at the end of January, then on to Chile for a few
months, maybe renting a flat there. Did you go to Valparaiso?

Now to the bit about men. I keep falling in love with them.
What can I do? Seriously, though, over the past year I've
recognized a need I have to relate to my own sex on a more
intimate, though not necessarily sexual, level. My best friends have
up to now always been women, and I have in general held women
in much greater esteem than men. But it began to dawn on me

that to relate only to one sex and to value that sex more highly than the other one was necessarily very limiting. Just as relating to men on a purely sexual level is very limiting. I also realized that any scorn I felt towards men (and I have felt a lot of it, often covert, in the past) would be played out in the relationships I had with my lovers. I would attract (and have attracted) to me lovers who would either be scornful of me or who would express those very qualities I would be scornful of. Not a fertile ground for seeding intimacy.

I guess through early experiences of my dad being critical, and of my being regularly bullied at school, the idea of trusting a man, or ever really being loved or accepted by a man (gay or straight), was foreign to me. Such men did not exist. Men did not have those qualities.

This year, I started to feel intuitively that something was about to change. When I met you in Guatemala, apart from finding you gorgeous, I knew things were really shifting. There you were, an adult, straight man, who accepted and loved me just for being myself. And liked my alter ego Jill, too. Remember the night when we went to the restaurant and I had an attack of manic hysteria after typing all day? Laughing uncontrollably and feeling I was about to pass out? I felt so stupid and expected you not to be able to cope with it, or even be interested in so doing. In other words, I expected rejection. But you neither ridiculed nor rejected me. You stayed, and in fact, sobered me right up by asking me what I felt about something that was bothering you. This is just one example, but it was great to feel so relaxed with you that I was able to let down my barriers. Certainly our different sexualities caused no problem.

When I returned to England in October, I noticed that my relationship with my dad had changed much for the better. He was really there for me in ways I had either not experienced or not noticed before. He spoke to me of his regret that he had not got to know his parents better as people, rather than just as Mum and Dad. We talked a lot. In fact, I found my mum, who I'd always got on with much more than my dad, sulking in the front room one evening, complaining that I'd paid her no attention. I did not react to this little dumping of guilt, I might add. I just explained the situation.

My dad wrote me a beautiful letter before I left England in November, saying he loved and admired me, and wishing me all the fulfilment of my heart's desires. So you see, Bjorn, it has been an amazing time. I'd like to say again that you have been an incredible inspiration for me and I love you for that. Charlotte's just come into the room, having fully completed her beauty therapy, and I think we're off for something to eat . . .

A huge hug and all the best for '92. Write soon.

Mark

CLOSE ENCOUNTER OF THE TRAVELLING KIND

~~~

The Dutch Air Stewardess

'I went to Mitad del Mundo,' said the Dutch air stewardess I am having a drink with in one of Quito's more expensive hotels. She is pretty and works for Air France, and she has taken a few weeks' holiday to come out and enjoy Ecuador. In the hour or so that I sat with her and a Swiss man whose acquaintance I had just made, her main topic of conversation was whether or not she should have a banana split.

'Go on,' I said, until I got bored with the neurosis of it – she wasn't listening anyway. 'They're very good. I love all that ice cream and fruit and gooey blackberry sauce. Was Mitad del Mundo interesting?'

I had never been there. Like many places on the so-called Gringo Trail, I simply was not interested. Conversations would often go like this:

'Been to Peru?'

'No.'

'Oh, it's the best. You should go. Machu Pichu is amazing, *the* most stunning thing in *all* South America, nothing to touch it . . .'

'Haf you been to Iguazu Falls?' (A German)

'No. I don't know Venezuela, Argentina, Brazil or Paraguay. But I really loved Colombia, what I saw – Cartagena was fantastic . . .'

'Have you been to San Agustín, Santa Marta, Ciudad Perdida. . . ?'

'No. I did sing in a piano bar in Cartagena . . .'

'Don't go to Rio de Janeiro, all that poverty and theft, I was robbed twice in two days . . .'

I had heard similar stories whilst I was in Barcelona.

'Have you been to Punta Arenas, Chiloe, Bariloche?'

No. *No. No.*

This was not the conversation I had with the Dutch air stewardess with the banana-split crisis.

'It wasn't anything,' she said. 'Just a monument and sign signalling the Equator, but I'm happy I went, to get a photo. I only stayed to get a photo, then I came back. You know, I don't know about this banana split. Should I have one . . . ?'

Jesus Christ, I thought. Simple things and all that.

THE SILVER STRAND
~~~

Alandaluz, January 1992

All along the sad coast road that runs from Manta to La Libertad the vultures stand and wait. There is mud and rubbish everywhere in this grey sticky morning and the trees on the hills are dying, their bellies swollen like starving children, their green fingers outstretched like begging men, and the hot breath of the sea sucks out all the air.

'What has happened to the trees?' I ask the gardener from the steps of my bamboo sea cabin.

'They have lost their hearts,' he says. 'And without their hearts, they die.'

The shrimp farms along this shore have poisoned the land with salt. I am sitting watching the sunset and the moonrise, watching the coming and the going of the tides, calling for my love to come, waiting for sweet water to replenish my parched garden that has known the salt for too long. In the mornings I watch the fishermen walk in the shallows of this dangerous sea, and throw their tiny circular nets. A line of pelicans skims the waves.

'There are times in your life,' said a wise woman to me, 'where all your energy will recede, like a tide going out, revealing what lies beneath. It is like a pale edge.'

I walk along this pale edge, along this ribboned sand, collecting blue stones. A white dog buries a bone, a black pig snuffles for clams and tiny jellyfish lie stranded and glint like glass in the path of the sea. In this desert beach that stretches for ever, I draw a circle, and I stand before the sea, with my back to the thirsting hills and I begin to dance.

I am in my centre. I exist in my own shadow. I dance my own dance. I sing my own song. I am my own red sun falling into the sea at evening and the bright fingernail of moon that hangs low in the sky. I am winter and summer, north and south. I am this smooth pebble I give thee, I am the kiss I place on your cheek. I am the starfish that once lay on the wet sand and dried at my window. I am this white shell, I am this piece of twisted wood, white as a bone. I am memory, I am prophecy. In my salty sigh is held each summer. I wrap myself round each rock, feeding it with my damp breath, this shell contains my sweetness. I am the sea, the powerful sea that no man can tame and I am the moon, the mover of the sea, that no man can understand. I am the temple and the poetry. I rule the tides and the tides of women. Listen to me, lie in my arms and you will remember. For you ran here once and ruled too, Prince of the Rockpools, with your seaweedy crown, when you heard me and my whispering sisters. I am the giver of dreams, I am the giver of silver. You played with my creatures, you buried my treasure. I loved you, Prince, you who stood at the edge of my kingdom, with your feet washed by my foam. O Prince of the Rockpools, child of the sun: come dance with me.

EVANGELICALS
〰

Baños

The hotel is big and old and wooden and run by a woman in her sixties who looks much fiercer than she really is. I probably feel guilty because I arrive with a beautiful young man who has just picked me up at the bus station and accompanied me here and I think everyone can see the ectoplasm of sex as it oozes out of us.

I hate to feel like that. Who cares what other people think anyway? As long as I am discreet. Behind closed doors.

But I do feel like that.

The beautiful young man comes and then he goes and I open my windows. I wanted a room with a view of the waterfall bursting out of the mountainside but I do not have one. The hotel is full. I can hear it though and at night it will be comforting for although I am not one to admit that sometimes I feel lonely, I do feel lonely. Sometimes. Like now.

Why did I come here? Oh, the usual. A break from Charlotte, to meet some new people. I don't really feel like meeting new people. To discover this town for myself; this town of thermal springs and many foreigners and horse riding which I have no interest in and restaurants and early morning mists; this town all the travellers talk about and where some end up staying. But not me. No, I won't end up staying here, it has no heart. It feels like a lot of people come and take from this town and don't give back.

I do not know how long I have been lying on this bed in this old wooden room, listening to the waterfall I cannot see from my window. But it must be mid-afternoon. I have discovered the eucalyptus Turkish baths and the swimming pool and the day is beautiful. I could go out and get a tan, I guess. But I don't want to.

Suddenly voices bring me out of my virtual catatonia. Voices, both of adults and children, as they swoop through my window like birds . . . noisy ones.

I know who you are before I even speak to you. I can see who you are from my window, even though I cannot make you out properly as you jump and play in and around the swimming pool.

Happy families.

I will go and sit by the pool and paint, pretend to paint, and listen. And watch.

Dad is tall and blond, late-thirties, kind of handsome but a bit too clean-cut and just beginning to go to seed around the midriff. And that unappealing smugness. Well, unappealing to me. And who am I to judge?

Mum is slightly mealy-mouthed and terribly nervous of the water. She twitches around her hearty husband and her cellulite twitches with her. She reminds the children frequently to be careful in the water, but I think she is reminding herself. The children are as happy as otters.

And sitting under the canopy beside the table-tennis table that seems like it hasn't been used for a long time, out of the sun, are Grandma and Grandpa.

Is it me or does this smack of just too much proscribed God? And who am I, such an unrepentant sinner, to judge?

This is one Loud Happy Family. Splash and squeal and laugh and shout. All Very Bigly. There really would be no room for anybody else, despite no lack of poolside chairs or water. Still I suppose you can do what you like if you are saved.

Well, Mark, you really are being judgemental, quite Old-Testament today, aren't you? And you haven't even talked to these people. How do you know they are Bible-bashers?

I just do.

'Where you from?'

I look up from my painting and into the eyes of Grandma. I would like to say the wise old eyes of Grandma, but I can't because wisdom is not what I see there.

'England. And you?'

'Oh, Alabama originally but we've lived all over the world: Bolivia, Africa, Spain. We are involved in missionary work.'

'What does that mean?'

'Well, Jesus called me to do His work over fifty years ago and we go into underdeveloped countries and help them to modernize and teach them about the Lord.'

Saving the souls of savages.

'And that's my son and his family. He leads missionary work here in South America.'

This woman talks and talks and not once does she ask me about myself. Even after I have asserted that I am not a Christian, born-again or otherwise, she tells me that Jesus can save my soul. Yes, once when she was in deepest Africa she remembers a poor savage black woman ill with a raging fever, whom she was tending ('Jesus loves you too') asking her not to step on an insect that crawled across the mud floor of her hut in case it was her grandmother's spirit.

'Who is anyone to deny another their beliefs?' I ask. 'It can be very dangerous to interfere with another soul's ecostructure.'

But I saw the eyes glaze over. The eyes that don't see. I recognize that look. I have seen it in the faces of Jehovah's Witnesses in my own family. And I know that this woman will not hear me, will not listen. Like she did not hear what the African woman was saying, even though her brain registered the words.

I have seen the adherents of many evangelical religions in many Latin American cities and towns. Those fervent young Mormon men with suits and short-cropped hair and name-tags, looking so upright, so decent, so saved. Many learn to speak Spanish and even the tribal languages, but they come to conquer not to learn. They do not believe that the native people have anything to teach them, and certainly nothing about God.

The family is leaving. Dad looks even smugger than before. The kids race for the changing room. Mum shuffles in after them. I remain silent.

'Well, I'm sorry I haven't been able to convert you,' says Grandma.

I smile tightly. You know nothing about me. You could spend months with me and not get to know anything about me. How dare you automatically assume that your life has more value than mine?

Didn't Jesus say somewhere that spiritual arrogance was a greater sin than murder?

CROSSING BORDERS 2:
ECUADOR TO COLOMBIA

~~~

'Colombia is beautiful,' said Amy to me on the telephone. 'It's so much more alive than Ecuador.'

'I'll come next week and meet up with you, on Thursday or Friday,' I shouted excitedly down the receiver. 'Ring me on Monday and we'll arrange where and when.'

At the time of this conversation, about midday on Saturday, 11 January, I was back in Quito in Jane's flat, completely out of my head on San Pedro cactus juice along with Charlotte, Marko and Jane, and dressed in a flowery print frock, enacting everyone's mother for them.

'Amy won't have believed that I meant it,' I said to Charlotte the following day.

Indeed Amy did not phone back on the Monday, but I had decided to make a trip to Colombia anyway. The usual warning signs that I needed to spend some time travelling alone were starting to appear. I would say things to Charlotte like 'Have you bleached your moustache recently, dear?' and even threatened (in my worst moments) not to write any more of the book. She was spending most nights at Marko's rented apartment in one of the highest areas of Quito, overlooking a fertile valley and where at night the mists would suddenly descend, then disappear as quickly as they had come. Sex had become a part of their previously platonic relationship.

I was staying at Jane's in the east of the city, with views of volcanoes, waterfalls and some of the poorer *barrios*, which, when the sharp clear sunshine strikes the mostly white and sometimes blue paint of the small tightly packed houses stacked on the otherwise green hillsides, take on a peculiar beauty of their own. And I was finding the behaviour of Jane's flatmate increasingly intolerable. He was an Englishman whose only passion in life seemed to be scaling volcanoes, and who would sulk and skulk around the flat in his heavy mountain boots, neither making the effort to speak to anyone, nor bothering (or plucking up the courage) to express in words, rather than in stomps, his obvious displeasure at the incessant arrival and departure of Jane's guests.

'I think you're fed up with Quito, Mark,' said Jane. 'Go and get recharged in Colombia. I had a fabulous time when I went, and nothing horrible happened.'

Amy and Jane's reports about Colombia differed radically from most of the stories I had heard or read concerning that huge land, birthplace of Gabriel García Marquez and two of the biggest drug capitals in the world:

'Be really careful on buses and never, but never, accept any bottled, or even canned drinks, or sweets from fellow passengers, they could be drugged and you'll wake up twenty-four hours later, in a hospital bed or a side-street, either way divested of every stitch . . . sometimes they even remove one of your kidneys . . .'

'People just get shot in the street, I mean, if you're in the middle of a drugs shoot-out, forget it, tough luck . . .'

'They don't do half-hearted robberies there like they do in Ecuador, you know, we are talking major knives here . . .'

'A lot of the people have a hard, dark look in their eyes. It's spooky . . .'

'Even the police will offer you cocaine, and then arrest you . . .'

'They have propaganda films on buses, showing babies' stomachs cut open to reveal smuggled bags of cocaine . . . Guerrilla terrorists kidnap you, and if you're released you'd better get out of the country quick via your embassy, because you won't last long otherwise . . .'

And the list goes on and maybe the stories are sometimes true or at least partly so, but each of us travels with our own energy and agenda of expectations, which I am convinced have a direct effect on our experience. Many travel drunk, doped, dreaming or otherwise not present. And if you are not there, you will not be aware . . . of people putting their hands in your pocket, for example. Also, people, like animals, sense another's fear, and that leaves a door open for the very things feared to enter. I always walk around new cities as if I know exactly where I am going . . . Well, nearly always.

Anyway, back to mid-January and Colombia. Charlotte and Marko went to the Ecuadorian coast for a week. I hesitated for a day in Jane's flat, playing Scrabble with myself, but the sound of the angry mountain boots clinched the decision for me. Six days after Amy's phone call, on a clear Quito Friday morning, I packed a few things in one bag and caught a bus to the Colombian border.

I was uneasy from the start, wishing I had not read so many guide books or listened to those people with their horror stories. But I would just have to put my ideas into practice and trust my energy. I took out my Walkman and put on a tape of Mercedes Sosa . . . 'All I ask of God,' she sings in her huge Argentinian voice, 'is that I never become indifferent to the future, war or love . . .'

All I ask of God is that I remain intact both mentally and physically as I make my way to this new land, I think. I begin to feel a familiar tetchiness and fatigue, and recognize it from my Mexico–Guatemala border crossing.

As we left Quito, there were whole pigs hanging roasted on the sides of the road and a trout seller walked along the dividing line of the dual carriageway, balancing his catch precariously on a pole over his shoulder. Occasionally we would pass a lorry or a building with Cementos Selva Alegre written on it. Jolly Forest Cement seemed the perfect example of the Latin American ability to get away with the most incongruous descriptions. At Ibarra station women, some Indian with plaited black shiny hair, others negro from a tropical valley nearby inhabited almost entirely by blacks, boarded the bus with baskets of hot sweetcorn – *choclos* – and fresh white cheese, and bags of *fritadas*, pieces of pork with maize.

I was too anxious to eat. We took to the road again, riding through the black tropical valley, an anomaly in those Indian highlands, and then climbing to the frontier town of Tulcán, almost three thousand metres above sea-level. A taxi brings me down to the border with Colombia. It is a short walk across a bridge from the Ecuadorian to the Colombian migration office. The officials stamp my passport very quickly and no one checks my bag – it all feels suspiciously easy. I am most protective of my bag, especially as I feel so exhausted, probably a resistant part of me desiring sleep instead of crossing this border and meeting the challenge of Colombia . . .

I am not tired enough, however, not to notice immediate differences between Ecuador and Colombia. Small Minis and Volkswagen Beetles give way to huge Cadillacs and Chevrolets, throwing me straight back to what I imagine the 'fifties and 'sixties must have been like. 'Thunderbirds are go,' I think to myself, and get into an enormous taxi which takes me to Ipiales, the Colombian version of Tulcán, only with more apparent wealth. One of my first impressions was that the people seemed to take more pride in their houses and land than in Ecuador. I change money with my Visa card, eat *arroz con pollo* in a café on the main square, then take a *cooperativo* to Pasto, capital of this department and the first main city after the border. The journey of two hours takes me through the most amazing landscape. The Andes appeared greener than I'd ever seen them in the mid-afternoon sun, and as we drove along the top ledge of a gorge with a sheer drop, I forgot to distrust my fellow bus passengers and their sinister cans of Coca-Cola for a moment in the face of the highly unfunny possibility of toppling over the edge. Beautifully kept farms grace the steep slopes of the mountains.

We overtake a huge articulated truck, grasping hold of the back of which is a young boy on a bicycle being pulled along quite happily at an alarming speed on these twisting roads. Salsa music fills the bus and I am surprised at how little it irritates me. It was the bane of all my bus journeys in Ecuador.

I wonder how Marko and Charlotte are getting on at the beach in another country, and worry a little about overspending and arriving alone at the bus terminal in Pasto. You are on your own now, Mark, you do not have Charlotte to project any of your little neuroses onto, and then pretend you have none. A melody, complete with all the harmonies, comes into my head, for a song I wrote and dedicated to my Swedish friend Bjorn in Antigua, Guatemala last summer. The bus surges towards Pasto and the Andes rise up at each side of me very greenly.

The bus station at Pasto presents me with no problems and the town itself is quiet and colonial. I book into a cheap hotel with enormous rooms, each with a telephone and a black and white television. Mine has a smell of polish, or is it insecticide? The low-voltage lighting casts an unreal glow and travelling salesmen sit together in shared rooms surrounded by piles of denim jeans and boxes. Along the pot-planted corridor I discover an enclosed bathroom, windowless and painted in cream.

'Yes,' I think, excited at the prospect of a soak after all the buses, taxis and (mostly self-created) border tensions, and after so many cold showers in Jane's flat. But the plug doesn't work and old water with hairs and scum comes up into the tub. So I make do with the showers, hot, but really quite public like in a boys' school, and painted the same clotted-cream colour as the joyless bathroom.

Do I leave for Bogotá tomorrow? Should I call the sexy (but I thought rather guarded) guy I had a quick encounter with in a posh hotel in Quito? He lives in the capital.

I go out for a walk, and decide to book a flight to Bogotá for the next day.

'Are you going to Colombia?' asks the travel agent.

'I'm in Colombia, aren't I?' I start to relax a little, though I do not so much walk as march down the street after seeing *Highlander II* at the cinema that night.

I fall asleep spent at about midnight in my big three-bedded room to the spooky sound of the black hotel cat with a chilling yowl that is almost human. About forty minutes later I jump out of bed from my sleep in terror, convinced that someone is in my room and about to attack me. I eventually ascertain that there is no enemy, only me, and drift back into unconsciousness. The telephone rings at 6.45 a.m. with the receptionist advising me of the time, wrenching me from a dream where I am asking myself whether I should tolerate Joni Mitchell's awful behaviour and rudeness just because she is a star . . . and depriving me of an answer.

In the *colectivo* taxi on the way to the airport, the radio news reports a drugs-related shooting of the previous night in Cali. I try to remain focused on the soft green of the morning mountains.

'I'm from Cali,' says my fellow passenger. 'Here's my address. Now you have friends to stay with when you visit the city of the most beautiful women in Colombia.'

I arrive trouble-free in Bogotá and another taxi takes me to the Hostería De La Candelaría in the *barrio* of the same name, where the houses look rather English with their tiled roofs, and where the streets have names such as Calle de la Agonia. It feels a bit like Hampstead, though I know of no Agony Street in London NW3. I eat *ajiaco*, a national soup with chicken and avocado, cooked by Omaira, a big black woman with huge joyous eyes, then take to my room to rest, after attempting another phone call to my man in Bogotá, who is and will continue to be absent for all the time I am in Colombia.

In the late afternoon I walk to the Plaza Bolívar and visit the market nearby, leaving my camera locked safely in the Hostería. I eat more chicken on the first floor of a *pollería* in what I discover later to be a very unsafe area. I was probably protected by the bliss of ignorance, but I certainly sensed an edge in Bogotá which I had felt nowhere else. It was very different from Guatemala City, huge in comparison, and anger was not, I felt, the main underlying emotion. Certainly not the anger of a country repressed and invaded by outsiders. Here I could perceive an identity existing in and of itself. Beyond the bustle and noise I captured a sense of both humour and audacity.

A week later in Cartagena, when I prevent a thief from stealing the camera of a dozy North American seated at the same table as me, the *ladron* will just pat me on the back, say 'OK, amigo' with a smile and then slither away.

Whilst I was eating my chicken, two clowns surprised me as they walked past the window. They were on stilts about fifteen feet high. The evening began to close in and I made my way back to the Hostería through the cobbled back streets of La Candelaría.

Roberto, a young Ecuadorian studying in Bogotá whom I met on the plane this morning, pays me a visit and we chat amicably for a couple of hours in my room. He tells me of his grandfather, a Rosicrucian whose mystical tendencies had been firmly quashed by the fervent Catholicism of his grandmother as she forbade even the slightest mention of things occult. But the old man would whisper to Roberto stories of magic and how as a young boy he visualized getting a blue rocking horse for Christmas without uttering a word to anyone, and on the morning of the birth of Christ, awoke to find the very same rocking horse awaiting its rider in his room.

As we are talking I lean on the glass covering of my dressing table, and it breaks leaving me spattered with Pepsi-Cola and splinters . . . I am a little worried about finding nineteen-year-old boys attractive, but thankfully talking is as far as it gets and the concierge, a rather aggressive mulatto man from the coast, orders a cab for Roberto and, when it doesn't arrive, calls the company again and swears profusely down the phone at them. 'Unreliable sons of whores,' he spits, and then proceeds to inform me of all the gory reasons why I should on no account go walking around the Candelaría after dark, not that I had any intention of so doing in the first place.

At breakfast the next day, served by an ever smiling Omaira, whose deep laugh I am convinced helps to keep the plants so green and healthy, I meet an attractive thirty-three-year-old Berliner called Sacha, who has all the sophistication of educated Western Europe (German mother) and a good helping of Latin American magic realism (Colombian father). He is writing a soap opera and reading a book in German called *Voltaire in Our Time*. He tells me lies are so much more interesting than the truth. I do not agree though I suppose it depends on your particular brand of truth or lies, no, I don't think I'll go to the bullfight this afternoon, thank you, I am a Taurean after all, but it would be great to have dinner together tonight and meet his sculptress friend Liliana, a politician's daughter who lives around the corner.

'She's into energies and psychic waves,' Sacha tells me.

Omaira clears the tables, Sacha goes off to his bullfight and I return to my room, at once exhilarated and exhausted by all these contacts I have made in Colombia in one day. What goes up must come down so I find myself slipping somewhat as I sit in the sunny courtyard in a deck-chair, reading a book Marko has lent me about a Peruvian shaman. I really do wish Amy would turn up. All she needs to do is ring Jane in Quito and get the details of where I am. She's probably in Bogotá. Let it go, Mark, if it is supposed to happen it will happen, I repeat to myself over and over again, the restlessness in my bones increasing with each affirmation. Oh, I hate this feeling of maybe we won't meet up at all. I want to control everything and have it all mapped out nicely. Why doesn't my man in Bogotá answer the phone? I bet even Sacha will let me down and we won't go out for dinner tonight. If Charlotte were here, I could concentrate on all her little foibles and moods. I don't like being confronted with myself right now. It's very uncomfortable.

I go out for some lunch, more to try and change the scenery of my mind than that of my stomach, still satisfied from breakfast. As I approach the Plaza Bolívar the strident sounds of a brass band reach my ears. The military is playing behind an iron fence in a big square near the plaza. None of the soldiers guarding the procession appears to be any older than about twenty, many a lot younger. But they are all rather stunning in their uniforms and standing proud. One boy looks more like a salsa dancer than a soldier with that swing of the hips. He asks a few of us 'si no les molesta', could we please move over to the other side of the pavement. I wonder why I am surprised at his politeness. A bedraggled, filthy and extremely deranged woman of about fifty appears, holding trash in her hands and dressed in ripped overalls, one side of which flaps open as she marches in time with the music, revealing a large flabby breast, bouncing rhythmically for all to see. She makes vulgar gestures which oscillate between a Hitler salute and something that says 'Up Yours' and marches beyond the line of soldiers where the public are not permitted to stand, performing her own number as she faces the military band. The boys, armed with terrifying machine-guns almost the size of them, remove her gently.

The band moves later into the open Plaza Bolívar itself, where I return after lunch (more chicken). This is when I notice the xylophones. There are all these macho young men parading around with their trumpets decorated with the Colombian flag – green and white stripes and a red border – and suddenly I hear a tinkle like bells, sweetly caressing the air. At the same time on a building opposite, anachronistic Nativity lights shaped into a Christmas tree blink on and off in the broad daylight, half red, half green, with a message of peace.

I find myself hoping that Amy would be in this crowd somewhere, my new New York friend with her thick mass of dark golden hair and her relentless search for the truth within herself. She feels so near I could almost touch her. I stand on some steps apart from everyone else and look into the throng, figuring she will catch sight of me if she is here. 'Miracles do happen,' I write in my diary back at the Hostería; we did not meet up that day but we would in Cartagena, and Amy would tell me that in fact she was in the Plaza Bolívar that Sunday at the very same time I was. Sometimes paths cross and sometimes they don't.

Sacha arrives back (much later than he said) just as I am about to abandon myself to the idea that no one I want to see will ever be there. He looks dashing in his Panama hat and jeans. We go to Liliana's. She is a woman of thirty-five with mad red hair that matches her fiery temperament, and bright staring eyes. 'Sit down, *setzt euch, sientense,*' she says. 'I'm just finishing some photographs.' On a table in her courtyard stand two nude models in an embrace which looks far more comfortable than it evidently is, judging by the relief on the man's face when the session is over.

'We have to take more photos another time,' says Liliana to the photographer, an Austrian boy in his early twenties from an aristocratic family who plies me with questions without waiting for an answer until I tell him to be quiet. And Liliana adds, 'I'm going out to dinner now, I've seen enough of you today,' to her novice photographer house guest, thanks the models who leave and says to me, 'The problem is the guy always gets an erection. I scratch that out in the photos.'

Sacha drives Liliana and me in her car out to a restaurant in the *zona rosa* area of Bogotá. I notice that there appears to be at least two armed guards per establishment. A quick shudder goes down my spine.

'This is Bogotá,' says Liliana. 'At night it's even dangerous to stop at a red light – thieves shoot drivers through the window, dump the bodies and make off with the vehicle.'

'Jesus,' I thought, consoling myself with the fact that my two new acquaintances had spent so much time in Bogotá and had arrived at their mid-thirties seemingly unscathed and certainly alive.

We talk over dinner of spirituality, Eastern and Western, meditation and the Dakini cards, which Liliana uses for herself.

'Charlotte has those,' I say, excited. 'We must do readings when she comes to Bogotá.'

Sacha becomes very irritated by all this illogical talk of truth-searching and mysticism, and Liliana, one of the most forthright women I have ever met, tells him he lives too much in his head and hides himself from view. When the bill arrives we have been overcharged and Liliana rants at the waiter in Spanish, at Sacha in German and at me in English: *'Que vaina es eso? Was ist das denn fur 'nen Scheiss*, they rip you off even in the smart places . . .' Then Sacha, who is quite merry to say the least from a day full of brandies but not from Liliana's temper, takes us back to the Candelaría at a terrifying speed through the city, driving on any side of the road as he avoids the bumps and potholes.

The next afternoon I have a flight to Cartagena on the Caribbean coast of Colombia – the first place below 1,500 metres above sea-level I shall have visited in over two and a half months. Sacha has said he would show me some of downtown Bogotá after breakfast and, as we walk through and from the Candelaría, he points out shadowy bars where hired killers can be contracted for a too-affordable price. Apart from being a bit dingy they look quite harmless in the daylight, I think, until I see a very frightening-looking man emerge from a wooden swing door with a deep scar on one side of his face and knitted eyebrows.

We stop by the university Liliana's father founded, then we look in a shop full of stylish leather goods. Sacha wants to buy himself what seems like a rather complicated vanity case. Do you really want to lug that around with you? I ask. We enter the street where the besuited emerald sellers conduct their business, talking animatedly on the corner in groups of three or four as people, cars and buses rush past and traffic lights change from red to green to red.

'*Esmeraldas*,' says a voice and a hand opens to reveal a glistening green stone. We walk on and I am swimming with a million impressions and clutching fearfully on to my camera case, why the hell didn't I leave it at the hotel, half-expecting at any moment to see a knife at my throat with accompanying macabre voice demanding I hand over the goods.

Each time I start to achieve the slightest relief from my tension, the front-page close-up photograph of a man with a knife embedded in his brain (and corresponding headline of how he survived for nine hours with it there) leaps out out at me from one of the newspaper stands. I keep very close to Sacha in the street.

'Inter-Andean integration is a curious thing,' replies the man next to me in the queue at the Post Office as I enquire of him how long my postcard to Jane should take to arrive in Quito. The self-created enigma Sacha, posts what seem to be several declarations of un-dying love to various girls around the globe. He skilfully evades any sort of answer to my question about whether he is in love with any of them. Then we go and drink the juice of the most enormous carrots I have ever seen and I photograph Sacha contemplating them piled up high in the window. We return past the beggars and the emerald businessmen, the newspaper vendors and the Military museum, to the Hostería, where I throw my things into my one bag, take leave of my entertaining and mysterious friend, pay my bill and catch a cab to the airport, where I post a card to my unavailable man in Bogotá as a last attempt at communication. My message says: I am in the city again in ten days, here's my number, do ring etc. But I obviously have not got the message. He wouldn't.

I leave Bogotá with the same feeling I had about the National Health Service in England: I had heard lots of dreadful things about it, but I was treated very well there.

Cartagena

I arrive in this ancient jewel of a city with a million balconies and the Caribbean Sea in the dark, my ears totally congested from both the change of pressure in the aeroplane and the radical shift in altitude on the ground. Disoriented, I ask the taxi-driver to take me to the Hotel Doral in Half Moon Street, and we drive round for ages, he obviously as lost as I, until we come to a Hotel Dorado miles away from the centre of town on the beach, where I do not want to stay, so we drive into and around town again, until we find the Hotel Doral.

There is a poodle with pink nail polish on its claws lying on top of the reception desk and an open-air patio inside from where the for-once-heartening sound of other travellers' voices drifts over to me, as they enjoy a beer in the sultry evening. The manager tells me there are no rooms available, could I return early tomorrow morning, and I leave feeling rejected, and envious of those inside with their drink and their company. My ears still filled with imaginary cotton wool, I take yet another taxi to the Bocagrande (Big-mouth) beach, and rent a spare, over-priced room with a cold shower on the fifth floor of a hotel with echoey corridors and noisy families. I put the fan on, undress, and lie down to sleep for an hour, my disorientation magnified by the noises of the city outside as they rise up to my room like the heat: laughter, traffic, salsa music from every restaurant . . .

As I eat a pizza in a nearby café later – Bocagrande is lined with fast-food places – my disorientation gives way to loneliness and fatigue, and neither the friendly smiles of the mulatto waitresses nor the Caribbean sensuality serve to abate these feelings: Why don't I have a lover? Where is Amy? Why am I staying in that horrible cheerless hotel? What did I bother to come here for anyway? And the street vendors sell their flip-flops and imported bandanas, and groups of coffee-skinned youths in Bermuda shorts saunter along the promenade, and the beat goes on, just not for me right now . . .

On the way back to my hotel, a man hisses at me from a dark doorway, 'Hey! You want a tour round town tomorrow?'

'No, thanks.'

'To the Rosario Islands?'

'No. Really. Thank you.'

'Then I have something *buenísimo* for your nostrils.'

'Absolutely not,' I say and we both laugh.

I arise early the next morning and go for a walk along the Bocagrande beach, removing my espadrilles and letting the soft sand massage my feet. The black women selling fruit are already up, large baskets of coconuts, papayas, mangoes, figs and melons balanced on their heads as they move languidly along the shore by the softly lapping sea. Coconuts hang heavy on lightly swaying palms and the warm morning breeze lifts up the hairs on my arms and legs. Ecuador seems a million light years away. A digital clock-cum-thermometer flashes 7.10 a.m. and 20°C alternately . . . it will be a hot day. I drink fresh papaya and carrot juice at a stall by the harbour and refuse to worry about the dubious ice the man has added to the delicious concoction.

I arrive at the Hotel Doral, downtown Cartagena, by eight o'clock. I am greeted by the manicured but otherwise grubby poodle and the manager, who has a room for me (with a shower). Two heavy-footed cleaning women, each with an eternal cigarette hanging loosely from their mouths, and that Caribbean darkness which borders almost on impenetrability, shuffle in to change bed sheets and mop the floor. I collect my things from the beach hotel and return to install myself. Although I am not half so gloomy as yesterday, vestiges of loneliness still wrap round me like morning mists as I sit and jot notes in my diary under a parasol in the tiled patio, one eye on the paper and the other typically peeled for a sign of any eligible-looking man. The hotel is on two floors and off the balcony of the second checked and flowered sheets of all colours blow gently in the wind to dry; somewhere a parrot keeps repeating the same phrase over and over. Other guests sit at tables reading or writing, the sun shines hotter and the two women go about their chores like slow-moving rivers.

At midday I go out into Half Moon Street, the sun now beating down inexorably on the city. I begin to feel much more in contact with my body after the months of heady mountains and I now bear myself upright in baggy drill shorts, a singlet, espadrilles and my Guatemalan panama hat. A middle-aged black man cries out to me with a smile 'que elegante caminas' – you walk so elegantly – and I meet a girl called Sue from the north of England (also staying at the Doral) and she has had her thick wavy blonde hair plaited with beads of many colours here in Cartagena, this town full of bead ladies and fruit ladies.

I lunch with Sue, who was robbed twice in Peru of all her clothes whilst travelling alone.

'Isn't it frightening being such a blonde gringa and travelling on your own there with all that theft and terrorism?' I ask her. I have thus far never been to Peru, because my interest in so doing does not match the tension that arises in me at the prospect of arguably Latin America's most trouble-ridden land. And I think the tension along with my lack of clear motives for visiting Peru could create a situation where I was robbed.

'Oh, I love a good adventure. And I didn't let them get away with it without putting up a fight. Then I bought new clothes . . .' And over the Chinese food, tasty with lots of French fries and more than a hint of Caribbean influence in the rice and black beans, Sue tells me of a shaman who visited her hotel room in Lima and talked to her of universal energies, humankind's link with the stars and how her life would change dramatically at thirty-three . . .

I tell her I wish Amy would call so we can meet up. Sue is also hoping for the arrival of a friend of hers.

'Maybe the fact we have talked about it will encourage it to happen,' I half-joke in the street afterwards.

On my return to the Doral, a message from 'Eme' in Santa Marta awaits me. Santa Marta is only four hours away by bus. Sue walks by and tells me her friend has turned up. I ring the number in Santa Marta and soon hear Amy's soft deep voice on the phone. I scream out loud, jumping up and down for joy, frightening the parrot and the old man who owns the hotel, from whose room I am making the call. When can we meet? Amy is excited too, but tells me she is not feeling too good, raised glands, lethargy, a sore throat. Well, I'll come to her. Or let's meet halfway. But she decides to come to Cartagena, she'll arrive around midday tomorrow. I go and sit in the patio and a tiny red-beaked humming bird with a green throat sucks at the pink flowers of a tree and I tell everybody how excited I am that Amy's coming, whether they care or not.

When I met Amy at Jane's flat in Quito on the last day of 1991, I was really in no mood to get to know anybody new. Gregory had paid us a visit after his week at the beach, and I had found myself talking and asking questions, and receiving no response (apart from the fact that he enjoyed the piece I wrote about him), until I stopped talking and asking questions and couldn't care less whether I received a response or not. When Charlotte and I returned to Quito from Cuenca on Christmas Eve, we picked up the keys to Jane's flat from our old *hostal* – Amy had left them there for us wrapped up in a photocopied photograph of herself in a canoe. The day she arrived at the flat, Gregory, who was fond of spontaneity and looking at people without allowing them to look at him, took a picture of her from the front balcony before she had even come in. He left shortly afterwards and we did not see him again.

Amy was twenty-eight and described herself as 'a nice Jewish girl from New York . . . State not City'. She had worked as an actress and stand-up comic in the USA, and as an assistant in a psychiatric clinic. Over the past year she had been travelling in South America. We talked almost immediately of our battles with various addictions . . . sex, food, alcohol, and I let her read some of my poetry, which she recited beautifully with her rich deep voice and the ability she has to let her emotions accompany whatever she is doing. What my connection with Gregory lacked in clear, direct communication was made up for in less than half an hour with Amy. She was planning to leave Ecuador in five days and, along with it, a sexually addictive relationship with an Englishman whose potential for violence and lack of willingness to admit any dark emotions scared her. In those few days, we shared many things – poetry and her home-made pancakes with maple syrup (she used cornflour in the absence of the wheat variety but they still tasted delicious), and she even witnessed me as I acted out in Jane's kitchen a frightened, demanding four-year-old boy, shouting at Charlotte for not being available, distancing herself and trying to control everything with her cooking. Amy sat beside me and whispered gently in my ear that really I was a little jealous of Charlotte's friendship with Marko and a bit afraid that I would be abandoned.

'I want Charlotte to fight with me,' I snarled.

But Charlotte did not want to fight. She wanted to get on with the dinner and have some peace. I got angrier and angrier, and just at the point where I had everybody's nerves in my hand, I laughed. Even Amy said she would probably have left had it continued. But that day, neither she, Charlotte nor anybody left.

After the phone call with Amy everything changes and most of the following twelve days become a whirlwind of energy and people. My senses flourish (without a lover) in the city which pulses with *musica tropical*, whilst protected by its old wall and soothed by its gentle sea.

Amy comes and we eat fat juicy shrimps and rice cooked in coconut milk in the air-conditioned art gallery restaurant, talking of everything and nothing. She tells me of a love in the Argentinian mountains and how she spent days alone writing poems to him in an ugly border town, paralysed by fierce emotions and unable to cross over into Chile, lest she would have to leave him and the passion they shared behind for ever. She says her poor health is a sign for her to return to the United States, that her South American travelling days are numbered. I become possessive later when she spends too much time talking with the other travellers, especially that good-looking young market trader from Essex. Amy is my friend here and I want her to myself. At night, a group of us grab a bus after popcorn and Coca-Cola cinema and go for a walk along the beach at Bocagrande. Sue and her travelling companion of six weeks, Sarah, are very shiny and happy on some San Pedro they brought from Ecuador. I am high in this land of cocaine and coffee, but on neither of these things. Amy and I come adrift from the others and from the beach musicians in pairs or groups of three who offer to serenade the tourists . . .

Barefoot, my toes dug in the sand, I thank the stars, the sea, the sun and the ground beneath my feet for carrying my message to Amy and bringing her to me and, though her feet are tired, she dances a sensual, graceful dance, as I sing 'Alfonsina Y El Mar', about an Argentinian poet who drowns herself in the sea: 'Sabe Dios que angustia te acompañó, que dolores viejos calló tu voz, para recostarte arrullada en el canto de las caracolas marinas . . .' 'Only God knows what anxiety accompanied you, what ancient pain your voice held silent, that you lay down crooned by the lullaby of the sea-shells . . .'

And Amy sings to me, regretting her tone-deafness, but that's not important, I say, it's the gesture that counts. Then she says about travelling, 'You know, Mark, we take our assholes with us' –

'But also our hearts,' I add. In fact, wherever we go we take the whole lot with us, it's just a bit naive to think that we can leave our assholes behind.

The next day a few of us go to the beach outside the Hilton hotel, recommended by Sarah as the cleanest one with wonderful toilets that double as changing rooms (unofficially). Amy keeps us all enraptured as she relates her experiences in the psychiatric clinic with schizophrenic patients, including a most extraordinary account of a large Jewish woman who would have attacks of panic accompanied by profuse sweating, convinced the Nazis were putting her into the gas ovens.

As Amy speaks I recognize a similarity between the work she did and the counselling I used to do. I keep quiet and let her talk; a vague unease comes over me as I sense that Amy does not want to hear what I might have to say. A coldness settles.

'I feel frightened around you sometimes, Mark,' she would say later. 'You are so loving and tomorrow I leave and you'll not be there. Then what?'

I reply that the challenge is to accept it and not block it off – after all I could say the same about her.

But has anyone come up with a guarantee that there's going to be a tomorrow in the first place? I haven't heard about it if they have, and so I feel I cannot afford to close off my heart from something so intimate and special. For me, travelling always intensifies friendship in this way. I am also convinced that the more open I am to intimacy when I have the opportunity to meet someone where it is possible, if only for a matter of days or even hours, a part of me heals, leaving a greater space to attract more of the same, maybe longer lasting, into my life.

We hire a big, blue inflatable banana, tied by rope to a speedboat, and after three-quarters of an hour of the man attempting vainly to start the motor and Amy becoming crosser and crosser at the whole scene including a second man grinning and running into town with a plastic container to fetch more petrol (I feel so irritated, Mark, I'm going to ask for my money back), it thrusts into action, and we are towed into the Caribbean at breakneck speed, all laughing and screaming and occasionally toppling off the banana. Oh my God, I hope there are no sharks here. And then the banana breaks and the rest of us pile into the speedboat whilst Amy does some water-skiing, very gracefully until she falls off and the owner leaves her stranded in the water for ten minutes whilst he takes the four of us back to the jetty. I tell him to go and get my friend, she isn't feeling well, and he grins and says she'll be all right, and I wonder if it's a little revenge for her impatience whilst he was trying to start the boat. And although I cannot see her face, as they approach I know that Amy is not all right and that she is crying. Back on the beach she tells me it is her mom she is crying for, a mom she never thought was there for her, whose food she did not want, and whom she found very difficult to forgive.

'I don't know if I want to forgive her,' she says.

'Forgiving is not the same as condoning or even forgetting,' I say.

We make a very good double act. In the Doral café we sit with Sarah and the English couple who had come on the banana boat expedition with us and talk outrageously about sex.

'I really would like to know what it is to have a dick, to penetrate someone,' exclaimed Amy over the fruit juices.

Niki, the female half of the couple, is a tiny, delicate-seeming girl of about twenty-two with a porcelain complexion. After about fifteen minutes of sex-talk, she stands up and shouts much to the bemusement of her mellow boyfriend who seemed to have very definite English ideas on politeness and manners, 'Yeah, I'd like to know what it is to have a dick too. Penetration!'

Amy and I go out by ourselves and eat maize pancakes with cheese at a street food stall, and a man takes a photograph of us together in the kind light of the setting sun against one of the old houses in a narrow street in the old town. We sleep that night in the same bed covered with one sheet in the sweaty Cartagena night, and even the family of cockroaches and the mouse that have taken up residence in my room do not disturb me.

Amy leaves the next day, back to Santa Marta, undecided as to an already planned walk with a friend to Ciudad Perdida (Lost City), in the homeland of the Kogui tribe, who have as little as possible to do with the outside world. Amy repeats that she is almost ready to return to the USA: her throat still hurts and she has little energy. I am so happy. I am happy she made the effort to come and see me in Cartagena. I am also happy to be alone right now.

It is Sarah's last evening in Colombia. Tomorrow she flies off to Miami to meet her mother. Like Amy, Sarah is Jewish, and predicts that her mother's likely opening comment upon seeing her will be 'You mean you've been away all this time and you haven't even got a tan?'

We go out to dinner with Martin and Niki (the timid girl of I Want A Dick fame), but beforehand I try my first and only line of coke ever. I am assured by my supplier as we gather secretly in my room talking in whispers, to perform the snort, that the effect will only last about half an hour, giving me a buzz and a heightened sense of self (I think that means ego). This takes place at seven-thirty in the evening. We drink gin and tonics in a piano bar at the top of one of Cartagena's plushest restaurants and listen to the playing of an old man, and I have absolutely no idea how he climbed up the almost vertical and extremely narrow spiral wooden staircase to his piano. Upon the request of my companions (not that I need much goading) I stand by the piano and sing several songs – 'Alfonsina Y El Mar', 'Summertime', 'Until It's Time For You To Go', 'Leaving On A Jet Plane' (for Sarah) and others, accompanied by the athletic old man, who just happens to have the sheet music under his piano stool. I feel on top of the world in this breezy attic room singing in my blue silk suit for my companions, and a Colombian businessman and his two English associates express their pleasure at my performance and invite us to a bottle of delicious Chilean red wine. We consume it in the restaurant downstairs where all the wealthy people of Cartagena appear to be on this Friday night, and where there is an open, dimly lit kitchen that is full of enormous iron pots and pans among which enormous black women manoeuvre, creating wonderful-smelling meals with pungent spices. We do not eat there because it is very expensive, so Sarah, who looks gorgeous in her navy blue Ghost dress, her soft olive skin glowing, thanks the Colombian businessman and his two English guests in perfect Roedean style and we take our leave. By this time it is about a quarter to ten and I am buzzing with energy and totally unaffected by the alcohol. We eat in a less expensive but smart restaurant and I discover Sarah performed a number on stage with Charlotte's brother Matthew when they were both four years old. It's a pity they won't get to meet tomorrow . . . another time. Martin and Niki are concerned about overspending but Sarah and I are well into the glamour of the evening and it doesn't take long to convince them to have a little spree – you'd go mad if you counted every penny. It is way past midnight when we finish and we are still talking in a more accelerated way than usual, at least I am, and I would not like to be with people whose company I was not enjoying after snorting a line of coke. I think it is very important to be happy in the environment if any drugs are to be taken.

Back at the Doral I cannot sleep, I am too hot in my room and sweating like the woman in Amy's story, all my glands have come up and I am still speeding away. So I clean up my room and fold my clothes at least five times, then at four thirty-seven in the morning I go out and sit in the patio writing my diary to the light of the bright half-moon and the sound of the chirping cicadas. An occasional car passes but apart from that everybody seems to be asleep; someone switches their light on; maybe Sarah is awake, should I go and see? No, better not, she's got a long day ahead tomorrow, or rather today. I work out what I have spent in Colombia so far, and I am horrified. I hope we've spent less than our proposed budget in Quito. I really shouldn't encourage others to be extravagant with all the nonchalance in the world and then sit up worrying about my own finances at five fifteen in the morning. I am definitely donning Jill's black Ray-Bans and my panama hat after I've said goodbye to Sarah, and taking myself off to the Hilton beach alone for one of María's 'fruta mi amor' chunky coconut, fig, banana, mango and papaya salads. Yesterday seems ages ago. I went to the telephone exchange and called Marko to check where Charlotte was – she hadn't phoned at that point – and when he told me she was on her way to Cartagena, without ringing me first, I just issued a stream of obscenities down the receiver with the door of the kiosk open and sweat pouring down my face. Amy, along with the rest of the callers waiting for a free phone, looked as if she thought I had lost it and the fan was whirring around in the kiosk and I asked Marko if they had had a nice time and he said yes. Then I decided to trust the Universe and cancel my flight to Bogotá where I had intended to meet up with Charlotte (the man might have rung).

I really must get some sleep now but I mustn't forget to write about travel snobbery, all that showing off about who can get the cheapest hotels and spend as little as possible in a day, no wonder some of those people have constant diarrhoea . . . Oh yes, and about that mean Englishman . . . What looks like quite a sexy guy just walked into the showers, does everybody get coked-up here and not sleep? How can those people go to that hotel in that other town and just snort the stuff day and night for months on end? What does that do for a person? What does it do to them? I suddenly remember an old client accusing me of having stolen a crystal ball she'd lent me and replacing it with a cheaper one. Why I should think that here I do not know, but I wonder, did she transfer her disappointment ('this is not the one') on to the ball when really it was me who wasn't the one she expected, when Jill answered the door. I hear someone coughing, a shower is running and the night porter is taking a piss. Soon the sun will rise; I am not tired; I might be horny; the waiter last night was sexy; I hope I didn't appear mocking; how can I be soft and direct when I am insecure? I'll sleep on the beach . . .

Sarah will leave in the morning and thank me for making her feel good about herself, and that makes me feel good. Charlotte will come to Cartagena later that day and one of the cleaning women will say to me with a wry smile, 'Ah, so one leaves and the other one moves in, ha ha.' Charlotte and I will visit a town on the Magdalena river, and stay in a hotel with a tree with vines where children can swing and which houses butterflies, birds and lizards. I will feel the huge penis of a young man in another town whilst watching a funeral take place opposite the window of the room we are in; then I will lose my nerve and leave abruptly. In yet another place where the buildings are all white, Charlotte and I will go out looking for the monkeys that screech at dusk in the trees, but we will not find them because we get lost and end up miles out of the way and the market trader Rhys and his travelling companion Phil a dentist and plastic surgeon, who we know from the Doral, will meet us in this place and Phil will check my glands and tell me there is absolutely nothing wrong with me, and no I have absolutely no need of plastic surgery of any kind, my face is perfectly all right as it is . . . I will vomit profusely on arrival back at Cartagena airport after a ten-seater plane journey where the turbulence played with the aircraft like the ancient gods played with humankind. I will go with Charlotte to Bogotá, back to the Hostería De La Candelaría, we will meet up with Liliana and read the Dakini cards – come on, Liliana, your turn to interpret the cards for Charlotte now, you can't just piss off after your reading. We will eat with her and her friend Edgar, who calls me an angel, borscht in a Russian restaurant where a handsome Russian man sings beautifully and congratulates me gracefully on my version of 'Summertime' . . . Sacha has left for the mountains for a few days, we shall not see him. Liliana, who is multi-lingual, will recite Lorca in Spanish and Rilke in German for us in the car on the way to her parents' *finca* outside Bogotá which has a huge bronze statue of the dancing Shiva in the bay windows and there will be fork lightning right outside the house in the afternoon and we will not go to a party in the evening back in Bogotá just to be polite and please Edgar even though he is very nice, because we are exhausted and we want to go to bed. We will leave with Lufthansa back to Quito the next day and the customs official in the airport will tell me that my Spanish is very Mexican with all that 'mande', we just say 'qué' here, and reprimand me for having a pair of dangerous scissors in the side pocket of my bag. Charlotte will tell me I look extremely relaxed and even beautiful in Bogotá airport waiting lounge . . .

THE FOURTH OF
FEBRUARY 1992

~~~

Jane's flat, Quito, Ecuador at about 2 a.m.

On this night we were to take the sacred cactus juice, I sit instead alone in bed. I am calm. Wait. Let me check. Yes. I am calm.

Yesterday we went to fetch Saint Peter's holy liquid which lets us in the gate. We wound around the mountains down into the mouth of the valley. The buildings we left high up on the horizon were like big uneven teeth. The taxi drew to a sudden stop. The road was blocked – a landslide – and we could not go on. We took another route, ignoring this first and potent sign. As we entered the city again, I wanted to leave the taxi and forget the whole thing. I felt an indefinable anger. Arriving at the doctor's door some thirty minutes later, we faced what we had known already . . . He was not there.

If someone is not there, they are not supposed to be there.

We should have been disappointed perhaps, but instead we were rather relieved. The curfew on sex was lifted (we attempt to do a three-day abstention from toxins and passions always before ingesting hallucinogenics), which brought more than one smile to the faces of Charlotte and Marko. I was meeting with a young and beautiful Swiss man for dinner at 6.30, which I duly did. We drank gin and tonics and a bottle of fresh red wine from Chile. We dined French and were the only ones there. He told me of his lover who is coming to visit him soon and who called yesterday ten minutes before he arrived back at his accommodation. So he missed the connection.

We just made love. Jane gave us her blessing, *claro qué sí*, he can stay, *mi amor*, and left flowers in my room. There was passion between us. He is quite the tallest man I've ever been to bed with.

Schuldgefühle sind verboten, Feelings of guilt are forbidden, *habe ich gesagt*, I said. But he got up and left. That was all right by me. Wait. Just let me check. Yes. It was OK by me, though I'd have liked you to have stayed.

I wiped my wet body with my red singlet and heard the man in the next room get up and go to the kitchen.

I am calm. Yes. Calm. I'd have liked you to stay but that's OK. I know you have a lover at home and that makes it different. I know it's not personal. I can feel your warmth even though you are not here, and yes, I'm calm.

Schuldgefühle und Minderwertigkeitsgefühle sind verboten, Feelings of guilt and feeling 'less than' are forbidden.

The Sixth of February 1992. Jane's flat, Quito, Ecuador, at about 3 a.m.

(AND THINGS ARE GENERALLY WORSE AT 3 A.M.
THAN THEY ARE AT 2 A.M.)

I am alone in bed. All is quiet except for the clicking of the Quito frogs somewhere outside the window.

Peter, you just left. I opened the door and you went out into the misty night. I would have liked you to have stayed. Now the Quito dogs, guarding the houses of the better-off here, are barking. Is it because you are passing by?

Tonight we did not make love, you and I. You made a decision to be true to your partner, he deserves the respect, you love him and he certainly loves you – that I can perceive across the thousands of miles of mountains and ocean separating you right now.

You said you'd like to keep and enjoy what we have.

You touch me and it's good to feel your warmth, but those strong slim arms will not hold me in the night.

I do not want you to feel *beschissen*, wretched, from guilt and wrongness if we make love for I know that it would be as bad for me as for you on some level. So I respect your decision. And am glad to feel your warmth, your honesty. But there is sadness in me. I want to make love; I'd like it to be with you . . .

There is too something stirring beyond the sadness; the knowledge you bring me something important. Something in your loyalty. The fact you say to me, 'If it were us, I'd be the same.' I respect your decision therefore and do not force the issue; and still I feel beautiful and loved when I am with you. I'm catching potent glimpses of something I want for myself, something not yet quite clear . . .

Still, I am sad you could not stay, and that we did not make love . . .

The Sixth of February 1992, 9 a.m.

Today woke up very sad. I hesitated to write this down, but the woman who comes here to clean twice a week said to me 'amaneció muy triste el día hoy'. And so I wrote it down. When I awoke I felt cold and angry at your absence. It's all right for you, I thought, you're all clear. What about me? Where are those strong slim arms that should hold me near? Well, you did hold me near and then you left. And talking of leaving, I leave in two mornings from now. What right have I to demand from you any more than you feel comfortable in giving? I guess I'm tired of waking alone in the morning . . .

QUITO: QUICKSILVER CITY 2
'THE GAP IN THE SKY'

~~~

And so I stand in front of this window for the last time. It is misty today in Quito. I cannot yet see the green mountains but I know they will come soon. Four white doves fly up for their breakfast. You are still asleep. I did not expect to find love in this city of I remove, I take away, to be standing here, watching your sleeping face, waiting for the sun. The birds eat from my hand, yesterday's bread.

What shall I hold apart from this? Jane's sunny flat where we danced and drank vodka (it was your country's Independence Day), and reading poetry (Amy's dark voice in the candlelight), and the four of us taking San Pedro on a magical morning. The eleventh of January. Eleven minutes past eleven GMT (it was six in the morning our time). North, south, east, west: we sat in a circle. Fire, water, earth, air. And that turquoise swimming pool where we dived and lay like porpoises (I first met Jane there . . . her blue eyes met mine and I laughed in recognition). All those yellow taxis, all those late lunches, conversations and coffee with Brazilian cake. Ah yes, we lived like kings.

On the last night of the old year, they set fire to the old men of straw in the streets of Quito, our fears and our desires burned away that night. We stood in a stranger's party and the three of us embraced each other and I knew something was changed (Gregory had walked away with a pack of cards that night: we did not see him again).

After that the electricity strikes began. 'Falta de luz!' you said. We were walking along the road to the hotel near where you lived.

We heard men shouting in the dark. On a skeleton building, there was a burning bonfire on the roof, to warn the hidden aeroplanes.

O look up, look up now into the bare sky. I am flying to the sun, you are flying to the moon. Sometimes we have to leave the old places, these crucibles where we were changed. Where do we go when we lift the cloud that hides us? Where do we hide when the stupor is burned away? What do we now see when we cannot sleep? The sun is up and eating the mists. The mountains bare their hard shoulders, the eucalyptus shakes her hair. A monastery bell is calling. O come out, come out and greet the new morning! How scared was I before to stand here in this pale intoxicating light, and look into the naked sky. Was I so afraid of my sacredness? Was I so afraid of my humanity?

A bird dips across the valley, and pulls apart the last fine curtain of mist. Not afraid to be bird. I blink and follow his flight, up and across and, like a winged key, I watch him open my new blue door.

4

BOLIVIA

BOLIVIA

~~~

White City

'Oblivion?' queried Lucinda, my one-time neighbour when I was back in London.

'No,' I said. '*Bolivia*. I want to go to Bolivia, to the mountains and hear the silence.'

'Oh,' she said. 'I see.'

I'm not sure she did really. I don't think I did that day when a pale clammy Belgian man leant towards us in a bus in Mexico and suggested we went to this far country. 'It is so quiet,' he told us. 'And the music is so extraordinary. There are no roads, you know.'

'What is the food like?' I asked.

He looked at me rather strangely.

'It's all right,' he said. 'Chicken, potatoes, you know.'

Yes, I thought, I do know and I know I don't want that.

But it was Bolivia I dreamt about, night after night. I called them my Bolivian flying dreams. 'I just fly over this amazing landscape,' I'd say to Mark. 'Over the Andes and feel the vastness of things. There is no one there, only the wind.'

Mark was not impressed by this.

'Get down to earth,' he said.

But here we are in Bolivia in early March. Having left our lovers behind in Quito, having been crying over our plastic breakfasts on Air France and sleeping in Lima airport amongst the coffee cups. We are curling our way down towards La Paz which lies sprinkled in a valley like a handful of silver coins in a farm worker's palm. We are staying in a hotel in a street that sells fiesta confetti and masks. Giant women in hooped skirts and little bowler hats run past the window. Young boys sing out destinations from the micro buses. The mountain cold has entered my bones. We are drinking coca tea and not saying much, waiting for our friends Andy and Susan to come from Argentina. Coca tea is one of the more unpleasant things I have put in my mouth in South America.

I walk down a street, a steep cobbled street, wrapped in darkness and I hear from a shut window an eerie sound of pipe and drum, unlike any I have heard before. It is like a march. I see no faces. On that first night in La Paz, we ate bowls of lamb stew and coarse brown bread and we were silent and exhausted and I was sick. Two dancers, their hair full of ribbons, practised strange steps in the corridor. I heard that music again, and I wanted to shut my ears. I knew it came from somewhere I was afraid to go.

'I have a very bad cold and altitude sickness,' announces Mark.

We are in the rooftop restaurant of the Sheraton Hotel on the second day, eating Round the World cuisine. Andy and Susan are not impressed by this lack of authenticity. They are arguing the merits of Argentinian wine over Chilean wine.

'This view is amazing,' I say, playing with my Hawaiian chicken.

'*I am very cold and I have a very bad cold and altitude sickness!*' shouts Mark. He is lying on the floor. He is refusing to get up.

So we go on the third day to the city of Sucre, which is warmer and lower down. Sucre is known as the White City: it sits amongst purple mountains and has a square full of balloon sellers and palm trees and students who walk around with their books at 3 a.m., chewing coca leaves.

'It's a bit like Oaxaca,' I tell Mark who has taken to his bed in a serious way. The maid is bringing him a hot lemon and Pisco drink called Chaufflay. I am bringing him an exotic French cough medicine. 'Except that these balloons are not filled with air. They are filled with water and the youth of Sucre like to throw them at you because it's Mardi Gras soon.'

'How unpleasant!' he says, inhaling from a steaming bowl of eucalyptus leaves.

'It's not that amusing really,' I agree.

Andy reels off some facts about Sucre. He is sounding like a Baedeker. Look at that so-and-so Indian from so-and-so tribe (You can tell by his hat), this is a *saltena* which is a Bolivian *empanada*, and do I want to go on a church crawl with him?

'I couldn't think of anything more horrible.'

'You are very lazy,' he says.

'I am not a tourist,' I retort.

'No, you are a lazy person who likes staying in hotel rooms,' he laughs and goes out of the room.

On the fourth day we hire a jeep and go into the mountains to visit a market town. So-and-so Indians go there and they sell so-and-so textiles, reads Andy from one of his fifteen guidebooks. On the way I fly into my Bolivian dreamscape, into the vast solitude and silence and alien blue and green. I feel as tiny and insignificant as an ant, as if I could be crushed by an invisible fist of purest air. My heart thumps against my chest. I feel very far away from myself.

We take a lot of pictures of ourselves on the road: looking very cold with altitude problems; lounging about the jeep, by giant cacti with flowers like white trumpets; and of five condors eating a rabbit (when they fly their wings beat the air like a drum across the empty valley). The market town is even colder and higher and we eat fried egg sandwiches and drink beer in a desolate bar. It is not market day. There are no Indians.

'Going to any churches, And?' I ask.

'Piss off!' he replies.

'It's not the arriving of course,' I remark. 'It's the journey through the mountains that is important.'

'O shut up, Charlotte!' say Andy and Susan and Mark. 'Let's go back.'

But I feel sad because I can't go back. Andy and I went to the vegetable market together and it wasn't the same: it wasn't Athens, or Portobello market, or that glamour deli in New York or the kasbah in Fez. It was the White City, where I had asked to be clear, to hear the silence. Where I had asked for purification. I feel sad because I feel alone. I feel wrenched, torn up by the roots and cannot transplant myself in this rocky soil. I do not belong there,

I do not belong here. I ring Marko in Quito. He is about to leave for Slovenia. I am saying goodbye and I can hardly hear him on the crackly line.

'How is Mark?' he asks.

'He's got bronchitis.'

'Have you gone to Lake Titicaca yet?'

'No.'

'Go to the lake,' he says. 'Vale la pena.'

'I miss you,' I say.

I ring my sister in Hong Kong. She is about to have a baby. I want to wish her luck but she isn't at home. I have a very frustrating talk with her amah in Spanish and Chinese English.

'Baby come?'

'Mr Korner he not home.'

'Quando sister regressa?' I yell. 'Que hora sister back?'

'She at dinner.'

'Ahseem, I give fax number hotel. Give to sister, por favor.'

'OK.'

'Give sister mucho lover, verdad?'

'OK,' laughs Ahseem from the other side of the world.

In the darkness at 2 a.m. I hear the invisible music again. Is it a wedding or a funeral march? I ask myself. Then I go to the window and I open it above the street. Men with trumpets and drums are walking past and playing a song of celebration, and young boys with red and purple neckerchiefs are dancing and cavorting before them. Where do you invite me?

On the fifth day we go to a ruined palace called La Glorieta. It is built like a giant Arab pastry with blue glass eyes. The empty rooms are full of graffiti and broken window panes. The army use it as a depot. Susan and I try to dodge the taxi driver: 'The Princess's portraits are this way!' he says.

'He is a real bore,' Susan shouts in a stage whisper when I find her creeping about the basement.

'Come on!' I say. 'This way!'

We run up different towers and wave at each other from the top.

I look over the garden where Andy is sitting writing notes by an empty fishpond. The wind is in the palm trees and their dead leaves are strewn at their feet like dry snakes. I try to imagine the princess who bought her title from the Pope in exchange for an Andean gold mine walking through this skeleton greenhouse picking flowers, watching the moon from the temple, staring into the grotto fountains. Did she see the mirror of her vanity there? Did she not know it would not last for ever? A trumpet sounds again. Did she envision how her palace would one day be full of soldiers and how a stranger would sit writing in her garden?

We can enclose nothing.

My ghostlife is slipping away from me.

I can hear a band practising, invisible, in the shrubbery. Where is this old music leading me, out of the garden and into the hills?

A week goes by. Marko flies home. Ruth has her baby. Mark starts to recover. Andy and Susan go back to Argentina.

'When are you coming back?' asks Andy at the bus station.

'I don't think I am,' I say.

'Maybe I'll come and see you in Chile sometime,' he says.

'Yes, maybe,' I say and feel hot sad tears run down my face.

Blue Lake

So while Mark was recuperating I went to the lake.

I meet three men: two brothers (one blond, one dark) from England and a red-headed miner from Australia. None of them wants to go back to their countries. I go swimming in the freezing lake with the dark brother who tells me about Africa. He is polite and charming and articulate but it is the younger brother I like best, the one with the flame-coloured hair. I like the way he burst out smiling when I looked at his hand and told him he was an artist, when I said to stop worrying about his father who wanted to be an artist too and had died of a heart attack, when something like happiness shone all over his face.

One morning we hire a little sailing boat with a white sail and row across this vast lake to the Island of the Sun and have a picnic. The blond brother rows when he feels like it. The dark brother rows well and is conscious that he always does so. The red man rows badly and gets furious with himself and angry with the water.

'Capitano!' calls out our young boatman to the youngest and navigates him through the rocky channels.

There is peace here on this island in the highest sailable lake in the world. Under these eucalyptus trees, up these Inca steps. I am reminded of Greece and I am reminded of Ireland and other lovely picnics by water. Two children bring their llamas. The dark brother is taking photographs, but has only paid one of the children.

'Pay them,' I say, 'or we will be followed all day.'

'Photo, photo,' say the children to me and wave their embroidered bracelets for me to buy.

'No,' I reply.

'Photo con llama.'

'I don't want a photo. Go away.'

I stare across the lake to the other island that looks like a sleeping woman. It is warm and the lake is blue as blue as blue.

'Photo!' say the girls again.

'Listen. I don't want a photo. I don't have a camera.'

'Si, senora, in your bag.'

'Look. Here is my bag, no camera, no photo, no buy *nada*. I want silence. And no goddamn llama scene, OK?'

The girls laugh.

'You are angry,' they say.

Yes, I think. I am angry.

'I want to be alone. I want to look at the lake. It's nothing personal.'

The girls do not move, they stay by my side. But that feels good. The llamas chew the spiky bushes, and the girls grow quiet and we all stare across the lake, across the blue blue lake towards the Island of the Moon. And the great silence of Bolivia heaves a sigh, and the soft wind blows.

I sat on the prow of the boat all the way back and stared into the dark depths of the lake for some inspiration. I saw no monsters. I saw no ghosts. I did not see my soul down there. All I could see in the water was the reflected sun.

That night I peeked my head round a small circus tent. It was full of Indians and their children sitting on wooden benches eating toffee apples. There was a raggedy clown and a dog who leapt from the trapeze into a Bolivian flag. Everyone was laughing and clapping. It was freezing outside, and the clown was terrible, he kept breaking mask and falling over his long shoes in the muddy floor and the dog-trainer girl in the lilac leotard looked very tired and the music was very loud and distorted. But when I look back, I remember something else from the blue lake. I remember the fiery smile of a young king, the sun in the water, two children standing beside me and the laughter of an audience that floated out of a small white tent into a freezing night.

Red Desert

For years I imagined that every journey was a journey of the moon: that you had to go back into your past, into your sadness, into your poetry and your dreams where your shadow story is written. But not all stories take that path.

The journey of the sun is different. It does not search, it cleanses. It clears everything away that you no longer need to let something else shine through, to admit light in a place that has only known darkness. 'Do not take my wound away,' wrote the poet. He was afraid that his verse could not stand the brilliance of day. I am too, when I travel over this huge landscape where only the wind lives.

Mark and I have taken a little train across the Altiplano with its fleeing goats and llamas, past the mining villages where children hold out their hands for sweets and coins, through the hills where the rocks have savage faces of beasts and birds, through the sulphur-yellow salt lakes, and into the rusty pink of the Atacama Desert. Into the red desert, whose hugeness is only broken by a dead tree or an abandoned house or a crooked grave.

Who came here before? I wonder. Who braved this loneliness? Who left their bodies to be dried like grass in this hot wind, held in this collapsing roof of tin?

And who returned to the city?

The sun sets the hills on fire. Amy once wrote to me about this desert. She said she sat under a full moon hoping that the universe would refresh her, hold her in its arms and take away her sadness and her loneliness. She watched the moon rise amongst the magical rocks but she remained sad and broken-spirited.

'Sometimes when I go seeking the comfort,' she said, 'I cannot find it.'

We are travelling endlessly through the night, a cold black night that is full of stars. I am covered in a blanket and crane my neck awkwardly against the bus window to see the constellations. It is not comforting, this sky at night, nor is the sun comforting by day. To be comforting would be to stay where I am known, to remain small and stuck inside myself. Sometimes you need to go to the places which are so immense they care not for man, so that you can find that part of yourself that is beyond the human, that is as timeless as the rocks, as vast as the sky, as primal as the sun. The place without roads and gardens. It could have been comforting to stay with my friends arguing about wine and churches, comforting to linger among the childhood palaces and the moonlit sea where my songs were born. But I want to be bigger than that, even at the risk of oblivion. I said I wanted to hear the silence of the mountains. I said I wanted to hear what silence sounded like, when all my old noise was taken away. So I listened and I heard a strange music that leads me now across this desert.

I listened and I heard the faint thump of my bigger heart that beat like a drum across the valley and I heard within me a higher voice that sounded like a trumpet amongst the peaks, heralding a very different event. I followed that music I thought was a funeral, a march of death or war, and it was a wedding, it was a dance of celebration after all.

INCIDENT IN LA PAZ

~~~

My head is full of air as I walk back through this breathless city to the Residencial Rosario. My first venture out after days of feeling sick.

Maybe it's this light, heady feeling which has encouraged me to dress so uncharacteristically today. That and the fact that I have always been told La Paz is safe. Panama hat, colourful Bolivian alpaca jumper (only tourists wear them), and purple sunglasses to shield me from the sharp light. Like I've really made an effort to blend in with my surroundings!

About two hundred yards from the *residencial* I happen to glance down. The bottom of my right trouser-leg is completely covered with a white liquid that I think, as my heart starts to sink, is paint. For some reason I do not bend down to see what it is, but decide vaguely to deal with it at the hotel. I carry on walking. Suddenly a voice, which I immediately detect as suspicious, snaps me from this whole out-of-body experience asking, 'Que te pasooo?' (What happened to you?) and a dark hand offers me a packet of serviettes.

For some reason I still do not bend down though I do accept the tissues and at the same time another man calls from behind me, 'Are you Spanish?'

'Si,' I reply, and the man says:

'Well, watch out! If they throw glue at you it means they are going to rob you! Don't bend down! It's the Peruvians, you know.'

The serviette man has made a miraculous disappearance by this time. I accelerate my pace back to the hotel, gluey-clothed but complete with all my belongings.

I wash the glue easily from my Chinos and the back of my sweater.

'You were lucky, it could have been urine,' said the hotel receptionist.

CROSSING BORDERS 3: BOLIVIA TO CHILE

~~~

I really am not sorry to be leaving Bolivia. A horrible bout of bronchitis has blighted most of my two-week stay here, my temperature soaring with hallucinatory condors. It seems to have taken ages to get better, though an altitude of three and a half kilometres and the corresponding lack of oxygen aren't exactly the kind of bedfellows your lungs would want for a speedy recovery.

Then as soon as I've started more or less breathing properly again, Charlotte goes off to Lake Titicaca in the company of three men and gets enlightened on the Island of the Sun and I stay in La Paz with cold bones and get a fucking migraine. Big deal, let's just get down to Chile.

And it is a much thinner me leaving Bolivia than the one that arrived just that fortnight ago. I've lost over a stone and my left eye is still squelching from the migraine-induced water retention. I hope it's not water-on-the-brain. I can't believe that the healthy, tanned young man who arrived back in Quito from Colombia less than a month ago was me. Oh well, it's no use dwelling on the past, however recent. My God, is that the train? I expected something rather grand and old-fashioned like the station, well OK, just old fashioned, this is Bolivia, but not this one-coach train that looks like it's lost the rest of itself. Oh no, it's completely packed. Good job I booked the tickets in advance.

'Do you trust the luggage here, Charlotte? Yes, I know I'm a bit neurotic about that, but I like to be in control . . . No comments, thank you, I'm not in a good mood, it's six thirty in the morning and I'm bloody cold.'

Not that the early morning is Charlotte's prime time either. She's practically catatonic until she's consumed inhuman amounts of black coffee, and about the only thing that provokes a response this morning (by way of laughter) is witnessing my pre-border compulsions. I am quite compulsive anyway, but these little tics increase in intensity whenever I am about to leave somewhere for somewhere else. Whether by plane or train, it's always the same.

'Are you actually going to come out of that room, Mark, or are you going to stand at the door counting for ever?'

Careful not to step on the cracks in the pavement. Touch the suitcases and count to a certain number, left, right, yes, now they can go. What if something awful happened because I don't get to ninety without taking a breath?

'Come on, Mark, get on the train. Stop touching each side of the doorway.'

Well, it's actually quite comfortable, no screaming children, thank God. Are we off already? Ooh, coffee, great! Now can I cope with the refrigerated ham and cheese roll? It's got that not-quite-damp moistness about it. I suppose it's better than nothing. I don't believe we're climbing higher.

'Charlotte, we're climbing higher. We'll be well over four thousand metres in no time. Will we still be able to breathe?'

'They say it goes up to about five thousand or so.'

'Oh, great. Listen, can you hear my eye squelching?'

'Yes. It's disgusting.'

'Just listen to that. What if it goes stagnant?'

'I'm trying to drink my coffee, thank you.'

I can't really tell where we are because there's so much mist. We must have left La Paz behind, though. Ah, it's clearing. God, what amazing plains. Just flat bleak land for miles. Our tiny train feels even tinier. How can anyone live up here? Does anyone live up here? Well, they must do because there are lots of llamas.

That girl at the front really has got the hots for that cute blond guy just behind her.

'He's very sexy.'

'God, Charlotte. What's wrong? I don't believe you just called someone sexy.'

'Nothing's wrong. It's just that I don't usually find people sexy simply by looking at them, you know . . .'

'No, I don't know, actually . . . Look, there she is again, turning round pulling all those pouty faces and trying to pretend she's just looking to the back. Jesus, I do things like that and I'm nearly thirty. I hope I don't look as desperate as that. It's terrifying. Charlotte, are you listening to me . . . ?'

Oh what? I really don't believe this. Dinner. It's only ten thirty. This braised meat's a bit dark. I wonder what it is. Oh, and Charlotte's favourite – Bolivian dried potatoes rehydrated, boiled and still hard.

'Do you think it's all right, Charlie?'

'I think it's absolutely horrid.'

We eat it though.

What now? This train is soooo slow. Impatience impatience. Just be in the moment, Mark, sit back, relax, enjoy the scenery. What's the hurry? Ah, llamas on the track. They really are very beautiful. They had them in Golders Hill Park near where I used to live. They were very fierce. One of them spat in my flatmate's face once when he was imitating them over the fence. They look happier here, mind.

How these landscapes amaze as they shift and change. Bare, dull-coloured rocks jut out now with cactuses bursting up suddenly. The tops of the hills have formations like faces and sometimes they look like they are screaming. Tombs shaped like little dogs' houses are occasionally grouped together, with crosses outside the small entrances. But there's no sign of life anywhere. No houses, nothing. Where do people come from to bury their dead?

I can't believe Charlotte is asleep. That really gets my llama, that does. She should be watching this wonderful scenery. Ooops, it's not about 'shoulds'. Don't be so controlling, Mark. Let the girl do what she likes, for God's sake . . .

'Charlotte, wake up and look at those incredible rocks, they're like tribes of people. I can see babies screaming in some of them.'

'Wh-what? Oh. God.'

'Yes, probably.'

We have now come down to a mere four thousand one hundred metres above sea-level and are waiting in a siding in a village full of adobe huts, until another train passes heading for La Paz. This is a one-tracked line.

I am talking to the cute, blond object of the girl-in-the-front's unsubtle desire, a twenty-five-year-old German called Frank.

'That girl really has got the hots for you, hasn't she, Frank? She's quite outrageous.'

'Latin American girls can be like that sometimes. I was living in El Salvador for some years during the 'eighties, and they liked the white, blue-eyed foreigners there. I'm not sure what I feel about that. They are very different from us. Not so liberated.'

(Yeah, yeah, yeah, get your trousers off, Frank, show us what you've got!)

'Wasn't it scary in El Salvador, all those bombs and shootings?'

'There were a lot of bombs. Sometimes they would miss and hit an old lady's house instead of a government building. We were OK. My father taught German there. Ach, you got used to it, really.'

I make a point of talking to people who give me the horn, because usually about five minutes or less into the conversation I turn off in all senses, and that stops me wasting any more time and energy fantasizing about them. I speak to a lot of people and get bored a lot.

At the Bolivian border town, moneychangers board the train and the lady behind tells me the rate is reasonable. It is the calmest currency exchange I have seen at any border. The girl-in-the-front gives a bag of sweets to a small girl with outstretched hands and a beautiful smile who comes to the door of the train. The skin on her hands and face is covered with warts.

'Quite quick with the old exit stamps, Charlie.'

'Yeah.'

Well, here's the Chilean border.

WELCOME TO CHILE — DRUGS DESTROY MAN.

I can't understand why it'll take us another six hours to get to Arica from here. Chile is so thin. Not that this is exactly an express train. Mind you, those people in La Paz did say that the other train (the proper big one) sometimes takes seventeen or eighteen hours and occasionally derails.

'What do you think "carabineros" means, Charlie?'

'Well, it means police in Italian.'

Well, the immigration officials are having fun with the foreigners' names. They can hardly pronounce the German ones. Still, who can? Oh no, please don't make that bloody joke about Sherlock Holmes again. I've heard that one all over the continent. 'Elemental, mi querido Watson.' Quite. Ha ha. I don't suppose I can blame them. They have to amuse themselves somehow. Why is everybody moving their luggage over to that table? *All the luggage!* Great, like I really want to unpack everything after preparing my bags so carefully, just so they can check there's no fruit hidden in them. It usually takes me about half a day to pack on and off. It's like a little ritual I do — I suppose some would call it obsessive, but I don't like to cheapen it by categorizing it as such. Why have all the inspectors got thick white cream all over their faces? Ah, the UV rays of course. Better to look like a clown than get skin cancer.

It has taken us over an hour to get through immigration. And that's quick says the lady behind me, a very noble-looking Bolivian, about sixty with bouffant black hair. She is talking to me about Bolivian music.

'A lot of people steal our songs, you know, and then make out they are theirs.'

'What do you mean?'

'Well, a lot of countries adopt our songs and call them their own.'

'Oh, That's not very nice.'

The toilet is not very nice. It is fairly clean but it's so close to the passengers at the back I'm paranoid they can hear every fart and this does not make for the most comfortable sit-down experience. They can't possibly hear anything anyway because of the noise of the train. Oh, so what if they can.

We are starting to descend from our lofty heights. More landscape changes. Saw some deer darting across a shrubby plain about an hour ago. No such life here, though. Just pink pink desert rock against a clear blue sky. Even the thorny now-and-then cacti with their bright flowers of white or red look hospitable in such wilderness. Gives me the horrors to imagine what it would be like being stuck out here with no water. Fatal, probably. Llama country seems light years away now. I might have a nap; Charlotte's still dozing. Oh, more food.

'Charlotte, food!'

'Oh.'

'Is this included in the $50 fare?'

'No, señor, only breakfast and lunch. You must pay the rest.'

Bloody typical.

We descend through the desert mountains into a startling oasis, a valley green and lush with those bare pink hills rising up at each side. They look gentler now next to the fertile land. Protective almost.

The teenage fatale has dropped off to sleep but so has Frank, so he's not even conscious to enjoy the lack of attention. Oh, not another stop.

'It's just the driver making a phone call to Arica, Mark, to say we'll be arriving soon.'

'How do you know?'

'Common sense.'

A quarter of an hour later, train-weary and relieved, with all our luggage intact and my left eye still squelching, we arrive in Arica by the sea, Chile's northernmost town. The balmy late-summer air is welcoming after bone-chilling La Paz. Everyone is impatient for their suitcases and bags as they are handed down from the top of the tiny train. Frank and his two German friends load their backpacks and disappear quickly and efficiently, the girl-in-the-front barely noticing as she talks animatedly with her friends. A woman tells us she and her family live in Viña del Mar, the hot beach spot of the Chilean wealthy.

'We're going to rent somewhere in Valparaíso for a while.'

'Oh. That's just a few kilometres away from Viña. But I don't like it. It's too bohemian.'

'That's why we're going.'

At this point we are unaware that 'bohemio' in Chile refers to drunk and disorderly nightlife with a good measure of sleaze thrown in. And at this point I couldn't care less. We board a black ramshackle cab for our hotel . . .

5

CHILE

CHILE NOTEBOOK

~~~

1. *Hotel Chungara, Arica*

At the Hotel Chungara, the rooms are small and functional, but there is a bath. Yippee! No plug. Oh well, I'll just use an inverted shampoo bottle with polythene wrapped round the top.

'People come here from all over the world.' The owner is a friendly man in his late forties. 'Chile is so much nicer than Peru. Tacna (the Peruvian version of Arica some forty-five kilometres away) is filthy; don't bother to go there.'

Despite its Indian-sounding name, there is nothing indigenous about the Hotel Chungara, nor indeed about the family who run it.

I am washing clothes in the warm Arica sun and thinking how totally different Chile is to Bolivia already. On a walk in the town centre, everything is so clean and fast-food places abound. And there are hardly any people of Indian blood. We pay what seems like an extortionate price for very mediocre food in a café with a German name.

'Foodwise, I'd rather Bolivia than Bavaria, Charlotte.'

The first of many times I hear Nilsson's 'Without You' in Chile is in the Hotel Chungara. It follows me around as I go from the shower to my room. I can't see any speakers. Did life stop in 1973 with the dictatorship?

'Come and have lunch with us today,' say the two sisters. One is the owner's wife and the other is visiting from Santiago with her extraordinarily tall fifteen-year-old son. They are all enjoying several bottles of lager each. I accept one and hope that Charlotte is not too long in returning from town.

'Ah, the Chilean women, they are very beautiful,' say the sisters. 'Chile is beautiful. The people. That's how it is. Chile. The people are lovely. The Chileans.'

One sister is almost ecstatic thinking about the beauty of her country and its people.

The lunch was a delicious lamb stew.

'Chilean food is so wonderful,' says a sister, and opens another lager bottle.

Charlotte has arrived just in time for lunch and is changing upstairs.

'I'll go and get her,' says the wife of the owner.

Charlotte tells me later that she just stood there and watched her change.

'We're all women together . . . *mujeres*,' she said. We would in time discover that it is the most normal thing for women in Chile to even accompany each other right into the toilet.

'We have German blood,' says a sister. 'Chile is very European. And the women are pretty. Chilean women. That's what they're like.'

'What's it like without Pinochet?' I ask.

'Well, I liked Pinochet. He did a lot of good for the country. For Chile,' says the owner.

'I'm glad he's gone. I'm a democrat,' says his wife.

'So am I,' says her sister. 'My husband is in the military. But I don't like all that. I like freedom. I like to make up my own mind. I'm a hairdresser.'

'The foreign press was always very negative,' says the owner.

I had not expected to hear anyone say that they liked Pinochet. The family seems to get bored with the subject, preferring to eat and drink. So I go no further.

After lunch the sisters totter off to the beach with their children, Charlotte goes to a different beach and I take another walk around town, marvelling at how the pink desert just drops to the sea like that.

The sisters are less gregarious when they come back. There are still some tourists in Arica as the summer season comes to a close, mostly Chileans from Antofagasta or Santiago. The local newspaper boasts daily cover photos of two or three 'lindas mujeres chilenas' as they catch the last rays of summer sun, and contains articles on the increase in vandalism in recent times.

Tomorrow we're off to Iquique, four hours south of here. I think I'll have a bath with the inverted shampoo bottle and clear my slight hangover . . .

2. *The Gypsy in Iquique*

There are ghost towns in the north of Chile. Old, deserted nitrate-mining towns with houses and churches still standing in the middle of the desert. And nobody there.

We do not visit any of these towns. But we do visit Iquique. Which seems like a ghost town – despite having a population of forty-odd thousand.

'Political prisoners were tortured there,' someone told us later.

At the hotel of our first choice, a very unfriendly woman tells us there are no rooms and slams shut the cast-iron gates. At another hotel a very friendly woman leads us to a musty, windowless room with high ceilings and shocks us with the price. We accept just for one night.

The sun shines hot and bright in the early afternoon as we walk along the coast to the centre of town. Everything is clean and quiet. Very quiet. An irrational feeling that I'll be arrested comes over me as we walk past the military barracks.

We lunch forgettably then return for a nap in the musty room. In the late afternoon I take a walk to the plaza. There are more people now. But I feel utterly disconnected. I put it down to all the oxygen after months in the high mountains.

A shabby young man with dirty long black hair reels towards me in the plaza and shouts to get my attention. Unnerved, I walk away quickly and enter the main shopping street where people hurry by and seem oblivious to anybody else. Despite this bustle the place still feels empty.

Two women appear from nowhere in front of me. They have

ravaged faces and are dressed in dirty white blouses with bright pink and yellow full skirts. I stare for a second too long and they are speaking to me:

'I'll tell your fortune, you give me what you want.' Deep-set eyes buried in wrinkles belie a youngish face and long spindly fingers with badly kept nails shuffle filthy tarot cards.

'No, thanks.'

The other woman grabs my hand and says she'll tell me my luck. I know I am letting myself in for something I do not want and I am hearing suddenly that someone has it in for me and, in order to do away with the evil intentions, I must take my money out and place it in the gypsy's hands. Which, despite myself, I do.

'Curse this money and rid yourself of the evil,' says the woman.

I attempt a rational explanation that the money is not evil and indeed that I can live for two or three days with such a sum. But she shouts and rants over me, rubbing her hands together as shreds of paper drop from her fingers. I am supposed to believe these are the remains of my banknotes, about seventy dollars.

'Right, that's enough. Give me back the money. All the dollars. *Now!*'

Unwillingly she hands me back the dollars and, after I have let her keep rather too many Chilean pesos, gives me a filthy small cloth cushion which she says will protect me.

I am furious with myself for having allowed this to happen. Feeling humiliated, dirtied, stupid, invaded, I enter a nearby shop.

'Everybody here knows the gypsies are con-artists,' says a woman who has pulled me aside and said she witnessed everything and was trying to find a policeman to no avail. 'They rip you off.'

'It won't happen again,' I reply. But it feels horrible.

I go down to the sea and throw the filthy pin cushion into the water. Protection!

A few months later I will meet a gypsy in Vicuña, an honest man called Milenko, selling beautiful copper bowls he handcrafts himself. I will tell him of my experience in Iquique.

'Scum!' he will say as he spits on the pavement. 'They give us a bad name. You come and visit my family. I invite you. We are good people.'

And I will see the film *Time of the Gypsies* three times in Santiago and think of Milenko . . .

That evening in Iquique, Charlotte and I have dinner in a huge restaurant in an old colonial house. It has taken several hours to recover from the unease the encounter with the gypsy woman left me with and feel clean again.

As the last rays of sunlight disappear, large black vultures descend, one by one without a sound, on the branches of the palm trees outside the restaurant window.

3. *Arrival in Santiago*

The bus station is hot, sweaty and full of bustle on this late Saturday Santiago afternoon as we alight from the coach after the dizzying twenty-eight-hour journey from the north. Yesterday seems years away. Into a taxi and to a hotel past grand old buildings through surprisingly quiet streets.

'You won't recognize it on Monday,' says the driver. 'It's always quiet at the weekends.'

I will have to get used to Chilean Spanish. It is very fast and the letter 's' is practically obsolete. But it's pretty and sounds like singing.

A familiar face beams out from a row of posters on a wall.

'Oh my God, Charlotte. Mercedes Sosa is in concert here next week. I have waited seven years to see her. It's her first visit to Chile in twenty years.'

I think I am going to like Santiago.

I am not in the hotel I want to be in. It would appear that the Residencial Londres is rather sought after. The man at the reception was very offhand, I thought, not taking reservations. Good-looking, though. Come back tomorrow morning at half past eight, he said. I am determined we shall have a room there.

At the hotel across the road I turn on the television to be greeted by an astrologer reading the chart of a politician (in his presence). I feel very at home. On another channel we are informed that Chile has the third largest rate of stomach disease (after Japan and Costa Rica) in the world.

'I believe it has a lot to do with the make-up of we Chileans,' says the doctor being interviewed.

Later we would meet a young Englishman with a guitar and a voice as sweet as the canned papayas so often served for dessert in Chile, and he would tell us of how he was hospitalized seven times in the first year he spent here . . . each time with stomach or intestinal problems.

And an overweight lawyer would confide to me one day in the sauna, 'The trouble with us Chileans is that we don't have an identity of our own. We so want to be European.'

Well, at least I'll have no problem getting hold of antacids for my periodic attacks of heartburn. And, I wonder, will Chile be the country where I learn to simply accept and love myself, period?

4. *Residencial Londres*

[i]

Pedro, the man I thought was so unfriendly yesterday, couldn't be more the opposite today. He shows us to Room 25 on the second floor where the sun shines through all afternoon and potted plants bring joy to the windowsill, and gives us a welcoming smile. The hotel is an old huge house with lots of wood and lots of foreign travellers. There are a few old ladies, resident from the time it was a boarding house, and a proud, efficient housekeeper called Estelita who has seen four owners come and go.

[ii]

'Where are you going to? Where are you coming from? Where are you going to? Where are you coming from?'

Co, a tall blond Dutchman, is warning me good-humouredly not to ask him any questions about his travel itinerary as he walks like a robot into our room. I am only too happy to meet his request. The same old questions become very tedious.

'Let's go and eat,' I say.

There are six or seven of us in the nearby Italian restaurant. We have ordered our food. I am wondering why it is so quiet. A group of fifty or so men suddenly arrive and take their places at a previously arranged table, which I (in my hunger) had not noticed. One man stands and addresses his brothers, and then turns to our table to welcome us: 'We are men of good who do good – a Men's Club.'

Agnes, Co's girlfriend, stands and goes to their table. She delivers a speech in very fast Dutch, occasionally touching her heart and saying 'Santiago'. Words flow from her for about two minutes. The Men's Club applaud her heartily, she takes a graceful bow and returns to our table.

'What were you saying?' I ask her.

'Oh, I jost invented de words,' she replied. 'It meant nothing at all.'

'What language was that lady speaking in?' asks the plump man with the cigar who has come over to our table.

'Dutch,' I reply.

'I was in Amsterdam last year and I never heard Dutch like that.'

'Oh, she's from The Hague,' I say. 'It's a totally different dialect.'

'She's all right, though, isn't she?'

'Well, goodnight,' says Agnes to the Men's Club as they leave. 'Say goodnight to your wives.'

[iii]

There's something about control in Santiago I cannot quite put my finger on. It is Sunday evening. Co has gone back to the hotel and

Agnes and I are walking round the city, letting our trousers fall down in front of restaurant doors. Some people laugh, but most look horrified, even indignant.

'What is your motive for doing that?' ask a young couple of about twenty. They have followed us into the park.

'We just felt like it. It makes us laugh,' I say defensively.

'If Chileans were to do that we'd be arrested,' says the boy, and maybe I detect a trace of irritation in his voice. I begin to feel like a naughty child who has behaved badly. But I said nothing because I really was not sure at the time what was the motive behind our dropping our trousers like that. Although it did make us laugh.

'You could have been had for "falta el moral",' (which I took to mean gross indecency) said Pedro back at the Londres.

'Oh, it was fun,' said Agnes simply.

But there is something about control . . .

[iv] Eating Together

There are six or eight of us in the lobby, trying to decide where to go for dinner.

'Chinese.'

'How much?'

'About three dollars with a beer.'

'I had Chinese last night. I don't want it again tonight.'

'There's a good chicken place around the corner. Five dollars with a beer.'

'That's far too expensive for us.' That one lived rent-free in London for a very long time and had an incredibly well-paid job. Shit, these budget travellers are a real bore. Won't even stretch to five dollars. Well, I don't want Chinese, cheap or no cheap. I hate democracy, all of a sudden. I'll go and eat on my fucking own. Ah, here's Andrew, a man with some sense.

'There's a restaurant, very decent, with rabbit stew and meat dishes. It's not far. About three dollars each with a beer. OK?'

Everyone heads out of the door and up the street. I'll keep close to Andrew who will talk about food and whet my appetite, because

I can hear snippets of travellers' tales of woe as we are walking. Sure, everyone has a story, I just don't want to hear you whinging right now about how dreadful Peru is for robbery, how much you saved last night on your hotel room compared to the night before, or how a taxi-driver ripped you off in Santiago, Quito or Lima.

5. *Getting Drunk*

I have taken to going out at night in Santiago and having a few drinks with new friends and acquaintances. And Charlotte, of course. Chilean wine is especially delicious in Chile.

'How are you doing?' I say to the Irish girl. We have all come out on St Patrick's night dressed in green and are sitting at the bar of quite a snooty bar in Bellavista.

'Oh me. I'm nicely polluted,' she roars drunkenly, throwing her head back.

She is not the only one.

Then she turns to me, sobriety seeming to have completely taken over her face, and says, 'Life is really a waste of time.'

She looks right through me and horror runs down my spine.

'Think about it – life is a waste of time.'

6. *Concert*

'I can't live if living is without you. I can't live, I can't give any more,' sings Nilsson on the radio.

'They killed me many times. Many times I died. But I'm still here,' sang Mercedes Sosa, many times.

I am reading a newspaper interview with Mercedes Sosa. She says she feels an enormous burden when she is referred to (above all, outside Latin America) as the Mother of America. Asked whether she maintains her communist tendencies she says, 'I sing about freedom.' Some of her songs have changed now because the world has changed.

But a lot of people appear to be resisting change in Santiago as they hold onto a past they deem more heroic than the present.

'When Pinochet was in power, we all had a common enemy. Someone to fight against. It's boring now,' said Kena, photographer and ex-communist.

'The challenge is to stop projecting all our anger, frustrations and fears onto the outside and work on the demons within,' I said.

'I know,' said Kena with a smile. 'But that's very hard.'

'Yes,' I replied. 'But what's the alternative?'

I am invited for supper to the house of an ex-boyfriend of a woman I had met in Quito. She is in Santiago to lay some ghosts. The people are long-haired (like me) and hippie-types (unlike me) who like to drink and smoke dope and talk about what a capitalist language English is.

'How on earth can a language be capitalist?' I asked my friend, incredulous. She had not thought about that before.

Her ex-boyfriend claims he is a communist and believes in free love. (I am starting to wonder whether I am, in fact, taking part in 'Doctor Who'. Will my Tardis be waiting outside after the party?) Mmmhh. Free love. Like, let's not take any responsibility for all the relationships we are creating and be really mellow and cool.

My friend says I have more common sense than anyone she knows. That does not come as comforting news.

I stay in the kitchen most of the evening and prepare the meal, mostly because I can't get off on the free-love vibe, man. My friend comes to help me a couple of times, but none of the communists share the work. After the meal there is singing, but I'm bored in spite of it. All the old songs come up about brotherhood and *campesinos* and freedom from the hand that suppresses. Some are beautiful songs. But it all feels so old.

Wake up, I want to cry to the gathering. Hey, we're in 1992! The hat is passed round for money to buy more wine. I am on the wagon, so I give my share and ask the ex-boyfriend to bring me some bottled water. He returns some minutes later. The wine is placed on the table.

'And the water?' I ask loudly, already knowing the outcome. I am friendly in my tone.

'Oh no . . . I forgot completely . . . It's just I . . .'

I stare at him for a few seconds and let myself think 'yeah, great caring for your fellow man . . . load of romantic wank . . .' and then add coldly,

'Don't worry about it, it's fine.'

I feel glad I made him feel uncomfortable, the boy who I could see would always have an excuse that someone would believe because he is pretty and Mummy's boy. His mother was there that night and I am pleased she too heard what I said. I leave shortly afterwards and my friend thanks me for being so direct.

'I'd forget any ideas of coming back to him,' I say to her. 'Unless you want your self-esteem to dwindle into nothing.'

A few months later in Ecuador, this woman would tell me she was not going back to Chile, but had decided to stay in Quito and accept a job promotion.

Mercedes Sosa played to a full crowd in the Estadio de Chile. Her enormous presence filled the hall and it was difficult to believe that this booming, powerful voice belonged to a woman of almost sixty. My skin tingled and goose-bumped all over my body as she sang *chacareras*, tangos and ballads, and I laughed to see her change her chiffon scarves red to white to turquoise. The audience sang along to many of the songs and I found myself wishing they would be quiet. I had come to listen to and enjoy Mercedes Sosa not the whole of Santiago. A girl in front of me kept shouting out inane responses to the things Mercedes Sosa would say in between songs. The indulgence irritated me.

'You cannot possibly have any idea what it means to us that Mercedes Sosa has come to Chile after such a long time,' Claudia said to me. 'You are coming for the music, but many people identify with her.'

Yes, and they all want a piece of her, I thought at the concert. And yes, I really was there just to enjoy her music.

A few weeks later we went to a concert by Silvio Rodriguez, the Cuban singer/songwriter. In contrast to Mercedes Sosa, Rodriguez sang in an open-air stadium five or six times larger than the Estadio de Chile. It was packed. He sang many of his famous songs in the first half and was greeted with rapturous applause. The second half was taken up by mainly new compositions and the audience seemed to become restless and even rather bored.

'He sang too many songs I didn't know,' someone said to me after the concert.

Too many songs that were not part of their experience, their own heroic past, the battle against the dictatorship. They could not sing along. At one point the crowd called out for 'An Urgent Song for Nicaragua'. He did not comply with the request. The song was simply not relevant now. He became irritated with the audience when they would not be quiet as he attempted to explain some of the current problems Cuba faces, and his song about all the young women who earn a meagre living by sleeping with tourists met with only a half-hearted response. The same audience who had at the beginning of the concert chanted 'Chile kisses Cuba, Chile kisses Cuba' seemed unable to listen to anything outside themselves or what they knew.

Isabel Parra, daughter of the late Violete Parra, is also a singer/songwriter from Chile. In an interview she said that she feels uncomfortable when people call her *compañera* now. She does not want to be labelled according to her past or to have to live up to the idealized expectations people project upon her. Psychotherapy, she explained, has taught her to rid herself of excess baggage, ideas and beliefs which no longer serve her so that she may develop into who she really is in the present. She pissed a lot of people off. But in her concerts she refuses to be drawn into performing songs that no longer hold any meaning for her.

'I can't live, if living is without you!'
It is easier to love the dead than the living.

7. *Smog*

'I have to leave this city as soon as possible,' I said to Ted over lunch in Santiago's bohemian Bellavista *barrio*. 'I'm beginning to hate everybody.'

Ted is a laid-back twenty-eight-year-old from the Bay Area of San Francisco who has the habit of surprising you with sudden bursts of insight totally pertinent to the subject in question, although it would appear he has listened to nothing you have said.

'Hey man, I think you're right, you know, I mean I've got to get out to the country too, man. It's like there's this bigger me, this me that almost seems outside of myself but that's part of me and when I'm in the country, man, I can just feel that bigger me, it like expands. The city just contracts that, man. Hey, I'm not really doing a good job of explaining myself here . . .'

'I know just what you mean, Ted.'

'Yeah man, it just like gets squashed in the city.'

I take my leave of Ted and go to pack my bag for the journey south. I meet our young friend Matt on the way and he tells me I am but a shadow of the man he met six weeks ago smiling and positive and just arrived. I bark and growl at the traffic and noise as we cross the Alameda. Maybe when I feel the bigger me again it'll blast out this stinking cold I have been unable to shake off in this suffocating smog . . .

WOMAN OF THE SOUTH

~~~

I am sitting in a café in Santiago by a square full of pigeons. I have just gone to the Post Office to scan the lists for any mail and I am on my way to the library.

In this café I notice the men are always served first, and the women like to eat large slices of white cake piled with cream. I am feeling very poisoned, I can hardly bear to drink my coffee.

When my mother got cancer, I got poisoned like this. I suffered all the side-effects of her treatment. Including her anger (it's guilt, Mark said). I witnessed her fight against the poison of chemo-therapy with all the ferocity of a bear defending her territory. (I was amazed by my mother's warrior strength.) The illness challenged the unspoken gap that had grown between us. In fact the gap between myself and most women. A gap that was as desolate as the rainy moor where my mother had spent her lonely childhood, and my grandmother her silent marriage.

The Village of Doves

There is a village in the hills outside Nice that is called St Paul de Vence. It sits like a stone crown on the top of a medieval hill surrounded by the pine forests and the snowy peaks of the Alps. I went there once. It was off-season and I was staying in a hotel, writing a story about the painters who used to go there, whose rough canvasses still celebrated the matriarchal culture that once worshipped the bull and the dove.

It was here that I met René who owns the café opposite the hotel, in this town now ossified by tourism. René is an artist and sculpts owls and cockerels out of broken glass and ceramic. His men have large cracked teapot heads and thin glass legs.

'That is all a man is,' he says. 'All head and legs. No arms, no heart, no body.'

It was here too that I met Yvonne one afternoon. It was pouring with rain and I was shivering with flu. I sat in the bar drinking a hot punch, made for me by the barman, of wine and rum, flavoured with cinnamon and clove. Yvonne moved slowly out of the shadows (she is partly paralysed). She sat down beside me and told me that it is in the moment of supreme boredom that life becomes most interesting. Yvonne is a natural storyteller, a weaver of tales. She tells me a story of how a stranger came here once and wanted to build a house which faced the four winds, so that every room he entered would have a view.

'A wall can be a view too,' she said and laughed.

I know about walls and waiting. I have been waiting for two days now with a curtain of rain in front of my window, blocking the view of the sea, feeling sick. I am waiting to speak to Yvonne's daughter who is an artist too. I am waiting to extract the secrets of this place where the dove houses are netted over and the magical white birds are mated with the vulgar pigeons of the town. In a graveyard I sat down, wrapped in a mackintosh, and smelt the clean air that is scented with wet cypress and earth, and I watched wasps fly in and out of a cracked tomb. The truth, I thought, is deeper and much darker than you imagine. At night I dreamt of African women who broke open wombs like seed pods which poured blood, and of huge-headed men like René's sculptures who came with knives to kill me. When I woke up I was paralysed, as if I was caught in a spider's web. I could not move and snakes coiled all about the lightbulb.

In the morning I went down and watched Pitou, Yvonne's daughter, walk amongst the breakfast tables arranging little vases of anemones and olive leaves. She has not painted for a year. On the stairway there are her glass paintings of stars and planets whirling through endless blue. She does not speak. She is thin and pale.

'Why doesn't she leave?' I ask her mother.

'She is afraid to go,' she replied.

There is a legend I know, it goes like this. The daughter of the Mother of Earth went wandering one day and as she bent down to pick some narcissus flowers, the Lord of the Underworld snatched her and took her down to his dark kingdom. The Mother of Earth so mourned the loss of her daughter that winter came all over the land: the trees lost their leaves, and the fields bore no harvest. Eventually the Mother went to look for her daughter and when she found her, the King of the Underworld said: 'You may have your daughter back but only if she has eaten nothing while she has been in my domain.'

'Have you eaten anything?' asked her mother and her daughter nodded sadly. She had eaten six seeds of a pomegranate fruit.

'You may have your daughter back,' said the Lord of the Dark World. 'But only for six months. The other six she must come down here to stay with me and be my bride.'

This is the legend of spring and autumn in a world where the gods are not departed and everyone keeps to their side of the bargain.

But this is not always so.

In St Paul de Vence I was reminded in the rain of the power of the angry mother and the displaced daughter. The mother like the earth, if she is not honoured, becomes dark, possessive and destructive, and the daughter hides in shadow and becomes too thin and fond of death. Now, though the legend says that the Mother of Earth grieved for her daughter and waited patiently for her to come back to renew the year, in a world where the fecundity of the female is not praised or held sacred (something once celebrated by a dance and a hymn to the corn), this creative power turns in against itself. The mother then grows jealous of her daughter's gifts. She does not want her to return to gladden the spring. Sometimes she likes to keep her wedded to the dark man, because she herself was so committed, kept in the shadow by her own mother and married off to Pluto.

I knew these things. I saw them in my own family, in my own society. I certainly witnessed them in my shiny magazine world: those bitter women and those young anorexic girls who wore black. I watched the legend grow sour each day. But I did not think it had anything to do with me.

Every winter I would buy a pomegranate fruit and let it grow dark as dried blood on a pewter fruit dish given to me by my mother. In my poems the pomegranate always appeared as the dangerous moon but though the power of this fruit fascinated me, I never tasted it.

Blanche

When we came back to London from Mexico that first time, Mark and I, I started to dream. I dreamed of eagles and albatrosses and swans with bound feet, I dreamt of escaping dark museums and abbeys narrowly with my life. I dreamed of towers falling and fire in the streets of my city and ashes falling that everyone pretended was just snow. I dreamt of planting corn and herbs in strange landscapes. I dreamed I plucked a silver key from a golden triangle out of thin air. I dreamed I flew over mountains, over maps, over ungovernable seas. And I dreamed of an Angry Woman Who Lived Under the Earth.

This dream woman was blonde. I managed to escape her wrath by my wit and usually by means of water. This woman was dangerous (she carried a knife) and demented. On one occasion she tried to kiss me.

'She sounds like the Woman of the South to me,' said Mark when I described her.

I laughed. Nervously. Now the Woman of the South is an archetype that does not occur much in our literature. She is the Dark Mother, She Who Destroys, she who comes spitting venom and rage, with her snaky hair and her tongue of flame, her madness and devouring sexuality. I borrow the term from Lynn Andrews who envisioned her in a jaguar temple in Mexico and from Carlos Casteneda who met her in real life in one of his adventures with the sorcerer, Don Juan. In Indian legend she is Kali, the Goddess of Death and Destruction. Perhaps we in Europe know her best as the Dark Fairy, the one who is forbidden to the charmed child's christening, the one who would tell us of sex and death. It is curiosity in the fairy tales that seeks her out, and it is curiosity in me that looks out for her, she who can destroy my sugary world.

Blanche Bennett is suffering from candida. Mark has told me so. Her belly is as bloated as an African child's and her hands are as cold as the Arctic snow. Blanche Bennett has every allergy under the sun. At one time she was thought to have Total Allergy Syndrome and was going to have to live in a bubble of purest air, cut off from the earth altogether. But she didn't.

I am standing in the Festival of Mind, Body and Spirit. It is May 1990. This small loud beautiful woman is hugging my friend Mark and saying she loves him and is thanking him for being on the planet, for sharing with her and helping her with her growth and her creativity. I am astonished. I don't know people like this who use such strange vocabulary.

'Have you squeezed your lemon recently?' she asks me and stares at me like an eagle directly right into my eyes.

'My what?' I ask faintly, blinking.

'Your lemon!' she repeats, crossing her legs while an orgasmic wicked look passes over her face.

O she means my clitoris, I think and laughed. I would like to say I laugh wholeheartedly but actually it is mostly in embarrassment.

'I am Blanche,' she says. 'I am going to listen to this wonderful person who is giving a talk about angels, are you coming?'

We sat through the lecture on angels. Mark in the middle, Blanche and I on either side holding hands. It disturbed me (all those armies of angels). Blanche disturbed me (all that female power). I felt angry. I went home and sat in bed with my typewriter on my knees, being confused. Then I typed out a piece of writing. I say typed, because I didn't write it. I channelled it. It was an instruction.

'It's not about the sword, taking up arms, New Jerusalems, the chosen, servants, ranks of hierarchy, even of angels, movements, prophets and the followers of prophets, nor their listeners.

Who fills the casket?

It is not about fighting and war but peace, not salvation, a resting place but a peace that comes with perpetual movement. Deep travel. Questions. In the question you will find the answer. Go deeper, underneath, in the forest, not by sea. Ask the forest and the bird. Go with him into the green clearing and he will come as the deer with the burning antlers. Show him the way out. He must go out. The forest is a good place to play but you must not hide there.

He can sing but cannot speak. I gave you the book. Fill it! You must listen: to cacophony. What sounds like harmony, is not harmony; that which sounds not as it is, is truth. Listen to the voice, give it words now! It is time to find words, although it is hard. Look into his heart, speak there: go deeper. Where you see, he speaks; where you speak, he sees. That is your task. Go now.

Dark choir. Not that but an older song. From the island where we kept our faith. There are gems, a lake of glass, a swansong, a tree in the wind. Mother is trapped, bound up by the tyrants but the tyrants shall fall out of the tower and the tower be burned. I shall not break thee. You are both once broken separately but now healed. Lame but can now walk. There is memory of lameness only, but necessary to remember to heal. The lance is not protection, not rescue, but a lance for the wound. The man and the woman that usurped thee are afeared of thee, for thy lands are everyman.

Take your brother to the platform. The tournament is beginning. Do not be afraid, there is no armour. I will protect him. Do not sit under the tree with oak leaves and jest always. Let him be blind and see: hold his hand. The fool will not always protect you in the palace of men. Keep your counsel; remember your womanhood. This will keep you and him. He is waiting in the garden where you found him. You cannot return whence you came. It is better that you are changed into birds. Fly up. Your lands are free. Remember your mother. For your father has betrayed you and married another who is false to her sex. She cannot bring forth children who sing.'

When I finished this, I was shaking. I did not know what it meant. Nothing like this had happened to me before. It was a weird scene.

The next week I met Blanche again at a concert. I told her of my channel. She told me of her trial (her daughter had been taken away from her and she could not get her back). Blanche's story is extraordinary and she will tell it herself one day. At that time, I wanted to tell it too. Let's write a play for television, I said. OK, she said. And that was that.

That autumn after I came back from Greece, I started to visit Blanche in her house in Chertsey (she hated the city). When I first walked through her bower of grapes and blackberries, I recognized the garden from somewhere but I couldn't quite say where exactly. I sat on her carpet by the fire (she was always cold) and drank fierce cups of coffee and we talked about her court case and the mythic and psychological significance of allergies. I told her I had gone past a wheatfield once in Suffolk and thought of her. I said, your land is blighted. You cannot even grow corn on your land. It is winter there because your daughter is not returned. You are like Ceres and your daughter is like Persephone. She is stuck in Pluto's kingdom. (I was rather pleased with myself.)

'There is another myth about the Underworld, you know,' she said. 'It is much older, from the time when women ruled the earth. An astrologer told me it once because he said Pluto dominated my chart.'

Blanche told me about Innana, the Goddess of Heaven, and her sister, Erishkageil, the Goddess of the Underworld, whom Innana goes to assist in the birth of her child. When Innana enters the

Underworld, she has to go through seven doors to reach her sister, and each one demands that she uncover herself. When she finally reaches the throne room, she is naked. Erishkageil treats her terribly. She hangs her on a hook and leaves her for dead.

'The seven doors are like illnesses,' Blanche explained.

'Yes,' I said. 'But what happens next?'

Well, Erishkageil is giving birth and is in terrible pain, so she gives Innana a break. She takes her off the hook and lets her go to find someone to help in the delivery. Innana returns to the sky. She asks her lover and her father to help but neither of them will even consider going down into the Underworld to save the awful, angry, vengeful Erishkageil from any pain. Finally Innana goes to her grandfather and he fashions two messengers out of clay from under his fingernails who manage to slip into the Underworld (without going through the seven doors).

Erishkageil is screaming her head off. No one will go near her but the messengers are not afraid. They go right up to her and bow before her.

'O wondrous one!' they declare. 'You who are so powerful and so beautiful. How can we help you?'

Now no one had ever called Erishkageil beautiful before or recognized her power. Instantly her agony is eased and she gives birth effortlessly.

'Is that the end of the story?' I asked.

'Yes,' said Blanche. 'Innana returns to Heaven as a star and Erishkageil rules happily in the Underworld.'

'And what about the child?' I asked.

'The child is not important,' she replied. 'What is important is that a birth happened in the kingdom of death.'

'And you are Erishkageil, I presume?'

'And perhaps you and Mark are my two messengers.'

Actually, although I like to think of myself as a messenger, in this case I think I had another part to play. If Blanche was the Queen of the Dark Place, the Woman of the South or what you will, then I was definitely her starry-eyed ignorant sister who fell to earth.

There are some people that you meet in life who just stand in your path and will not let you pass unless you confront them. I call them Bears in the Corridor. You have to get past them somehow, you see, because, as they advance towards you with their claws out, you realize that they have come out of a door that you must go through. You can see the sun there. Blanche stood in front of me like a bear with a sore head, in dire need of honey. It soon became apparent that our 'play' was a foil for some other drama to be enacted. Something far more personal, more primal, more matriarchal than the neat classical myth I had chosen for the plot.

Now I was always a daddy's girl. I always loved men, the company of men, their jokes, their dialectic, their bravado. I was charming in the company of men, and clever. I liked working with them, and wearing their clothes. With women it was always different, difficult. I fell out with women. Talking with them made me uncomfortable. I disliked the way they desired men and hated them at the same time. The way they talked about babies and diets. And feminism always seemed to me to be more about separatism and superiority than any kind of equality. Most women bored me rigid.

But not Blanche.

Blanche Bennett was one of the cleverest women I had ever met, and the most talented. She was poet, singer and visionary. She did not hide her vision with drink or with a pretty life (though she had in the past). And her clear sight made her suffer. For she did not side with the men like me, so she was not protected by their systems and their sentimentality. On the contrary, her battle with lawyers and doctors and her daughter's powerful grandfather constantly had her on the defence.

When I met Blanche I realized I could no longer afford to stay entirely in the company of men any more. I could see that my world was malfunctioning. I could see that I was dysfunctional. Blanche challenged every single aspect of that pretty witty world I once lived in. She stripped away all the things I hide behind: my controls and good fairy roles – Little Mother to the Lost Boys, jolly jester of the court, honorary member of the boys' club. I took off their uniform bit by bit. I grew my hair. I was forced to become intimate: to lay myself open. I started to get allergies myself. I realized that my love of cooking and of markets was not a love of eating. It was an obsession, and this obsession hid a deeper wound. You see, I had always been surrounded by women with food problems: anorexics, bulimics, and Blanche, with her severe reactions to food, was in a long line of women I had known with eating disorders. But it wasn't until I met her, until I walked through that seventh door naked as a baby, that I realized that these were mine too. As a child I had refused to eat constantly, I even rejected my mother's breast. All I wanted to eat was sugar.

From the very day I was born something in me had rejected the female power in preference to male control.

Blanche and I fought, quarrelled and wept and read poetry far into the night. We grew furious with each other, and jealous, and we sang (the three of us in three-part harmony) in the kitchen, in taxis, all the day long. She was my sister. I loved her and I hated her, but I did not fall out with her. I could see the shining light in the door behind her as perhaps she could see the midwife in me.

Blanche Bennett did not come with us when we left England, though we asked her to, both times. You have to write your book, she said. I have to complete other things.

When I came to Ecuador I wrote her a letter. I wanted to tell her about the city of Cuenca which she would have loved, and about a man I had met called Marko with green eyes. I wanted to tell her a story about a girl who grew up in a house of copper and one day met a woman of iron. How this confident androgyne finally unbuckled her sword and paid her homage, and was walking through a door.

Dearest Blanche,
When I first met you, you told me the story of Innana and her sister (whose name I cannot possibly spell), how the Queen of Heaven, the star Venus, fell into the earth and discovered its

riches. *I always thought this myth brought us together. I to bring light and to honour the birth of your child, your creativity; you to show me the value of the dark, the fecund womb, the treasures of the female – her patience, her receptivity, her terrible anger when not held sacred.*

I don't think I remembered this enough all the time: what is so clear in a story is never so straightforward in real life. We are people after all, not gods: though surely the gods do live in us, the Queens of the Heavens and the Underworlds, the women of the North and South, the dancer, the warrior, the priestess and the poet, the woman who makes the soup, the girl who dreams of wolves and stars, the lover who takes us to the garden, the wise old crone who brings us death. I know they are all there, waiting to be found, discovered, set free.

I have set my sword down: I used it to cut myself free from my masculine swaddling bands. I took my father's heirloom, and separated myself from the legacy. I was afraid: in a land of raped virgin forest and enslaved tribes, I was unwilling to be so unprotected in my own geography. But I took off my armour. I knelt on one knee. I waited.

'I'm sorry, I don't normally attack people,' said Marko. 'But I had to talk to you.'

'Oh, that's fine,' I smiled. 'I wanted you to.'

I am flying up: flying up to breathe another air, to discover fresh water, new fire, pure earth. Perhaps in my flight, in our myth, in our singing with Mark, in all our friendships, new and old, in Quito, in London, we are all freeing the gods for each other, putting them back where they belong, out of their cages (the books and the museums) and into their real hunting ground, in heaven, on earth and within ourselves.

If I am flying, I know you are too, even though we may be going in different directions. I like to think of you, striding out from the dark place that held you captive, singing your own song, bicycling through the winter lanes, publishing your poetry, dissolving your chains, preparing your garden. Sometimes when it's

*very difficult, when the way up seems so steep, I hold you in my
mind. I think, 'What would Blanche say to this? What would she
do?' One night I dreamt I left my house in your safekeeping, and
when I sold it (I was in another land), you told me not to worry:
you would get rid of all the furniture for me.*

*So you see, sweetheart, though I wasn't perhaps there as you
wished always, though I pushed away your child too roughly, ran
away from your warrior, confused pity with compassion,
undervalued your work, was ungenerous in my heart and fell foul
of flattery, it was all a mirror. I only hurt myself more. As I put
away my sword and open my casket, I can honour myself, you and
all the imprisoned feminine. I can go to open the door.*

*I write this in peace and acknowledgement. It is, as I said, an
explanation by way of apology.*

Fare ye well, brave sister, I salute thee as I lay down my arms.

With love

When I left the kingdom of my father, I did it with the help of other
women. Wise and noble women like Bridget and Josiane who
taught me about spirit, and dramatic angry women like Blanche
who taught me the value of the dark. I went out of the forest, as
that channel instructed me, I listened to the other voices all tumbled
together and tried to make a song of them. I took Mark to the
platform and we wrote this book together. I did not stay in the
palace of men and play the fool (I left my job). I flew up (to find
my spirit). I remembered my mother, my earth as I struggled to
remember my own womanhood, buried away deep within the
darkness of me.

'My womb is a sterile wasteland!' I cried out when I was on magic
mushrooms. I don't think it has to be.

But unless we live in a world where the earth is honoured, we
will find only barrenness, unless there is balance between the male
and the female, the dark and the light, we will be laid waste.
The mother will destroy those who destroy her. We have to feed
our spirit, we have to give back to the earth as the Dark Fairy

must be invited to the christening and the daughter must be the bride of the Underworld. Because we did eat the six seeds of the pomegranate.

We did take away.

The City of Sugar

It wasn't until I reached the city of Santiago de Chile that I realized what my encounter with the female underworld finally required me to honour and admit. The Woman of the South may bring back your holy fury, your passion, your madness, your rich creative power, but most of all she is there to remind you of where you once belonged. You who are so dispossessed.

Santiago was the first city in Latin America to remind me of my own. It is full of ghosts and machines, of neurosis, of distraction, of addiction and eating disorder. Though it was familiar, I awoke each day with a feeling of terrible alienation.

This is an extract from my diary, written before I left for the south, in an autumn that felt it should be spring:

I am invisible. I walk invisible. My eyes burn. My stomach bloats. The lights blink. Take away, take away city: hotdogs, instant coffee, and large, pink artificial cakes. In the supermarket where I go, there is a shelf of diabetic jam called Diet Control. All the apples are the same size. Very shiny. The bread is always purest white. It is very efficient. When you cross the road in this city you have to hurry. There is just not enough time before the cars will come again. The lights shine: red, green, red, green. Quick, quick. Take away city. Take away what? Replace what? Who me?

In the coffee shops where I go (the ones that do not sell instant coffee) the women are like strip-bar girls. They wear sex dresses: violet, red, violet, red. They put a small glass of pumped and icy

*water directly into the hands of the men in suits who stand, and
hold their stare. But I cannot see into their well made-up eyes. A
woman in a café sighs and walks away (she did not understand
my order, it wasn't on the menu) and another woman falls asleep
at the till. Another woman is filing cards in a library. I am
watching them. They are all invisible.*

*'The reason that so many women in Santiago wear those
clinging clothes, is that it's the only way they get attention,' said a
man I met (he was from New York). Mark says at the photocopy
shops, the women devour him with their eyes like trapped tigers.*

Thank God for you, I say, that there is a machine in the way.

*I am angry, I am poisoned. I give up everything (well, it is
Lent, I say). I give up cake, chips, cigarettes, beer, false food,
fried food, all those chemicals, all that artifice, all that sugar. But
still I am bloated. Still I am trapped. I hunger but nothing will
succour me.*

*I listen to a tape of Laurie Anderson singing. So hold me, Mum,
she sings, in your long arms, electronic arms, your petrochemical
arms, your military arms. I burst into tears. I am so exhausted I
only want to sleep. O sleep, sweet sleep. In the mornings in the
shuttered room it is hard to wake up.*

*'The daughter of Fidel Castro is anorexic,' says Mark (he is
reading an old magazine in the hotel lobby).*

*'Fidel Castro said: the revolutionary knows no family. Well,
how can you nurture what you refuse to see?' The revolution and
the regime does not notice the women, only the system, only the
men who run the system and the women who acknowledge the
men. This is a city of women who devour cake and those who
abstain with lust in their eyes, and cars that do not stop, and gods
who have gone.*

*The dogs are sleeping undisturbed, wrapped round the trees in
the Alameda.*

I have a dream. There is an animal at my window, half owl, half cat. I feed it cake. But it does not want cake. It wants red meat.

I am invisible.

I buy myself a purple man's jacket from a second-hand store.

I am less invisible.

This is a city of tired women and cats who hide in the shadows and shop windows.

I have a dream: I am poisoned by a current at the metal floor of a pool of water. I crawl about the streets of the city like a snake. I need help to get back to my room but I cannot ask anyone for help. They are all men, and have eyes only for other men. I am invisible. My pain is not their concern. I cannot even ask my father for help (he is waiting at the lobby of the hotel). A man is planning a party. He is licking his lips at the thought of all the young dancing boys he will invite. 'It is important to ask the women too,' I tell him. He does not hear me. I am furious and this anger helps me climb the stairs to the room where Mark is waiting.

This is a city of silent cats.

This is a city of silent woman.

This is a city of silence.

But there is so much noise covering up the silence I cannot hear it. I cannot hear you. I cannot hear you. I can only feel the black space, the emptiness, the absence of you: the space you left behind.

It is autumn but I think it should be spring. In my country, it is spring. Isn't it?

Mark said: the gods will not come unless you call them. So I called, I stood in the shower and I howled for you. Mother. Mother, where are you? I cried like a baby for its milk, and heard the seabirds crying in the wind.

O Mum, hold me in your arms and rock me, hold me to your breast and feed me, your hair of wheat, your breath of milk, in your apple arms, your cornbaby arms.

Tell me there is birth as well as death.

TIGERS AND TYRANNIES

~~~

You have a tiger's eye on your windowsill. Do you watch it, or does it watch you, in the forests of the night?

Last night before a concert a dark woman leant over to us in a café and asked what signs and animals we were.

'I'm Gemini and a Monkey,' I said, quick as a flash.

'Very clever,' she said and looked at you.

'Taurus and a Tiger,' you replied, more slowly.

'O!' she exclaimed and leant backwards as if to move out of the way. 'Watch out for that paw!'

You are fiercer than me. I can turn upside down and make people laugh and think with my quickness but you are a tiger with a tiger's paw and when you walk, clearing all that stands in your path with your fieriness, people feel naked and challenged. Sometimes they run away.

I have felt your paw many times as you have swiped me out of the way, swinging through the air, amongst the leaves and branches, teasing you and chattering. Sometimes I have felt it in the wind and laughed and sometimes I have felt the full blast and the claws and been angry and chastised. Sometimes I called you tyrant, and sometimes you called me victim. And sometimes we were both right.

But as we have walked along this path together, you with your burning eye and I with my dexterity, I have learned the difference between tigers and tyrants.

When we arrive in Santiago de Chile after a twenty-eight-hour bus ride across the desert, the first sign I see says '*Santiago está baja*

Control – Santiago is under Control.' It is an advertisement for Pisco.

We stay in a hotel in the centre of the city with polished parquet floors and high ceilings. We have decided to start the book here, and take turns with the typewriter. So on some mornings I sit by the open window overlooking the courtyard drenched in the hot autumn sun. It is not as easy to write as it used to be when I had deadlines, that old control of work, to help me.

Not to mention the alcohol.

When I get stuck I talk to the other travellers who congregate round the green leather chairs in the hall, waiting for the phone or watching the afternoon soap operas on television, pretending it is going to improve their Spanish. They are all so active with their schedules, I am starting to doubt my quiet life. Shouldn't I be like them? Shouldn't I be going out and doing things? I might never come back to Chile. Perhaps I should go to Isla Negra and visit Pablo Neruda's house ('You have to see it if you've read his poems'), to Viña del Mar for the day, to Patagonia for a week, up to the statue of the Virgin on the hill, off to the ballet in town, and then I could write postcards all about it.

'Look,' says Mark, 'you don't want to go to Pablo Neruda's because it is just a house. You don't want to go to Patagonia because it's too cold. You don't want to write to anyone because you have nothing to say. And as for going to the beach . . . !'

'I know, I know,' I say, 'the terrible tyranny of the tan. But what do I want?'

He laughs.

'Do you want the typewriter?' I ask.

He doesn't laugh.

'What the point?' he says and gives me a thunderous look.

The worst tyranny has nothing to do with other people, or tourism. It is to do with the self – the tyranny of originality. I can't possibly do/say/write/sing that. It's all been done before.

But 'it' has never been done before. Because I have not been alive before. Tyrannies make everyone out to be the same (fit in, know your place, do not disturb the status quo). And they keep us small, thinking we have no song to sing of our own. Nothing to add.

Tyrannies stop us asking the real questions about our value: who needs an outer tyrant when we so clearly control ourselves?

No es mi culpa, as they say in Latin America. It's not my fault. Isn't it?

It's more than my job is worth, as they say in British NCP car parks. Is it?

Whenever I ride the shiny subway in this city, I get this irresistible urge to sing *very loudly*.

Before I came to this narrow land, I had a stock liberal response to political dictatorship. I thought that any regime that is not based on nineteenth-century parliamentarianism or the American Constitution was immediately suspect. Even though it is two years after the dictatorship, we hear a lot about Pinochet here, the man many still affectionately call Pinocchio.

'He got the economy going,' they say.

'The metro is so beautiful!' they say.

'We were glad when he came,' say the German family we go to stay with in the south. They still had his portrait on the wall. They told us the agitators had thrown firebombs into their garden when Allende was in power, and Estelita, the housekeeper of the hotel, said Santiago had been in chaos and there was no transport and there were queues for everything.

'But the country was deliberately destabilized by the CIA,' I pointed out to Mark as he suggested that perhaps the situation was not as black and white as we liked to think.

'She had to walk for hours in the cold and dark,' he said. 'What use was that knowledge to her?'

We also hear about the dreadful suppression of the 'seventies ('They asked for trouble,' some say. 'It was nothing compared to Argentina,' others say). We go for lunch with a writer I once interviewed when he was an exile in Berlin. All the people who sat around his barbecue in Las Condes returned too after the dictatorship fell. They all had their dark tales to tell (they did not tell them that day). You can hear stories everywhere if you seek them out: of the musician who had his hands chopped off, the students murdered in the football stadium, the intellectuals tortured in the desert town of Iquique.

Something inside of me has started to feel uncomfortable simply condemning the actions of this regime out of hand, as I would have before. Though I cannot condone any atrocity, I cannot pretend that I have played no part in it on some level. I cannot ignore the fact that tyrannies can mirror the part of ourselves that has abdicated responsibility, in return for comfort and an easy black-and-white point of view.

When I left England it was in the aftermath of the Gulf War, the conflict in which Saddam Hussein rose as the Arch-tyrant of the Apocalypse ('Did you realize that Mabbas the Antichrist, is Saddam backwards?' my friend Jo would ask me in New York).

'You can't expect a dictator to surrender gracefully,' I remember my brother saying, quoting Mrs Thatcher at the family lunchtable. 'You have to rout him out.'

'I think it's a waste of energy battling on the outside and blaming everything on one man,' I said, quoting Mark. 'This war is an invitation to look within and deal with the Saddam Hussein we have created in ourselves and in our homes.'

All the male members of my family grew silent and moved away from the table when they heard this, and went to read the war reports in the Sunday papers.

'Women love dictators,' I continued. 'They give our life drama and intensity: someone else to blame for all our woe. Tyrants stop us looking at our addiction to pain and our reluctance to stand up for ourselves.'

All the female members of my family grew silent, and moved away from the table when they heard this, and went to do the washing up in the kitchen.

RESIDENCIAL LONDRES
– SANTIAGO – CHILE

BREAKFAST – AGNES AND CO

VERY MUCH
AWAKE
– SELF-PORTRAIT
WITH PAINTING
– SANTIAGO

BEIGE IS BACK! SPRING FASHION SHOOT, WITH ANDREW – ELQUI VALLEY – CHILE

ROOM 33, RESIDENCIAL LONDRES – WITH RESTING TYPEWRITER

BAÑOS DE LA VIRGEN
– BAÑOS – ECUADOR

THE TRIBUNAL,
WITH BRIDGET
– CUENCA – ECUADOR

SO WHAT'S NEW? – JOSIANE
– CARTAGENA – COLOMBIA

ON THE BEACH
– CARTAGENA

EARLY MORNING
– SANTA MARTA

MARK GETS BEADED
  – CARTAGENA

MARK AND MORE BEADS...

HOT! HOTEL DORAL WITH JOSIANE

ECOLOGICAL DISASTER – COLOMBIA

LAST GLIMPSE OF THE ANDES
– TAXI WINDOW – BOGOTÁ

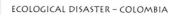

HOSTELERIA CANDELARIA WITH JANE

MINE'S ASTRAL! – BOGOTÁ

LOOKING BACK,
LOOKING FORWARD,
LOOKING NOW

LAST DAYS IN SANTE FÉ DE BOGOTÁ
– CALLE DE LA AGONIA

Which left me.

Which still leaves me.

What tyranny have I created for my perfect state?

'It's not the bully who creates the victim, it's the other way round,' quoted Mark to me. 'If the victim removed his head from underneath the dictator's foot, he would fall over.'

Sometimes I have been a victim and sometimes Mark has been a tyrant (I called him the Stern Emperor) and sometimes I have enjoyed it. I enjoy the attention: better this than none.

Why don't I have the courage to argue back with him?

Why do I still relapse into childish silence? And prefer the pity of the world to my own power? When I know that I will be kicked like a cringing dog?

Is this out of comfort too?

Am I still so desirous of approval?

So afraid of being alone?

(O Daddy, Daddy, notice me!)

After three months in Chile I realize I can no longer hide behind my old fashioned ideology (a mix of natural idealism, and a Trotskyite pose adopted when I was a student as a reaction to my narrow middle-class upbringing). I realize I can no longer afford to take sides. I know the truth lies somewhere uncomfortably in between the black and the white, in the difficult world of paradox, and that I can no longer mutter democracy when I no longer even vote, or ignore the fact that certain things have 'worked' due to the Chilean dictatorship, such as education which has made the people more open and equal and more informed than in any other Latin American country I have visited. This may not have been Pinochet's intention but it is the result of his rule. A part of the infinite plan.

I used to have a stock liberal response to the heavy-handed politics in my own country too. But now I think I have to see from a higher perspective and not just react by passing an easy judgement, not just offer a 'politically correct' opinion in the same way I might once have worn a designer label.

In hindsight, the insistence on individualism by a 'tyrannical' Prime Minister *was* in the end about freedom, although not the sort the politicians or the men in power had in mind (the much-hated Poll Tax made many drop out of The System and erase their names from the governmental files for ever). The cutting back of the Health Service was not about a government battling against socialism (which was dying anyhow) or salvaging an ailing economy but about forcing people to become their own healers.

The changes that 'tyrannies' have brought about throughout the world have been far more radical than any of the tyrants imagined: the power has been returned to the people. And I don't mean that in a romantic 'Come the Revolution' way either. I mean we have been forced to take responsibility for our lives: the victims have been asked to remove their heads from beneath the tyrant's foot as the parent state was taken away. Johnny has been made his own master.

It is not easy to live without tyranny to blame, nor to live in dangerous health without our little illnesses to stop us feeling our true power as individuals. For when the statues of the despised tyrants have been pulled down and the liberation parties are over, the harder questions then begin to arise.

What will I do with all this free time? Now I have no outer controls? No one to hate? Now I have nothing to prove, no approval to win? How can I write my protest song?

Sometimes former victims do not wish to acknowledge their part in the tyranny, they do not want to forgo its protection, or the sympathy of the world, and move on (on to what?). There was a lot of silence in Santiago as some refused to admit the past, or others to let it go. A taxi driver sighed that people still did not go out much in the city at night, even though the curfews had ended long ago.

'The dictatorship is in people's heads still,' a Chilote jeweller will say to us in Ecuador when we return.

I saw how two bright and articulate women were genuinely

shocked when Mark sent back his badly cooked steak in a restaurant and refused to pay for it.

'We never send things back in Chile,' they said. 'We accept everything.'

'It's perfectly all right,' said both the wineshop assistants when I took back a bottle of corked wine and asked for a replacement.

'It's horrible,' I insisted. 'Taste it.'

To my absolute amazement, they drank the wine that was yellow and rancid and said it was fine.

'Look,' I said. 'I'm not angry, it's a horrible bottle of wine and that's the truth.'

But they still denied it, though they let me take another one.

I don't think truth can be denied in this schizoid way any longer. Resistance is not the appropriate response to the truth-bringer in whatever situation, to the swipe of the tiger's paw that says: Get Real. Wake up. Grow up. Take responsibility. Stop hiding. Get out of your head and into your heart. Get out of that fairy castle. Get out of the machine. Nor is it a gut reaction to leadership ('You have to trust me when I tell you something,' Mark shouted at me in the bank in Oaxaca when I queried his mathematics, 'because one day it might be a matter of life or death.')

Because the tiger is not a tyrant: he is something else.

'Jill is something else,' I said.

'Jill is a phenomenon,' you said.

Jill is total tiger. Warrior queen, she strides through your dark and hidden rooms, letting the sun in and confronting you with the truth: with one fierce stare of her black Ray-Ban glasses, and a disdainful smile of orange or pink or purple. Or black.

'Pyjama people are boring me to pieces,' says Marko.

We are in Jane's bedroom in another reality. We have been acting out family psychodrama with the help of the hallucinogenic San Pedro. Mark has been in blue silk pyjamas spitting and smoking cigarettes and threatening to piss on the floor, I have been in vanilla silk pyjamas laughing hysterically and telling Marko to take some responsibility as father to these anarchic children. 'Come outside and have a beer,' was all he could say. Marko says the people in his country don't have emotional problems.

Suddenly Jill enters: she is wearing Jane's cousin's blue flowerprint frock and strides about waving a pink hat.

'Shall I show you mother?' she asks and stands towering above Marko.

He leaps physically backwards, in absolute horror.

'No, no,' he says. 'Not that.'

Jill is the epitome of female power where none of it has been given away. Which is why she is frightening to both men and women who have abused their femaleness. Jill does not take on other people's pain, she does not have liposuction, she does not fake orgasms, she does not cook chocolate cake and pretend it is love, she doesn't hate herself or her body, she has no neurosis or eating disorder, she does not retreat into the shadows, into her insecurity, into her victimhood. She does not submit to cruelty or tyranny because no one would dare insult her with any. And when she stands there she confronts the very part of you that you have deliberately anaesthetized, handed over to the machine, to the control of the inner dictator. Get real, she says, get human.

Once in the Café Colon where I was having breakfast with Marko after my return from Colombia, Dark Jill appeared in total black. 'O dear,' I thought.

'Have you ever had *hongos vaginales*?' she asked Jane sweetly.

You bastard, I thought. In Colombia I had been suffering from thrush and cystitis and this was not the conversation I wanted to have with my lover right now over *pan dulce* and *naranjilla* juice. I could have happily thumped Jill at that point but something in me took heed. Jill, like my body, knew there was something that was amiss in my sexual relationship, something that I had not kept precious: where I had forgone my humanity and replaced it with hunger and addiction.

O yes, behind those dark glasses is a stare that knows exactly the nature of the infinite plan.

I have learnt with my monkey cleverness and trickster wit to be friends with authority for years: with my father, my teachers, my editors. They gave me licence, like the king to the jester, but they did not allow me my full power. And I never took it.

I never argued back. I never sent their false food from my table.

It has taken me a long time to remove my victim head from beneath my protector's foot. And it has taken me a long time to see the difference between the mechanical system of the tyrant that crushes people's hearts and permits us to be less than we are and the fearful symmetry of the tiger that removes the masks and the comfort zones we all like to hide behind, when we refuse to see the god in ourselves and others, when we refuse to acknowledge the very complicated truth. When we shut down our hearts and forget to listen.

Once when Marko insisted to you that all women were bitches and all Ecuadorians were monkeys, when he painted all the gods in a week with a Rotring pen and some coffee essence, you rose up in fury:

'Do not play with the gods,' you wrote. 'For they may come. And they are not always nice. And they are certainly not there for your naive amusement.'

You wrote that I knew the potency of the deities, male and female, and that I was lithe and alive and knew too the power of moons and my juices and, though I probably defended my lover against this tirade out of misguided loyalty, I was proud that you respected me, as much as I respected you.

I have learned to trust the courage and authority of the tiger. I think its power is given to those who can defend the kingdom of the heart because they know it comes from a higher leadership. The roar of the tiger is there to challenge us when we give up our true territory as human beings.

Lest we forget.

And as I run, chattering above in the trees, asking questions, getting on your nerves, I now know I have a higher role too, in my contrariness and my challenges: in my acrobatic mind.

I am the wise monkey who can turn upside down and keep the dialogue open.

I am the ape who can look at the king.

NIGHT THOUGHTS
– SANTIAGO DE CHILE
~~~

I'll just have another game of poker dice with myself before I go to bed. I really ought to be writing something for the book, instead of wasting more time throwing these useless dice and seeing how quickly I can get five aces to come up. I hate it when I have to throw more than twenty times, shit, I really hate that. Bloody hell, Charlotte returns tomorrow morning. She said on the phone she doesn't want to stay in Santiago – well, what about her fucking Spanish lessons she's supposed to be having with Claudia in exchange for meditation sessions? Oh, I'm not even going to mention it to her, fuck it. I'll just make sure I stare vacantly into space the next time we're out together in a restaurant or at a gathering where the people are only speaking Spanish . . . Mind you, the pollution's really been getting to me here, but I don't want to just keep pissing off every time I find things about a place I don't like. It's a pain in the arse. Anyway, I do like Santiago. I'm enjoying myself here. Bollocks, why did that die just have to fall off the table onto the floor, now I have to fucking bend down and pick it up. Thought about going back to fucking Ecuador today, and then on to Colombia. It's easy in Chile but I didn't come all the way here to spend my time in a rainy city with winter approaching. Missed England as well. Then Charlotte gets a really long fax from some friends and family at a dinner party, but none of the bastards send their regards to me. Well, sod them. Who wants to fucking go back anyway, it's always the bloody same. You want to share your experiences with your friends and family and they try to look interested for about ten minutes but the fact that they're not and that they don't even know what you're fucking on about, or on, half the time, well, it's depressing. Then you suddenly realize, shit, I'm back here and it's all the fucking same and I want to go away again. I'm looking forward to seeing Charlotte tomorrow and having a chat about what's been going on. Oh, what a load of crap, twenty-eight throws to get five fucking kings, I'll never beat my record now, and I'm only half-way through the game. Oh, sod it, I'm not wasting any more time with this shit. Charlotte spoke to Marko on the phone and he's going back to Ecuador in May, or rather early June. I thought it was great but she was her usual `it's not quite good enough' self about it, she'd hoped it was earlier. I don't know what she wants. Or what she expects. I don't think she does. Oh, bollocks to it. The book's not going to be finished by May anyway. Jane wrote and said she can't come till August now. Come where, that's what I want to know. And that's five bloody months away. Anyway, I'm going to bed now and if the bastard who was banging on the door down the road and screaming last night at two o'-fucking-clock in the morning repeats the performance again tonight, he'll get this empty Nescafé jar thrown at his miserable head for a nightcap.

CROSSING TO CHILOÉ

~~~

Puerto Varas – Lake District – late March

I am in the south, I left the city. I left on the night train and was rocked to sleep in a mahogany cradle. I awoke to blackberry lanes and hips and haws and a silvery light and gardens full of apple trees. Herons were waiting in the fields, standing and waiting for the fish in the water. I was in Chile but I was in a different place. I know this place.

I am staying by a lake, with Ursula, Esther and Siegfried Apel in their papa's old schoolhouse, and eating breakfast with them (black bread and salami and homemade gooseberry jam) and I sleep in an attic under a big feather quilt and the Southern Cross.

'There is no such thing as bad bread,' Siegfried tells me in his garden alpen hut and other Lutheran proverbs. One afternoon Esther brings me yellow apples on a plate and gives me a drink of firewater flavoured with murta which is a wild berry that grows on the slopes of the Osorno volcano. It is crowned with five spikes which form a pentacle, like the pips of an apple if you cut it widthways.

'You can always recognize the murta,' Esther says, 'because it has a spiral on its head.'

I am in the south to stand like this pentacle, with my two feet on the ground and my arms held out to the wind and my head lifted to the sky. I left to feel this. I had a dream before I went. I was feeding a seagull that hovered over my head. I was in a ship at evening. I fed him white bread and salmon and dried mother's milk.

'You need to feed your spirit,' Mark said.

I left to feel this, to feel connected to the earth, to let the spirit come from the sky. Let my birds come, I said.

I was in Chile. But I was in a different place. I knew these gardens (with their white geese and their giant cabbages) and I knew this island as soon as I came to it. I knew its bracken, its pines, its desolate heath, and its coloured houses, its mud, and the evening smell of firewood and salt and water.

I had been here before.

The Bridge

It is Sunday morning and raining. Down by the steep hill I walk towards the bridge. Three chickens stare at me from the white window of a house. Three men are walking across the bridge with two oxen: the oxen are afraid and rebellious. One of them has a stick. He is guiding the oxen with it and the two other men tug the oxen with ropes. The oxen are reluctant and bang into one another. The men are laughing at this lack of control they have over the beasts. They are talking to the oxen and the oxen are staring at the road. Two small girls cross the bridge with a large pink umbrella. They look at the three men and giggle and put their hands over their mouths. The river is full of rain and fish. Except for the laughter there is complete silence and the rain falling. Steam rises from the wet backs of the oxen. I am walking across the bridge.

The Fisherman

'You are from England,' the fisherman said. 'And you love the sea.' I smile.

'What do you do here?' I ask. 'Are you working or are you on holiday?'

'My work and my pleasure are the same thing,' he replies. 'I am a fisherman.'

Eduardo is a fisherman from Viña del Mar, which is a resort town in the north but he has been fishing here for a year in the wild part of the island. He has a big scar across his chin and green eyes.

'I love the sea too,' he says and tells me how he and his

companions fish for sardines at night. You put a light into the water and they come, hundreds of silver fish, and you move the light into a spiral. They follow the spiral right into the net, then as they enter the centre, you lock it with a special key. That is how you catch sardines at night.

Eduardo is very surprised when I ask him if he likes to eat them. I tell him they are delicious with bread and lemon and a glass of strong white wine.

He says this is not a good year for fish because it is a leap year.

'The sea is always about luck,' he says. 'You never know each day whether you will find everything or nothing.'

When I crossed to this island, diving birds bobbed in the still, coloured water. I saw sealions playing and giant seaweed drifting by, deep down, mountains of clam shells on the ancient seabed. And then in my own drifting I noticed something out of the corner of my eye. What was that? I turned round and everyone is standing on the bridge of the ferry, and pointing silently. I look out. A spout of water, a glide of black, a wing of tail.

Whale!

Tha' she blows!

I saw my first whale on the way to Chiloé.

The Island

I am sitting in a restaurant, painted blue and green, that sits on stilts overlooking the grey water, eating soup by the singing wood stove. The rain is sliding down the windowpane. I am watching the drops like a child: which one will get to the edge first? Small heads of rams and bulls and goats with blue eyes stare at me from the walls. A stone mermaid swims on the mantelpiece.

Eduardo told me it is different here. 'Because an island is not like the continent the people have their own customs. They distrust outsiders. Those who do not respect their way are not let in.'

So it is with islands, I think, and I like that, a place that has its own self. Down by the harbour the women sit and knit pale jumpers in a large wooden shed that smells of wool and earth and smoked clams that are threaded like necklaces and seaweed bundled like lost octopus arms. The fishermen come in with boxes of magenta crabs and sea urchins and conger eel. The sea-kestrels scream at each other, carrying little silver fish in their sharp beaks. Kra-aak, kra-aak. Click-click, go the needles among the soft voices of the women.

I don't think the invaders or the dictators would get past these sea-witches. What charms do they knit into these tough yarns? What rough magic is held in these fish and birds and figures, woven from marsh grass, that hang from the rafters of this restaurant? Nothing that can be taken away, or fit into a box.

Like the sea, like the sea.

The Estuary

'Home is where you are,' Mark used to say.

'Home is where you belong,' I said, and he did not agree with me.

But I know there are places where I belong and others where I am a stranger. I have made many hotels my home and many towns and many mountains and said, I can be anywhere, even in this filthy city, yet still these wild places call me home: the salt marsh and the estuary and the island and the briar and the seabirds' cry.

The tide is out. I am watching clampickers. A little dog is keeping them company. Gulls and oystercatchers are out in the channel too, finding the stranded shellfish. The mackerel sky is full of their noise.

Is it in my blood? My family are from wild and salty places, the Arran Islands, the Cornish cliffs, the Yorkshire moors. Or is it from my childhood, all those summers on the Kent marshes and the Suffolk coast where the boats sleep in the gardens? I have spent a lifetime watching cockle collectors with their big spades and naked feet disappeared in wet sand, with the sea gone out. Or is it that there is a pebble in my heart that is so stubbornly Saxon or so Celt that no travelling will remove it? How can I ignore the tug of this tide, this wind that smells of the sun in strong salt grass, this silver wind that lifts my spirit up like the kestrel above the shining flat water, that makes me want to run like a hare in spring through the spiky gorse and fight currents, jump, leap, like the salmon, finding the source, the dying and the breeding ground?

Do we all have our secret places of belonging known only to ourselves? Where we may reclaim ourselves? I don't call this place home because I am comfortable within it, or safe. I call it so because I am part of it, and it of me. Like these houses which have wooden walls like fishes' scales, like the fish have scales that reflect the pattern of water. It is my element. Home is not a place where we can stay. Home is a terrain where we can roam freely, in harmony, in our natural habitat.

I have travelled to many places and lived in many rooms and the words of that North American Indian on a Sacred Run across Europe always come back to me: 'The eagle is still the eagle, and the owl is still the owl.' And if this is so, then the owl must fly by night and the eagle live in the mountain. He who adapts, survives, this is true. But if we can go beyond survival only and into choice, if we can choose the geographies for our hearts and souls and bodies, if we can go where it is appropriate, where it is true, then I, kestrel, hare, salmon, I choose this wild salty place as my spirit's hunting ground.

THE ENCHANTED CASTLE

~~~

I have just said goodbye to a woman: she has a notion she can help save indigenous people, the dispossessed and the unspoken for, and give them their land back. She is a photographer. But sometimes she is a nurse who looks after premature babies in incubators and life-and-death cases in intensive care. She tells me she feels helpless when Japanese businessmen cut through the forests like heartless samurai, and she feels she can say nothing to the dying who face a similar figure dressed in black and carrying a scythe. She is angry. But she is locked up and afraid of death. She holds the delicate babies to her starched white breast and wishes they did not have to grow up.

I said goodbye to a man I loved a long time ago: he was clever as a shiny pin, he was young and beautiful, a golden boy when I knew him, who wore velvets and wrote poetry and was adored by women like an Elizabethan courtier. I used to imagine him composing sonnets for that virgin Queen, wearing her ring. He is not beautiful now, nor is he young. 'I am in the wrong hotel,' he laughed when I saw him last. He never nurtured his talents, but went instead to live in a big dark house where no light comes, where he breeds swine and keeps a woman he loves far away from the valley she loves, from the sunshine and the green. She pines for it. But he keeps her in winter and the dark next to the black sea. He does not want her to be disappointed.

I said goodbye to a couple a year ago: when I first met them I thought the man was so very beautiful. He is like a minstrel, I thought, with long golden hair and his sweet music; he is so gentle and seems to adore this small pale woman at his side, this dark woman. This woman is so sensitive and so special she cannot even breathe the same air as us, he explains to me. She cannot eat the food you lay before her. The tall blond man is this invalid's companion-at-arms. He thinks she is the Princess Who Can Feel a Pea Through a Hundred Mattresses. He thinks his Ariel song will bring her back to life.

'I will save you,' says the Minstrel Knight (who is really a prince in disguise). 'Stay where you are.'

'Don't go into the wood or the wolf will get you,' whispers the Swiss nurse and pulls a red woollen cap over the blue heads of the babies and the dying men.

'Beauty will never come to this castle, I will make sure of that,' says the man who thinks he is a beast in disguise.

I am walking towards the town of Puerto Varas, where the German settlers came and built their gingerbread houses by the lake. There are red-cheeked children in woollen hats selling apples and fishermen pulling up their catch and the smell of woodsmoke in the air. It is a landscape that I know well. I lived here once upon a time when I read the fairy stories of the Brothers Grimm and Hans Christian Andersen. I would like to say that I had found my way out of those magical forests of the past. But I have not.

Though I wave farewell to many enchanted people, I do so from my own fairy castle.

Which is why I have known so many who were still locked up in the fairy turrets of their 'happy' childhoods. Why I am witness to the snow white women lying asleep in glass coffins, poisoned by their mothers, the young men kept in bondage by being given impossible tasks by their jealous families, and genius trapped in a forgotten heirloom. I have seen whole courts asleep held in a spider's web. All waiting, all waiting beautifully for their redeemer to come. Waiting for the Princess to come, waiting for the King, their father, to recognize them, waiting to be transformed from goosegirls, frogs and willow trees, into human beings, into royal beings, into stars. Waiting for the bold child to steal the golden eggs and the singing harp to make us rich at last. Waiting for the simpleton to walk past with a donkey on his head to make us laugh again. Waiting and becoming angrier and more pale and no one dares come by and rescue us with their selfless love.

This is a story about a brother and a sister and an enchanted castle. We all have our stories and this is mine. When I was young I read the story of Byrd Helen who ran widdershins (that is against the sun, into her shadow) into Elfland, and never came home. Her brother, Childe Rolande, waits on the green for her return. He calls for her across the valley. But she never comes back. He so mourns her loss that he decides to go into Elfland to rescue her, into the dangerous land where no one speaks the truth and all the food is damned.

I always imagined myself as brave Childe Rolande. When I met someone I felt was imprisoned, I went to meet them in their shadowland. I smote the heads off enchanted beasts, I refused the poisoned fairy food but when I came to the Dark Tower and presented myself as their redeemer, they did not recognize me. They turned and banished me from their sight. I did not realize that what my pale sisters saw was not their dear brother but a reflection of their own anguish.

I did not know, you see, it was not another but my lost self I had to save. It was myself sitting there, sadly by the windowseat, all alone, waiting for my lost brother, with an iced-up heart and a ruined voice, captive in Elfland where everyone is a liar.

Fairy castles are built of love and shadows. In the space where love is taken away, we put a brick, a brick of defence, to protect our injured hearts: and so we build our towers, brick by brick, with our stones of anger and sadness, to hide us from harm, from the wolves, from the dark man, from Death, from the furious woman with silver teeth, those who took our love away. But it is not the stepmothers or the deaf kings who actually put us there: it is ourselves. And so it will never be the charming Prince who will rescue us, or the Youngest Daughter with the Golden Hair, she who sweeps ashes, who will know us. It can only be ourselves.

If we dare to go out after dark.

You may ask me how I got to know this and I will tell you. When I was young I read the story of Byrd Helen who ran widdershins into Elfland. When I was young my brother whom I loved more than anyone else in the world was sent away to school, and our garden in Kent, the place I loved more than anywhere else in the world, was sold. My life completely changed with these two events, my interior life. I found myself in a dark city with no escape and no one to love me and play my games with me. When my brother came back from school, he was changed too. I knew he hated it there but there was nothing I could do to stop it. My brother had gone for ever, and so had the place I called my home. So I stayed in Elfland.

'Why aren't you responding,' Mark shouted at me. 'You just go off, into another place. It makes me feel violent.'

I cannot hear him. I was sitting in the Edelweiss Café in the Chilean Lake District. I was eating apfelstrudel. It was nice in there and warm. But I have gone somewhere else. This always happens when I feel threatened. I freeze, my heart stops, my mouth shuts and I run into a safe tower. But something in Mark's look stops me this time from going through that familiar door.

'Don't you realize,' he says, 'how your silence affects me? You always say I am shut up in a fortress, but what about you? What about you?'

I turn round and stare at him. Who is this? Whose eyes are these, looking at me? What are you saying?

It's time to go home, he says.

When I was young I read all the fairy tales about brothers and sisters who were separated and kept captive against their will, who were pushed into ovens and turned into swans and whose hearts were frozen by the Snow Queen and they haunted me. Because I knew they were true. Even when I grew up I never let anyone get near enough to me to be my brother, just in case they were taken away one day, and I never let any place be my home. If anyone came too close, I pushed them away, if I felt too attached to a place, I walked away. I miss no one, I would say, I belong nowhere. I am the Cat Who Walks By Himself and all places are the same to me. I've struggled bravely on my own, shielded by this romantic outsiderness, and I've railed against any system (like a school) that bullies people and changes them and crushes their hearts, and I've hated cities that do the same. Oh, all my life. But it never released me from my tower and it never changed my story. Because hating never does.

If you are stuck in an enchantment, if you are held hostage in a castle of silence and loneliness, you need a storyteller to re-tell your story, to give it back its true ending. A spell can only be broken, as any reader of fairy stories will tell you, by another kind of magic: by the simplicity of trust, of courage and finally by love. You need a storyteller you love and you trust because you have to know that your story is their story too and that your liberation is their liberation. By the telling of a tale are all the characters and the narrator freed. In the remembering is the healing.

Suffering, you see, is never solitary. It always affects others. As Mark says: 'There is always a payoff.' Every time you refuge yourself in a fairy castle, you revenge yourself on someone: for not listening, for not being there, for not understanding, for being cruel, for loving someone else, once upon a time. You make them stand at the moat and look up at your locked window, at your noble pain. You make them pay. Those who you would love so dearly. You deny them your heart because you think yours was so denied. Once upon a time.

When I was young I loved my brother more than anyone else in the world but when he was born I was so jealous of him, I stopped talking. I dreamed of ways I could push him downstairs and kill him.

Fairy castles are fairy prisons. When you hide in a fortress, you do not simply shield a part of yourself you would rather forget (your innocence and your guilt), you steal away another's liberty.

When you put a baby in a glass box or a woman in a big castle or let a man kneel before you in full armour, you prevent their shadow from falling behind them. Everyone has their own shadow and in that shadow lies the direction of their sun. You may call it rescue, you may call it protection, but it is in fact denial.

The Swiss photographer could not allow the pure Indian tribe to prostitute their land; the poet could not set free his Virgin Queen to desire as she wished; the Minstrel Knight could not let the Fragile Princess get better (for who would he save if she became Queen?); the Princess did not risk the Knight his unheroic anger. To release all those ugly passions. All that darkness. All that childhood abuse and hurt. All those tears. All those secrets.

And I, in my Rip Van Winkle sleeping, in my Rapunzel solitude, what did I prevent? I did not allow my brother his right to battle. I neglected to teach him the secret of warriors which I had learnt. I knew that you can only have courage if you have a heart, you can only stand your ground if you have a home to fight for and someone you love to defend. But I, in my own dispossession, with my hidden jealousy, I denied him this knowledge. I made him suffer.

I cannot go back and change what happened to me at nine years old when I flew against the sun and went into the Dark Land. I cannot atone either for the shame and guilt I felt for not helping my brother, the powerlessness that made me turn away from him and not listen to his pain any more. In my own misery, I pulled up my drawbridge and shut my heart and would not admit his tears into my turret. I could have said something to comfort him. I could have said something to the adults whose ear I always had (for my brother was silent and I was always his spokesman). But my voice went dry and I pushed him away. What was the point when there was no garden to play in anyway?

But I can say something now. I can change this scene as I stand before the door of my castle and I hear Mark say in this lakeside café,

'I cannot bear this lack of communication.'

I turn round and stare at him. I turn round and stare directly into my brother's eyes. Into the wounding: the bullying, the homesickness and the isolation that I refused to see before and I don't turn away, not this time.

'I'm sorry I hurt you,' I said. 'I didn't realize how it affected you.'

I'm sorry I ran away that bright spring day and hid in a place where you could not reach me. I knew what was happening to our garden and I knew what would happen to you when you were sent away. I didn't tell you. I abandoned you and I saved myself. Forgive me.

'I love you,' I said.

'I know,' he said. Let's go home.

SONGS FROM THE GLASS BRIDGE

~~~

Song One

It is Easter. Mark and I are in the south of Chile, staying with the Apel family. They are very puritan and not very fond of the extravagances of chocolate. I am in a quandary as to what to give them for a present.

'Perhaps I should get them some wine,' I say to Mark as we pass the local grocery store (we have been invited for lunch). But the shop only has cheap boxed wine.

'I'm sure it will taste all right,' he says.

'It offends my Venusian sensibilities,' I declare pompously and laugh. 'I will go into town.'

I walk along the lake which has been scowling a bit like my friend for the last few days and like Siegfried, the eldest brother, aged eighty-two. He has taken leave of woodcutting and is staying in his room listening to Schubert quartets. Horrible, he pronounced of the Swiss accordionists who gave a concert last night (there was an electricity strike and one woman yodelled in the darkness to keep our spirits up). 'Papa would not have been impressed,' he announced when we escaped at the interval. He took equal umbrage at our playing the old man's harmonium this morning. *Death and the Maiden* drowned out the *St Matthew Passion*, and Ursula was forced to retire downstairs.

But today is a lovely day: the lake is as blue and as clear as glass. The two volcanoes raise their snowy faces to the sky. I feel exhilarated.

When the family come back from church I present the wine I found in town. I couldn't help my sense of humour: one bottle (red) is called Casillero del Diablo and the other (white) is called San Pedro Llave de Oro: the Devil's Casket and St Peter's Golden Key.

'I wonder what these will unlock,' whispered Mark wickedly into my ear.

We sit in the warm wooden kitchen with the iron stove and big wooden table and stripey cats and we eat the Easter lunch of lamb and garden vegetables and Peruvian eggs and apple and *murta* pie. And we drink the devil's wine, except for Mark who has given up alcohol (Siegfried is horrified that my friend can refuse this gift of God to man). Suddenly all the secrets tumble out about Papa. The fine upstanding schoolteacher whose military portraits we see all round the house turns out to have been a terrible tyrant.

'Strictness is all right if there is love,' says Esther. 'But there was no love.'

'Do you miss him?' asked Mark.

'On the contrary,' she replied.

The sisters tell us hysterical stories about the guests who have come and gone through this *hospedaje*, and we play dominoes together and then we start to sing. They sing old Prussian war songs and we sing old music hall songs from the First World War (the family were from Dresden). I sing 'Lorelei' and 'Tannenbaum' which I remember from my German O level class and Mark sings 'Alfonsin y El Mar', and the force of his voice booms through the old schoolhouse and I feel the Apel sisters will be quite blown away on apfelstrudel wings.

I love this family. I love the way they have such pride in what they do, how it fills the house the way the smell of the hip jam curls up the stairs. I like their orderliness and simplicity: how Siegfried stacks the firelogs in the rain and the sisters bring us fruit puddings while we are working and tell us we must get some *frisches Luft* before it gets dark, and I love the way they sing now, like two young girls liberated from Papa's stern conducting baton, their high pure choral voices echoing around the room. This Easter Sunday has nothing to do with sacrifice: of the children to the father, the lamb to the knife or the hearts to the machine. It feels like something else is going on between the old enemies of Europe, some third alliance that is unspoken for, like a hand held over the ghost trenches.

Sometimes you can talk for ever and nothing ever changes. But when you sing, something transformative does take place. I have seen it happen. I remember another starry night in Greece in a different year when I sang an Irish song and was astonished when the islanders all joined in, humming the tune with me.

'It's a song about a man who falls in love with a woman's dark hair and walks a dangerous road,' I explained.

They smiled because they knew the song already.

I remember singing an English lullaby for the Señora's grand-daughter in Guatemala. I remember Mark singing 'Summertime' in a Russian restaurant in Bogotá. I remember us singing 'Here Comes the Sun' to a sad Canadian doctor on a train on the way back to Santiago.

I remember the smile that crossed the faces of the audience and an invisible hand that crossed over the divide, over the seas and the borders that no good intention or political strategy could ever bridge. And I fancy at those times I can hear the sound of ice breaking.

Song Two

I am back from the south in Room 25, Residencial Londres, Santiago, sitting at the window. Mark is having a shower. I hear an amazing voice soaring into the blue sky from an upper room.

'Remember me.'

Who is this woman singing so operatically on this Santiago Sunday?

'Remember me.'

It is the swansong of the suicide queen Dido about to fling herself off the cliffs of Carthage. All for the love of the Trojan general who is about to desert her.

'Is that a record?' I ask Mark as he walks into the room dripping in a very scanty towel.

'Is that a woman?' he asks.

The voice belongs to a dark lithe Irishman with owl's eyes. We meet him as he bounds up the wooden backstairs of the hotel.

'O my mother's from Ireland,' said Mark. 'From Port Laoise.'

'I'm sorry to hear that,' he said.

'Where are you going?' I asked him.

'We upstairs breakfast on a different social level,' he said and disappeared.

Andrew is a magician who sings in a different voice from the one he speaks with, and he is fond of disappearing like a rabbit from a hat. At the age of thirty-nine he disappeared from Dublin, leaving a career as conductor, concert organizer and restaurateur for life on the road in South America. He is about to magic himself now onto a cargo ship to the San Fernando islands. He invites us to go to Valparaíso with him. In a dockland bar, while he waits for his papers to be stamped, he recites a poem. It is about an old tinkerwoman who walks the old bogroad and longs for a warm stove and a dresser of Dresden china. When he recites there is a passion and a fire in his eyes, and I love him for that straightaway. On the way from the bus station we start singing, we three. We try out our old repertoire and Andrew slips effortlessly into the bass line.

'When you come back,' says Mark, 'let's go busking.'

His watchful eyes look at my friend's outrageous suggestion with a professional dismay but something of the magician's love of surprise get the better of them.

In spite of the men's nerves and my PMT we go singing two weeks later in the metro Moneda station at 6 p.m. Our favourite song is 'Molly Malone' and it fills my green Andean hat with pesos straightaway. We try and keep a straight face. 'The Boxer' is less of a success. Andrew says he hasn't worked out the harmony for that properly. 'I am a mathematician,' he says. 'I am not an artist.'

His conducting hand keeps us all in the right time in the river of shoppers and bemused office workers but when he sings the part of Molly's ghost, his eyes raise to heaven and his hand becomes imploring for this fragile girl, for the cruel fate of this queen of shellfish. And all the mathematics fall away.

Twenty minutes into our medley, the blue-coated transport police walk towards us.

'You can't sing here,' they say and blush.

'*Qué lástima*,' I say. 'What a shame. Don't you like music?'

'Everyone likes music,' they reply. 'But it's against the rules here. You can go outside.'

Outside in the Avenue O'Higgins a thousand gaily-painted buses snort past and the rush-hour crowd pushes past. We decide against our open-air venue. Mark counts out the money.

'Let's go and celebrate at the Nacional,' says Andrew (he is fond of a waiter there).

On the way he puts a protective arm around me and sings us a song about an ambitious mother who marries her ugly daughter off to a ne'er-do-well and only realizes it after the wedding. It is one of the funniest songs I have ever heard. My moon mood disappears.

Andrew comes and Andrew goes. He conjures another passage on a ship, this time to the Easter Islands.

'I got this for you,' I say when we meet to wish him fair passage, and I give him a giant bulb of garlic I bought from the witchy women on the island of Chiloé. He is quite surprised by this unexpected gift, pulled from my hat, just like that. He looks at Mark and me with excitement in his eyes, and we plan that day to go travelling to the Elqui Valley. 'We'll get a house,' I say recklessly. 'And winter in the desert.'

A month later, suddenly in the rain, Andrew appears through the doors of Room 33, Residencial Londres, Santiago, bearing gifts: a tape of the Easter singing for Mark and a necklace of shells for me. I throw my arms round him. He says he has to go back to Europe and he and our new French friend Marianne discuss over lunch the most economical ways to fly to Spain. I try to cover up my disappointment.

'Come to the desert,' I whisper softly in the magical place where I hope he can hear.

He does come. We spend almost four weeks, one of the happiest times of my life, together in the Elqui Valley. We cook and we sing and we argue about Carmen who he thinks is a bitch and I think is fabulous. He sings us Elgar's 'Sea Songs' and the songs of tragic French heroines and he throws up his eyes and supplicates to a God that has never known Newton's compasses. We sing 'Teddy Bear's Picnic' in three-part harmony as he stirs our breakfast porridge and he teaches me an Irish jig in the dining room to the great amusement of Maria, the *dueña* of the hotel. In the day while we write he sits in the path of the sun from the time it arrives over emerald hills and goes behind ebony hills, leaving in its wake a sky bathed in purple and gold. He is plotting his return to Europe, with plans that change like quicksilver.

'I'm going to America.'

'That sounds fun,' I say.

'Or I could come back with you and stay in Colombia.'

'O yes,' we both say. 'That sounds even more fun.'

'But after the jungle in Ecuador . . . all that mosquito repellent.'

'What happened to Spain?' asks Mark.

'Provence is definitely a better place.'

'Good for the dairy products,' I add (Andrew is not impressed with the lack of fresh cream in the desert).

'Or I might go back to Ireland.'

'Forget it!' we chorus. 'Definitely Provence.'

'Via America,' he insists.

'Via America and find us a house. We'll meet you there one day.'

I like the idea of Provence because it is the land of Cathars and troubadours and because it is the gateway to furthest Africa. I tell him the story of Blondel and Richard the Lionheart, how the singer walked all Europe to find his captured king. He sang up at all the castle towers until the king recognized his song and was set free from his lonely captivity.

'It's a metaphor for us all,' I say grandly. 'We need to establish our courts.'

'Well, that's great, like,' he replies. 'Bien sûr toute suite encore un autre demain dimanche lundi mardi . . . All French fluent, you know. My family are all white and they have been for centuries.'

One night we go to the next village because it is their saint's day and we dance in an adobe courtyard under a net of stars and a sickle moon. Young couples ride up on shiny chestnut horses and tie them under the pepper trees in the square. We drink the local Pisco and watch very drunk men dance the *cueca*, the national dance of Chile, with women with dark hair, waving handkerchiefs over their heads like the tails of peacocks. Andrew points out all the characters of the village with shining eyes: he says it reminds him of the annual dance in Ireland where all the marriages are fixed. He can transform such a scene into a ballroom, as he turns each dish into a feast and even that surly waiter in the Bar Nacional No. 1 (the one who insisted to Mark that Chile was the best country in Latin America because of its superior telephone system and its absence of Indians) into a prince in disguise.

He can tell a story like no man I have ever met. He can weave a tale that starts in Dublin and ends in Africa, full of people I will never meet and houses I will never see. But somewhere else they all live in me: the mad aristocratic woman who paces the room and shouts obscenities, the poorhouse where the old men died alone because the nuns were forced to care for those still living, the fishing island where the flies lived, the piano teacher who was partial to onion sandwiches.

'I am not an artist,' he insisted to me over a bowl of *cazuela* one lunchtime.

I interrupted him.

'You are a magician,' I said. 'A man who heals with stories and with singing. I know no better definition of an artist than that.'

He is silent and his owl eyes watch me, I am never sure whether in anger or in delight.

It is the last day before Andrew leaves the valley. I am writing in the vineyard in a throne of crimson plastic. Mark is in the bath and singing an Yma Sumac song for Jill's South American tour. Maria is washing sheets at the back and singing a Mexican song, her voice cracked with emotion, and Andrew is ironing his linen shirt and singing in his high clear voice, the voice that goes beyond this grubby world of geometry.

'Remember me.'

As if we could ever forget.

Song Three

It is our last night in Santiago. We have gone to a *parrillada* in Bellavista for our farewell meal. Andrew flew to Miami today. All our bags are packed and waiting by the door of the Residencial Londres, Room 33. Neither of us wants to leave Chile. We are quite silent.

Mark leaves the room suddenly, and I look around at the other diners talking over their grilled meats and dark red wine. Most of the tables are occupied by flashy Chilean businessmen, waving their hands. In the middle of the room are a couple who are not talking to each other and next to us, a table of loud hysterical women (I think they are Spanish). It's an ordinary enough scene. But one thing catches my eye. A young waiter, he can be no more than eighteen, is standing just by the entrance. He is holding a baby in his arms as if this were a natural part of his duties, along with clearing the salt and pouring the wine.

Mark returns.

'He's here,' he says excitedly.

'Who?'

'The singer I told you about.'

A black Peruvian singer, tall and very handsome, about forty I'd say, strides into the room with a guitar. Everyone looks up. Everyone stops talking.

He stands in the middle of the room, surveys the scene and bids some good evening. Then he smiles and starts to sing.

'I can't believe he isn't famous with a voice like that,' Mark remarks.

'Maybe that's not why he's singing,' I say.

I look around the room. It is quite changed. No one in the room wants the singer to go: the girls at the next table who turn out to be Portuguese and Argentinian have all calmed down (one of them has burst into tears), the couple who turn out to be Brazilian have woken up and are smiling at each other, and the besuited moneymen have turned round to face the singer and are joining in all the choruses, and we who were just before so sad and distant, are now joyful in each other's company.

Once, before I knew in my heart that singing could create an invisible bridge between people, I read a book about cellular biology. In it the scientist wrote that a knowledge of separation is in all living things on earth but it is the rhythm, the pulse, the heartbeat that is in all living things also that keeps this wound healed and the connection with the universe alive. So whether it was the beat of a one-celled organism or the rapture of a nightingale or the boom of the whale undersea, it was the perpetual call of these voices that summoned the sun and kept the heart of the world beating.

No one wanted the singer to go this night because we knew, as he walked through our lives, a magic was happening. He was remembering us, calling us to a place where we might earth our natural rhythm and catch in the crack of our voices, in that loop you hear in all the folk music of the world, the higher song, the divine music of the spheres.

The singer stamps his foot and throws back his head in the beat of the *cueca*, or *mariñera* as they call it in Peru, the dance where the man and the woman invite each other to their lands, holding aloft, above them, their flags of peace and surrender, calling their beasts across the valleys and the plains, calling what is rightfully theirs home.

'That man is a troubadour!' cries Mark in admiration.

'Yes,' I say, looking at my friend who loves to sing more than anything in the world. 'And he is also the king.'

DISARMAMENT

~~~

I am in the valley of Elqui, cooking potatoes in the ashes of a huge fire outside my room in the Hotel del Sol. The sky is ablaze with cold stars and there is a silence here that only the desert can give.

Brigitte, the nurse and photographer from Switzerland, is telling me about her Chilean friend who was tortured for his underground activities and how she fights for justice by documenting the indigenous tribes who live in the dwindling forests of Canada, Colombia and Chile. Her eyes shine with outrage as she plays with her Swiss army knife in the flickering light of the fire.

'Put your knife away,' I say to her gently. 'You will cut yourself.'

This morning I left Santiago in a rainstorm. I was shaking as I climbed into a taxi and waved goodbye to my friends standing in the middle of the traffic in their plastic, coloured capes. I hardly noticed the seven-hour journey north. When I left that wet and dirty city, I had walked away from a combat that had engaged me all my life.

Now there are many kinds of purification in this tainted world, as there are doors to be cleansed and bridges to be crossed. 'Healing,' as Mark once said to me, 'is not curing. It is a chance to start again.' So the struggle with my negative soul did not end when I left the white walls and blue swimming pool of Antigua. Old voices still howl within me and I have to strive to keep patient and not give in to that black ego that demands attention like a mewling infant. But it does get easier. Though the forms of addiction come in different guises, I can recognize them when they present themselves. The enemy is no longer invisible.

Did I say enemy? Well, there we go. You see, one of the detox stages I did not go through in the angry country of Guatemala where the military is much feared and the resistance is hidden behind closed doors, was disarmament. Disarmament came much later and quite suddenly, here in the once-upon-a-time dictatorship of Chile.

I met a woman called Marianne. She was a wise woman from Brittany, a professional masseuse who had been travelling for twenty years. She had learnt weaving in Guatemala and lived by the shores of the Atitlán lake for almost a year. 'I love water,' she said when I met her. This is a woman who could cure a sick soul, I thought. I laughed and felt myself move towards her instinctively as you might go towards the shade of a tree on a hot day. Three weeks later I met her again, she had been to the Elqui Valley where Mark and I were about to go. Our paths crossed for two days. In the Residencial Londres, in the pouring rain.

We went for lunch and she told me a story about heroin. When she was eighteen she and some friends in Thailand decided they would take heroin for the summer. They started one day at seven o'clock, the next day at five, then three and so on. After five days they were completely hooked. One morning they got up and went to their stash outside and found it had gone. They were thrown into complete panic because they thought the police had discovered it and were now watching them. Terrified of being caught (for the penalty in the East for drug offences is always severe) they decided not to buy any more. They went cold turkey instead. 'You cannot imagine the agony,' said Marianne. 'For two weeks of heroin, it took one week to detoxify.'

A week later, they saw a boy come to the place where they once kept their stash. 'It was not the police after all,' said Marianne, 'but a boy who wanted to sell it. That boy saved our lives.'

'What is heroin like?' I asked her.

'It closes you in,' she said. 'Totally. It is like you are in a small room, disappeared into yourself. I could stare at my finger all day long and be in paradise.'

I know this feeling well, I have been locked in a small room of my own for some days now, oblivious to everything and everyone, even to my own fate. I don't care. I just stare out of the window, watching the rain.

There is a burned-out shell of a building opposite, a ghostly neo-classical house that has a giant For Sale sign outside. But this house will never be sold, because it is here, they say, that all the interrogations during the regime were carried out. Only the moon lives there now, and the occasional teenage drug addict who stands at an upper-storey window, staring vacantly into space.

Or perhaps she watches me.

I am in a place of forgetting but I cannot remember what I am here to forget. I ask Marianne for a massage and ask secretly that her strong hands will awaken the will and the magic that seems to have fallen into a deep poppy sleep. As she runs her fingers down my spine, like a skier wedeling down a mountain, I see in my mind's eye a golden warrior and a dragon snake breathing fire, standing on either side.

That night I have a strange dream; I dream I am at the top of a white mountain. There is so much UV in the sunlight I can see through people like X-rays. 'Look,' says a blond boy. 'I am so protected, you can't see me at all.' I ski down the mountain and my skis fall into a fixed path. I lose control and fall into a pile of broken crab shells. A man comes past and picks me up and takes me roughly to the bottom of the mountain through three sets of doors which he blasts open with force. There is a general at the descent awarding prizes, and a giant snake whispering in my ear. I try to wrench myself from both: from the mound of yellow chemicals that the general is forcing me to accept, and the slippery advice of the snake. 'This is poison!' I yell at them, as my eyes begin to burn like fire. 'You can always use it later,' urges the snake.

'But don't you see how this is killing me?'

I wake up in a sweat with my whole back aching and the right hand side of my face feeling as if it were corroded by acids.

'The general is within you,' said Mark when I tell him the dream.

'And that snake is not a good snake. A snake can be a snake in the grass, the snake of temptation. Think about it. You're always going on about peace and how I am so Martian but you are the one who is always dreaming about war and soldiers and escaping capture, how there is nothing left to fight for. Maybe you like it in the war zone.'

I am furious with my friend. I am angry that he is always commanding me and I am so subservient. But I do not move out of my numbness, my heroine silence. I know in my head he is right and I am foolish and uncourageous but my heart is failing me. I am stuck. I am about to leave for the desert and have to say goodbye. I do not want to go but my friend blasts me out of my hermit shell with his anger and forces me through the doors and we are hurtled down to the places where all the wars start. To the land of the closed heart. Where the child guerrilla learns his art.

O how ridiculous is this battle we keep fighting with our dictator father, and with our absent mother. We cannot keep fighting this way any longer; the tyrannies and the subterfuges, the army that invades, the secret agent who campaigns for liberty. This is a struggle that will never end. Unless we declare peace for ourselves and walk away.

'The soldiers and the guerrillas are the same thing,' said the Señora in Antigua one day. I did not agree with her then but I do now.

The blond boy in the dream was a friend in Santiago called Ted who came from a town in California called Eureka. He told me once how he had taken up mountain climbing because each time he scaled a rock with his heart in his mouth, he blasted his way through another fear barrier. 'Man, we live our lives covered up in fear,' he said. 'We just get stuck.'

Every time he came back from the mountains, he felt a little freer, and a little more courageous. Moved through another shut door, into a bigger space.

Octavio Paz, the Mexican poet, once wrote that in order to escape the stifling confines of society, women had to attempt some kind of jailbreak. But to be truly free, I know I have to set fire to the prison as well.

I would like to think that when I go to sleep tonight in the quiet valley of Elqui that my long career as martyr to the peace movement is finally coming to an end. (O campaigner for truth and liberty, caught in the crossfire of newspaper opinions and dinner-table argument, how you loved to fight!) I would like to think as I sit by these dwindling embers that my fear of the conquering militia and my admiration of the noble resistance will now be replaced by a true warrior and a golden snake; by a will that loves and a wisdom that heals.

Disarmament is the hardest inner process of all, because battling and resistance, attack and defence, is sometimes all we know – our only chance of becoming a hero, someone that matters in a bombsite world. But the battleground within, like the courtroom within, has to be demolished. Because if you don't dismantle the structures, blast your way through its strategies and its traditions, war will always find a place within you, as there will always be cases to be tried.

So I shall linger no longer among the locked-in heroines of that small room, among the opium eaters and the lotus eaters: I shall remember what I came here to forget. I shall raise my new sword and breathe my new fire and I shall destroy the walls that contain me still. O little home, o home sweet home, where my heart failed me, o home sweet home that witnessed my wounding, o home sweet home, where I advanced and retreated, and was always defeated. I destroy thee now, and set me free.

THE TIME OF STONES

~~~

The Copper Mountains

'We come from a long way,' said Ted. 'Man, so far, so far. I am just a feather from a big bird from far away, and that bird is my family.'

We are waiting underneath the eucalyptus trees for a lift. Pomegranate seeds are spilt at my feet. We are on the way to the thermal baths in the mountains outside Santiago, eating empanadas that burn our mouths. I am not sure we are going to make it.

Eventually we are picked up by a gravel truck, and we stand in its huge emptiness like charioteers as the metallic wind hits our faces and we roar past the green rushing river. The sun is already falling from the sky by the time we get to the lowest bath which is like a giant orange swimming pool. We stand shivering, naked in this copper water with the warmer currents bubbling through the gravel at our feet, and we watch the goats leap from ledge to ledge on the snowline. This valley is cold and dry and mineral and looks as if it runs with fire.

On our way back a miner gives us a lift. He is a happy man, this man of the deeper earth. We buy a fresh goat's cheese from a friend of his who lives in an isolated smallholding with shiny horses in the garden. And we devour it hungrily in our hands. He leaves us in the dark to catch a bus back to the city. On the way out of the car, he gives Ted a piece of copper ore. I am quite jealous.

We are visiting the commune today high up in the Elqui Valley where they perform a fire ceremony that they say will give back the energy to the earth. We stay and have lunch of lentils and rice and sharp oranges and spring water. Along the refectory table everyone holds hands and blesses the food and sends out healing to the world and we all pick angels out of a book from Brazil. Mark's is the Angel of Peace, mine is the Angel of Patience.

'Infinite peace, my arse,' he growls into my ear.

In the garden outside the adobe walls of this refuge, a horse ploughs the soil and a silver dog in a halter of string waits by the gate. A baby with blue eyes walks towards me and holds my hand and a little dying cat rubs herself against my breast, her whole thin body shakes with purring. There is great peace here with the sounds of the running water and I imagine if you had infinite patience, this would be a good place to stay. But my gods do not live here: they do not come from the east. I do not follow gurus or want to live in a place with rules, or imagine that a starship will rescue me from this damned earth if I am good and holy and abstain from the pleasures of the flesh. I cannot be where there is no delight in the beauty and art of man.

'What do you think?' asked Mark as we climbed into the car, longing for cigarettes and chocolate and coffee.

'I was not impressed by the sad cats.'

'They were given reiki every day,' he said. 'And they have lived longer than is usual.'

'I know,' I replied. 'And that's fine but sometimes love is different.'

On our way back we stop off at a place called La Huerta, which means orchard, to buy herb teas. We walk into a private walled garden by mistake. A radiant woman with blue eyes welcomes us and talks to Mark excitedly underneath the shade of some giant bamboo. Her daughter grins at me and I buy some of her cedarwood perfume. And I laugh with happiness when I hear her say: 'In my house everyone is free to do as they wish.'

The sun is setting. Though the sky is grey, there are huge bowls of golden sunlight on the tops of these strange mountains that are the shapes of sleeping panthers, and snakes and salamanders and tortoises and embryo birds. 'I think I'm going/Homeward bound,' sings the radio in the car. The river runs white through the bamboo and boulders and weeping willow, and the vineyards are yellow and orange and look like a twin river of flame running through this narrow valley. Those that are bereft of leaves stand with their arms outstretched. Before I thought they looked like crucifixes, now they look like men taking wing. The white egrets are flying home to roost down the valley and we are going home to a fire and wine and a stew and as the first star appears, the sky is a lake of silver before us and behind us the still small peaks above the snowline in the far far distance are turning red, deep pink, copper in this falling day.

The Road of Iron

In the small town of Vicuña by the square of the giant pepper trees, I thought about the meaning of stones. One night in a restaurant, just as we are leaving, a man, a dealer in gems, gives Mark a piece of raw lapis lazuli. I go out to the toilet and hear caged birds singing in the darkness. I have drunk too much red wine and feel disturbed. I wish I had been given a piece of rock too.

'Why didn't you wait?' asked Mark. 'He was going to give you some too.'

'I think he was looking in his pocket out of good manners,' I replied. 'And besides perhaps lapis is not my stone.'

The time of all stones unturned is come, as Mark once wrote in a poem. Perhaps now the stones we are given are an indication of the qualities we need to give back to ourselves and to the earth. We have to know we have these qualities to offer because any feeling of lack creates a need and neediness creates a gap which can never be bridged, a hole that can never be filled. When we grasp for love and attention, when we tear down trees and only consume, we take, we do not create. Our world becomes barren. We do not see the silver of the sea, or the gold of our proud kingdoms. Perhaps Ted needed copper to know the metal of Venus, to know his own beauty and feel beloved in order that he might fly his own path. Perhaps Mark needed then the lapis, the magician's stone, to know his own transformative powers, his alchemical art, in order to sing his own song.

This is the time of gifts, I wrote in my notebook on that night when the sky was a glass carpet of stars. What have I been given? I empty my travelling pockets. Here is an African copper coin given to me by a child in England ('So you can remember me,' he said). Here is a piece of crystal given to me by a Romanian tarot reader in New York ('To keep clear,' she said). Here is the little golden owl with lapis eyes which Mark gave me in Santiago to live in my buttonhole as a reminder of my wisdom and my inheritance. Here are the three silver coins which Kena, my Chilean friend, gave me to throw the I Ching so as not to forget the loveliness of change. And here is the egg of combarbala given to me by a mapmaker travelling through this valley.

'Time to plant a new garden,' I thought when he handed it to me with a shy smile. 'Time to plant my seed.'

When I am about to leave Chile, I will add to this collection a piece of raw iron given to me by a man called Christian and his wife, Maria Paz. I do not know then that this metal of luck and warriorhood will help me to cut myself free from my childish self-pity and rage, help me defend my insulted womanhood and enable me to see with a crusader's clarity and the commanding vision of the eagle.

Each of us is given the stone we need, at the time we need it. The stone that has been taken away by the greedy claw of man and machine and now we can replace. I did not need the connection of copper, nor the magic of lapis to bring to my world, I needed a weapon and a strategy. I needed an iron will.

I laid down my father's sword a long time ago but now I pick up another. This is not the sword of destruction, this is the sword that divides my night and day, and protects my territory and my treasure, this is the sword that hangs by my side, as I walk, and sometimes stumble, along this hard strange road, with the changing sky above me.

PRACTICALLY PATAGONIA

~~~~

I saw Borges once, the great Argentinian poet and fantasist. I saw him recite a poem in the forgotten language of the Anglo-Saxons on British television. Borges was very old then and blind but the expression on his face was one of youth and ecstasy. No one interrupted him, the audience was spellbound, even the interviewer kept quiet. I was amazed because, though I did not know what the poem meant, I could see that the poet had accessed a land not afforded by his own, where he could walk like a warrior.

'*Qué lástima!*' says the bank clerk in a toast-coloured jacket.

I am in Puerto Montt waiting for Barclaycard to OK my money order.

'What a shame you are not going to Punta Arenas.'

'I know.'

'It is very beautiful by boat,' he insists.

'I know,' I say. 'But I'm not going.'

'Hola Slovenia, this is Chile!'

I am ringing Marko from the Telefonos del Sur office.

'This is Ljubljana, where are you?'

'I'm in Puerto Montt.'

'O nearly in Patagonia!' he says with excitement in his voice.

'Yes,' I say. 'I'm in Practically Patagonia.'

But not quite.

I am in the seatown on the border of one of the landscapes I have dreamt about for many years. I can take a boat there, I can take a bus there. But I don't want to. I know it is beautiful, the Antarctic light and the ice floes and those strange colours that only exist in the furthest south. But I have travelled enough. I have consumed seas and mountains and cities until I am full and just right now I don't want to see anything else.

I am changing as I sit and write in this attic room, at the end of the Andes, on the edge of Tierra del Fuego. Last night I dreamt Mark and I swam under a besieged castle and opened a metal door with three silver keys that opened into a room of air. Some people who had also escaped, joined us there. Then Mark and I opened another door and travelled by car through a polluted land where there was no air to breathe and when we came to a chasm, we leapt into nothingness, into a pale fiery light.

Each of our journeys through Latin America has been about moving: moving on from the smog of Mexico City, from the chaos of Bogotá, from the history of Antigua, from the pyramids of the Yucatán, from the roaring Pacific, from the turquoise Caribbean, from the purple mountains of Bolivia, from the red deserts of Chile. It was always time to go, to find the next place, to see something different, to challenge a new inner geography by walking another terrain. But now it isn't.

It's time to change elements.

So it is not the cold or even weariness that makes me stop here in Practically Patagonia, it is simply that the next journey is about fire. And the land of fire is not a geographical place but another dimension.

I knew this today when Mark played a piece of music to me. It was a song sung by an extraordinary women's choir from Bulgaria. As I stared out of the window onto the moody tin-coloured lake, the lake that is like a dark mirror, a voice soared up and it sounded to me as if she were standing on a tall cliff overlooking the Black Sea, with a chorus of women behind her, calling all her ships home.

I felt something grab me in the heart and the guts in the same way it had two years previously, when I had run through Chapultec park in Mexico City with Mark in a storm.

The song did not make me yearn for that eastern sea, to find those Bulgarian cliffs. But I did want to be able to sing like that, to stand

and call my ships home from the invisible sea. And as I stood, looking over the glassy lake, listening, I suddenly didn't know where that cliff was, whether it was on the outside or the inside of me, or the ships and the song and the sea, and all the women. And that was a strange feeling, all that land being inside of me.

The Whale

I once met a man who lived in a derelict mill in the old whaling town of New Bedford whose passion was for the sea. When he talked about whalers it was with the same expression Borges talked about Anglo-Saxon warriors. As we bicycled around his giant attic, he told me he wanted to write a book about the monsters of the deep, those octopuses that had grown as big as leviathans with the nuclear waste under the Atlantic.

He wanted to sit in a submarine for six months and wait for them. He was going to persuade the Navy to let him go there.

'But do they exist?' I asked him.

He smiled and looked at me with his Irish eyes, the eyes of a trickster hare.

'That is not the point,' he said.

When I crossed the sea to the island of Chiloé and saw my first whale, I remembered him and his imaginary sea-creatures. I realized that though I had never seen a whale before, whales had always swum in my mind's ocean, in much the same way as the ships must have always existed for the Bulgarian women singers and mermaids for the Chilote women knitters. And that if I held something inside of me, it would be mirrored on the outside.

Ugly or beautiful.

I realized that in all my travelling, I had been reclaiming land in a dimension that had been forgotten by my culture, and that, in order to travel there, I had to destroy all the barriers that blocked its access, the bars that held its treasures captive. In order for the animals to return to the forests again, I had to open the zoos inside me. In order for the gods to come back, I had to open my old museum doors. In order for the seas to be unpolluted, I had to destroy all the factories and machines within, I had to knock down all the historical statues and demolish the safe houses. I had to close the schools and burn the churches and let the cities be covered with ashes that looked like snow.

The land of fire is a land of spirit: a land that is not destroyed when women keep it protected and held sacred inside of them, neither by a communist regime, nor a political dictatorship. Nor by any kind of systemized destruction.

But I do not have the traditional ways to track the animals of this world, I do not have the drumbeat to call the spirits, as I do not have a knowledge of birds, or the corn, or the wind.

So I have had to call them in a different way.

And I have had to call them because I have not held the sacredness of this earth within me, I have not honoured myself and, like everyone else, I have begun to pay the price.

Burn-Off Day

We are back in the Residencial Londres, on a bright autumn morning, gathering for breakfast on the second floor. The second floor is ruled by a woman of about sixty, with a pile of shiny coiled hair, called Estelita and a tiger cat with a limp called Eliberto. Estelita has the grace and dignity of an empress. When she serves you your humble white roll and cup of milky Nescafé, it is as if she presents you with the breakfast of the Sun King himself.

I am sitting with the big black-and-white cat on my lap, the kettle singing on the paraffin stove, reading a letter from my mother. She writes that she is now completely cured of cancer, and also that she will not now come and visit me:

'There is me thinking this could be the only escape in the world, but lo! Chile is suffering from ozone problems and has the highest skin cancer and cataract problems in animals due to a catastrophic volcano in Mexico a few years ago. So there is no escape. *Doom and Gloom!!!!*'

The conversation at breakfast is no more optimistic: we have all been reading a report in *Der Speigel* downstairs of the horrific nuclear poisoning in Russia. Mike, the New Zealander, is telling us about the Slip, Slap, Slop campaign in his country that warns unaware citizens to protect themselves against the carcinogenic ultra-violet rays.

'Dark sun,' mutters Mark darkly. 'If you can't go outside, you are forced to go in. There is no other way.'

'I've had quite a few skin cancers removed, yeah,' continues Mike. 'Yeah, in New Zealand you go to the doctor and they freeze the cancers off, sort of style, yeah. Burn-off day's Tuesday at my doctor's, so I just go and he freezes them off, know what I mean, yeah?'

Brigitte is railing against the Japanese businessmen who consume and do not replace the life of this continent from the tequila cactus of Mexico down to the seaweed of Chiloé. I tell her I once went to a conference in Kyoto that discussed the future of consumerism and ecology. I met a fashion designer there who lamented that the Japanese insisted on using throwaway wooden chopsticks every day, and had razed their own woods and fields to landscape golf courses. I remembered how we sat in a noodle restaurant and we discussed how the Western imagination was ruining the spiritual aesthetic of the East. 'Look,' he said, pointing to the traditional wooden window, 'once everyone could look at that light falling through the slats of a window and feel enriched by those patterns. But this is disappearing now. So fast.'

The West has destroyed the East as much as the East has destroyed the West. North and South, greed and ignorance is much the same at whatever cardinal point. But Eastern spirituality has fuelled the flagging spirit of the West as Western music has given the suppressed ego of the East some individuality and youth, native medicine has brought healing back into the mechanics of modern medicine, North American biochemicals cure African children, Africa gives Europe a new dance and a new costume . . . The interchange goes on. We are not separate. We live in the same world. We are all responsible for closing the gap. But I am not going to sit here in the Residencial Londres arguing the point.

I am entering the land of fire. I work on another level. I have to. I remember the Chilote women knitting their spirit-tracks into the sea-jerseys, I remember the mesh of light that fell from the window in Kyoto. And I think there is another way to mend the gaps that we have left in the earth, in the sky and in the sea, and in ourselves, those gaps between heart and soul, body and spirit.

Last month when I was waiting for a train from the south in Temuco, I went to eat lunch in the market. An old Mapuche woman came in and sat at my table. There were plenty of empty tables in the restaurant but she came and sat right next to me. She ordered nothing to eat or drink. She said nothing.

'Why have you come here?' I wondered inside myself.

A boy turned round at the next table and smiled at me. For a moment the world stopped spinning and I was caught in a golden net between the lovely elfin boy's smile and the old woman's silent presence.

The old woman got up and left, as quietly as she came. I got up and left too and as I walked through the emptying market towards the station, I saw the boy again standing on a cart of seaweed coiled like snakes, looking after two oxen. Waiting like a guardian.

Everyone is leaving to get on with their day on the second floor. Estelita clears our coffee cups. Eliberto jumps off my lap to lie in a stripe of sunlight on the parquet floor. Carmen walks into our room with a pile of perfectly ironed washing. Luis calls someone to the telephone from the courtyard below.

Mark remains behind, deep in thought.

'You may think I'm bonkers,' I say to him, 'but I just had this idea that if we asked all the grandmothers in the sky, they could knit the sky back together, they could darn the hole in the ozone layer.'

He turns and smiles, and keeps silent. But he does not laugh at me.

The Red Tide

When I was in Chiloé, a fisherman said to me: This is the time of the *marea roja*.

The *marea roja*, the red tide, is a natural occurrence in the Pacific Ocean. It happens once a year. Some Mexicans call it the sea's menstrual cycle. During this time, the sea becomes intoxicated, and likewise everything that swims and breathes in it. The shellfish is poisoned and debris is washed up on the western beaches. No one can swim and no one can fish. The sea becomes a dead zone. No one may enter.

It is the sea's way of cleaning itself.

The earth is cleaning itself more slowly and more dangerously. There is no shore we may wait upon until the poison time is over. So it is very hard to escape the contamination, to find another way to breathe and eat. Everyone is affected.

A little boy I knew in Greece called Alexander once stood upon a chair and flung up his arms to the stars. He told us, myself and his grandparents, as we sat in the kitchen, that a big fire will come and throw the roofs off all the houses. All the windows will fall in and the planets will whirl about and the plates will whirl, around and around . . .

'. . . And then all the flowers will die,' he ended softly.

'Why?' I asked him.

'Because there is no water,' he replied.

'O you children want to take on all the problems of the earth,' said my mother. 'You all want to be stars. It was so much easier in my day.'

Alexander, aged four, worried about the amount of Es in his food. When I was a child, I knew nothing about chemicals. I did not have apocalyptic visions. It was much easier in my day too, when I drank water from the tap and lived in the safety of a garden, protected by seasons and teatimes, traditions and rules, all the structures of a polite society. I chose not to hide behind these any more.

But the time chose this for me also.

Some people believe that as the earth purifies itself, in this tide of toxins, space ships will come down and lift them off, so that they may avoid this cosmic chemotherapy. I don't believe in spaceships, or the chosen. Spaceships and aliens are for those who are so alienated from their earth, they cannot believe the higher levels of dreaming and spirit exist here or in everyman. I think if the land is within us, so are the stars and all the cosmic forces.

In the old days, everything in nature and in the sky had gods and guardians. These were their protection and ours. But as we advanced beyond our scientific knowledge we left those gods behind, we scorned them. We thought we did not need them. And so we played with all the elements like greedy children and took away the power of the mother. We stole her jewels, insulted her animals, and played with her fire. We ignored the sacredness of things and we demolished the guardians like the Chinese demolished the temples of Tibet. With brute force.

We thought the means justified the ends.

But now we pay the price for loving history and forgetting the gods. History says that the world changes because of kings and politicians and generals. But it doesn't. History is just a celebration of ego. If you look carefully at the real shifts that happen, you will see that the world changes as man changes his attitude toward the energies contained within its gravity. It is a measure of his lack of respect and his neglect of spirit. It was gold that changed the continent of America; it was lead that poisoned the Roman Empire. It was opium and wine that killed off the poets, the poets who were once priests. And it is the Red Tide that now changes the face of the world as dramatically and completely as the Black Death changed Europe in the Middle Ages.

The Island of Stone

The island of Chiloé reminds me of an island in Greece where I spent all my summers, and the women of the storytellers who used to sit on the steps of the ancient road that led from the inky sea. This Greek island appeared unprotected: it had no fences, no guard dogs. It was like a woman; receptive, welcoming, dreamlike. Its houses were built like wombs inside, its wells were rounded like a woman's belly and the dovecotes still had the triangle carved into them which is the sign of the divine vulva, the female earth goddess of the Mediterranean.

Then the modern world crept in.

All the inevitable things happened to the fragile structure of this island. The road was demolished and replaced by an ugly grit road. Concrete was used for the houses. Athenians bought up the land. The women and children watched television. No one danced in the cafés as they used to. And the boats which brought all these new materials goods now came to a harbour which polluted the once-empty beach.

But some things did not change at all. Contrary to prediction, not all the children left the island for the city, and the tourists did not come in their hordes.

Fifteen years later I went back to the island and the boy who played a wild violin and kept bees and sang so beautifully in church is now the priest. The families have electricity and a doctor: their lives are less harsh and, thanks to the subsidies of the EEC for crops like olive trees, they are richer. And his church is full on all the feast days.

Before I came to this bigger continent, I went to a service there when the church was filled with basil branches. The children carried the candles, and the women stood by the chairs around the sides, and the men cut up and handed out the bread that is still baked in the side of the mountain, and everyone praised the fruits of the summer. It was a saint's day but I forget the name of the saint because it was something else that was being celebrated here: the relationship between man and his earth.

I'm glad I went to the island for all those years and saw, in spite of history, it retained itself. The islanders welcomed the new power, but they did not abandon their God. They let in change but they did not sacrifice themselves to it. They went on worshipping in the old way.

The women may not sit as they once did, spinning their white spindles on the steps, but they sort rice, and when clean packaged rice comes, they will knit and even if the wool is not pure or from their own sheep, they will carry on knitting, and even if they have no grandchildren to knit for, they will still weave each other stories: they will still sit there and watch the sun fall behind the ruined monastery and they will smell the thyme on the hill and the donkey will raise its head to the sapphire sky and they will hear its strange lament, and they will say, 'Today was a yellow day.'

Today is a red day.

I envy the women from the island, knowing these things: the way they grow basil in pots by their gateways and thrust a handful into their families' hands when they return to the mainland by boat. I envy the Chilote women who hang up their marsh baskets and the Bulgarian women who can sing like that. I wish I had that sacred legacy that comes to them so naturally. I wish I could dance the wedding dance I heard once in Bolivia.

But I come from a different culture. A culture that took away and did not replace: so I have no natural protection when invaders come to my territory, no guardians, no spirits, no cactus fence grown over centuries.

So I have had to suffer the full brunt of the *marea roja*: I have had to bear witness. I have borne witness to the cleansing of the earth. I have witnessed the exigencies of ego (the fall of politicians, the collapse of my own brilliant career), I have witnessed cancer and AIDS, I have witnessed depression, addiction, child abuse and sexual violence, every illness of the modern world. I have suffered allergies, I have eaten poisoned food and food cooked without love or spirit, I have partaken in weddings where there was no celebration. I have listened to music where there was no under-

standing of the deep mysterious power of song that the poets call
el duende, and I have seen kings hidden in towers and women who
starve themselves so much their periods stop, I have seen young
men fly away so far from the earth that they burn themselves
against the sun and children who are kept frozen under ice. I have
lived in a world where the grandmothers do not knit or tell stories,
where a lack of humbleness and respect has reduced their wisdom
to ashes.

I do not wish to live there any more.

Patagonia Regained

'What is this song about?' asks Mark.

'It's about the grey sea,' says Marko, whose native language
shares some of the Balkan tongue of the Bulgarian women's
folksong. 'And cuckoos. It's a wedding song.'

'The Black Sea?' I ask him, remembering the women and the
ships.

'There is no sea in Bulgaria,' Marko laughs. 'It's landlocked.'

Marko may not know about the sea but he has been to Patagonia.
Very shortly after we meet back in Quito, he gives a slideshow of
the photographs he took there, traversing the length and breadth
of this land I never went to. As I sit by a roaring fire in his *posada*
watching the flickering wall, I understand why I didn't visit this
place he calls the turquoise frontier.

His Patagonia is like a pristine vision of the earth before man
came and destroyed it: the purple hills and green lakes and ruby
sunsets and the pre-historical faces of the sea-elephants and the
giant blue cathedrals of ice, are fierce and clean and heroic. There
is no one in his pictures, except for the black-and-white dog who
led him through the mountains. But if you look carefully man is
everywhere, in the faces of the rocks and stones and water, in the
expression of the ancient sea-mammals' eyes. All there, buried in
the geography like new men waiting to be born.

We understand different territories: I can sing of the valley and the sea, and he can sing of ice-floes, and Mark can sing of the jungle and the volcano and Marianne can sing of lakes, and Blanche can sing of winter lanes, and Andrew can sing of the island where they tie the cows' legs together to milk them, far away in the Pacific Ocean. I know I have all these territories inside of me but I cannot stalk them all. I can walk those that are native to me, that I belong to, and I can travel with the others as they stalk them for me, and I for them. These are our gifts to one another. And sometimes when we meet in those we all know, we laugh in recognition and we greet each other, like long-lost friends.

I have travelled away from my country for over a year. As I have travelled down the backbone of America, I have tried to recover parts of myself that I thought were lost for ever: my kicking womb, my silvery soul, my jaguar heart, my spirit birds. I came to reclaim them here, at least I have begun to.

I cannot give you basil for a lucky journey because I do not know the god of basil, I cannot knit you a jumper to protect you from the monsters of the sea because I had no grandmother to show me, I cannot sing at your wedding, I do not know the tunes.

But I can tell you a story, and one day I will show you my dance.

As I step over into the land of fire, as I cross the bridge, and as I close the gate, as I sit overlooking the green velvet mountains of Quito, I will tell you what I have seen.

Today is a red day.

Once upon a time, all the lands belonged. All the earth was joined together but when the seas came, the lands were separated and it was the storytellers and the singers, the dancers and the weavers who kept all the lands joined by invisible threads. The wise men and women from every tribe, even though they spoke different languages, could talk with each other, in another realm where there were no divides or barriers. As the earth was joined to the sky, so was that whole remembered world connected with this broken, changing one. There were no holes or gaps because as soon as one appeared, it was healed and replenished. These bridge-walkers kept the vision of a complete earth in their hearts and in their memory and by their singing and in their medicine was this world kept in a balance.

No one told me this story: I taught myself.

6

CROSSING
THE DESERT

RETURN TO QUITO

~~~

Jane's Flat

1 JUNE 1992, 3.15 A.M.

Outside the Quito dogs are barking. The gold lights of the highway on the hill opposite contrast with the silver lights in the smaller streets. They are like foil-covered chocolate coins on a Christmas tree. Most all the houselights are off. I sit at Jane's desk in her living room. On the sofa, under posters of Colombia and accompanied by a teddy-bear, sleeps a seven-year-old Scots girl and she sometimes talks, says things I cannot decipher. Her parents are asleep in their bedroom. Charlotte and Marko are in the middle room. And Jane is in her bedroom.

Charlotte and I arrived from Santiago yesterday at midday and it was a bronzed and excited Jane who met us from the airport. She danced up and down outside the exit gate and we danced up and down by the baggage claim.

'All these signs are freaking me out,' said Jane in the taxi on the way to the fruit and vegetable market. 'Marko rang this morning at seven announcing his arrival. Then Amy called too. Oh, Marko doesn't know you're here. I'm afraid I had to tell a big fib and say I had no idea when you were coming. I felt awful. But he'll be here.'

In the market my heart and stomach leapt for joy at the bright yellow papayas all fleshy and fresh and so different from the tinned ones of Chile. Oh, and those wonderful purple onions, we'll be able to have a salad of those with mozzarella, tomato and coriander. It's all so exciting.

'Chile was amazing,' I say to Jane. 'But the food isn't so great.'

We arrive at Jane's flat full of light whence we departed those four months ago. During the afternoon we read poems and pieces to her and she shows us her paintings of the Galapagos, beautiful, funny and full of colour. She only started painting four months ago.

'I'm so overwhelmed. I want to cry. I haven't felt like this since you two left,' she says and rolls an enormous joint in the thin paper of the *Guardian* weekly. Then she adds absentmindedly, 'I wonder what Marko will bring over from Slovenia.'

Marko arrives at six o'clock. He is tired. Absent. Jet-lagged. Yes, that's it, jet-lag. Absence through jet-lag. I am trying to stop my heart from sinking. Patience. Peace.

Though I could not help but notice how he held Charlotte so briefly. And did not look into her eyes.

All has been far from peace in the land that was once Yugoslavia and is now a deathtrap not even the Red Cross dare to go any longer. Marko is from Slovenia, an oasis in the desert of war.

'His country is not at war,' I say to Jane in the flat downstairs where she has gone because she cannot stand to hear Marko recount tales of babies being murdered and old women armed with machine-guns as he lies in the hammock, his very long legs hanging over the edge. Not looking into Charlotte's eyes. It is not his war. He has other wars.

We drink champagne, toast our reunion. The evening disappears and Jane excites my taste buds by telling me about Joe, a hunky gay Scots guy who is staying downstairs for a week or so. But I do not feel as elated as I did in the afternoon. Marko goes to bed. We follow on shortly. I am exhausted and excited and poisoned by the champagne and strong aguardiente Marko has brought from Slovenia.

I cannot sleep.

Outside the Quito dogs are barking . . .

QUITO: QUICKSILVER CITY 3: 'I LEAVE'

~~~

I am so tired of saying goodbye to those I love (will I ever be there to welcome you home?). I am travelling on a bus out of this returned city, past the ramshackle suburbs and the dirty green hills where the rainclouds sit like elephants. It is election month and the names of politicians shout from the walls of houses in red and black, red and black. There are dahlias in some of the gardens. I saw dahlias when I first met you: the flower the poet said was a reminder of pain and happiness that one fiery heart bequeathed another.

I do not want to stay in this city any longer. I am reminded too much of what we gave each other here. I still see us standing arm in arm at that corner of the avenue that night when a crowd appeared through the mist and the lights shone blue and yellow and green and everyone was dancing on glass. It was fiesta week. You said, 'Are they the aliens or are we?' I still see you there in Jane's bedroom lying on that sunlit blanket of rough animals, where you first held me and tamed my wild cactus hair and taught me the way of the rose garden. Last night a child with golden hair gave me rose petals to eat. 'Make a wish for me,' I said. You did not see her, nor did you see me. You were locked away somewhere else, wishing on another star.

Now I am travelling south to a spa town with the taste of flowers and ashes in my mouth. I do not know where you are going. You did not tell me. You only said, 'This place is a prison for me now. I watch only for planes in the sky once more to take me away.'

'This city,' I said, 'is a mirror. The prison is always within. And no plane will set you free, my love, nor starship come to discover you here.'

I do not find it hard to go today. Because I do not love prisons or history. It was in this quicksilver city, in this city of all change, that I cut those bonds that once held me too, my puppet strings, and here where my spirit flew through a blue door and my feet began to walk a green earth. So I know what I must do: I must walk on past that sad gaol, that comfort of aliens. I know how I must leave, how I must grieve, how I must let you disappear into the mercurial mists. I cannot be separate from these green hills, so I cannot fly away with you or hold you in that dark place. I belong here.

But when I boarded the bus on this wet and smoky day, where the men sold thin gold chains and the women warm white bread and three children sang in high sharp voices at my departure, I remembered roses and dahlias, and I wished to God that this seat had not been empty, and that you were still travelling at my side.

O I am so tired of saying goodbye.

IT DOESN'T MATTER
WHERE I AM
~~~

I am by the sea. Come to dissolve something heavy. Come to remind myself of who I am. I forget sometimes (it's fear, you know). Grey it's been the last few days, well, since we got here really. What do I mean by here? Here is a place by the sea, ecologically sound with bamboo and straw huts, three meals a day, semi-vegetarian, frogs in the shower, a bitch with six puppies and thin breasts, a donkey with chewed-off ears, bright red land crabs, lots of people I don't want to talk to, some I do, grey sky, grey sea, Charlotte, me.

I am by the sea. Sitting underneath a wood and straw canopy. A very concentrated American boy sits under the next canopy. Why can I not be so concentrated? After all, I have a book to write, well, finish. Here come some people I definitely don't want to talk to. I'm not even going to describe them. There is a beautiful grey heron on the beach. The first one I have seen in the south. The first grey one, that is. I've seen lots of white. Herons. That dreadful German girl really got on my nerves this morning, whingeing. 'It is impossible zat all ze showers are bissy,' she whined at Charlotte. 'How long are you here for? Oh, it's expensive, zere's no sun. I can't leaf.'

O fuck off. Yes, sometimes it's just fuck off. But I'm not going to describe when it's not.

I am by the sea. Not describing. Come to dissolve something heavy. Over there is the Island of the Hanged Man. This morning the sun graced us for two hours with its presence, then the Hanged Man looked all glorious and white and shiny. It's probably birdshit that does that. But it was quite lovely, I thought. Actually, the

American boy is quite lovely, I think, but all that Peace Corps concentration gets on my nerves. I've changed position now, so the sea's at my side and I can see all the bamboo and straw huts and the big red gladioli shooting flamily up in all that green.

In the ecologically sound centre.

I am by the sea. Looking at the green and yellow creepers on the sand, stretching towards the water. I will look back fondly at this time. I will think, this was a blessed time. I may forget the grey sky, or more likely it will cease to be important. By the way, the German girl who whinged and couldn't leave, left. Her name was Charlotte too.

'There's major victim going on there,' I said to my Charlotte.

'Well, goodbye and good riddance to my victimhood!' she retorted.

I am by the side of the grey sea, under a grey sky. It doesn't matter where I am, by name. I am come to dissolve something heavy. Come to remind myself of who I am.

I forget sometimes.

BAÑOS DE LA VIRGEN OR SWIMMING POOL, SOUTH AMERICA

~~~

I am floating in a warm pool in Baños in early morning. People are moving past me, slowly in the rising steam, resting on the stone steps like sea mammals, drinking the water that tastes of rust. It is quiet, even the children are silent. We have put the mud from the mountain on our faces and it has dried the colour of gold in the sun. Mark sits in the cold rushing river holding on to a bar, looking like a charioteer in a shining mask.

We come here in the mornings very early before breakfast, in the misty spa town under the waterfall, where men stretch large skeins of toffee from hooks and jewellers from Chile sell magical silver rings.

Mark's mother walked barefoot to the baths this morning. She says Ecuador reminds her of Ireland, and the statue of the Virgin, of the altar in her childhood home which was the only shining thing amid the dirt and the confusion. She told me how she brought flowers to it every day, wild flowers from the riverside, and was sometimes beaten for it.

'The earth is crying,' she says as we watch the water tumbling down, rivulets from the bare rock. Something in me feels very quiet and humble when I hear Bridget's stories. I am amazed that suffering has yielded such wisdom and clarity and so little self-pity. That in spite of the poverty of her past she is so generous and open-hearted. I feel I want to throw my arms round the stoical child-who-once-was. But of course I can't because she isn't there any more.

'We have ruined the world because we want to avoid pain and sorrow,' she said. 'For our comfort and our convenience.'

Above us in the curling steam of the yellow baths stand a family from the mountains who have come here to wash. Shiny faces, wet hair, gumboots, father, mother, six children all in identical checked ponchos from the same bolt of cloth; whispering to one another and smiling.

The eldest son is swimming and they point at him as he frolics in the hot mineral water. Is he the only one who learned how to swim? Or the only one whom they can afford to let swim?

The family stand transfixed at the activity of all of us in the water, their eyes open wide with awe and joy and something they used to call innocence.

At a table I wait with Mark's mother. It is evening and the rain is falling. I am eating a plate of radishes. Mark is building a wood fire and a Frenchman, a melancholy man, asks us whether he should open a restaurant or not, and what name it should have. There is much banter in several languages across the table. Mark sings a song and the sad man tell us about his house in the jungle he calls the monastery, how he hopes people will come and rejoice in the spiritual life with him.

'I have no children,' he says. 'But there has to be fecundity in my life, otherwise I just concentrate on myself and do not give back. I am caught in a cage.'

I know about cages and being stuck in a dread place you have not even names for: the place where no love lives. How it is that you can never hide from your emotional past, even in the strangest forest thousands of miles away. How that memory of bars ('for your own protection') and punishment ('for your own good') comes to haunt you, years after your prison guards have left the door open.

A black dog once guarded my pram in the park: so no stranger could approach and tell me there was a different world outside this one I was trapped in. And I seem to have spent my life trying to get past him so I could play under those singing trees.

But tonight I want to be as still as Bridget. I do not want to dwell upon the insult of that dark cot for ever, raging on a small stage, changing nothing, giving nothing back.

'There is more to life than psychological process,' said Mark. 'And more to life than survival.'

And indeed more to life than my small self. Besides, how could I ever presume myself innocent? Because, even if as a child I were blameless, I still carry the sins of my father or my mother or my past life, or my culture that once robbed the land from these quiet Indians: sins that cannot be washed away so easily, even in these warm springs and this endless rain.

Something has to be cleansed on a much higher level so that we can remember awe. So that, even if in our memories we still suffer mute hunger and loneliness, we can feel nourished and loved by the milky heavens. And thus be brave enough to take out, to voice what cruelty we have borne witness to. And end it for one and for all.

A scarab beetle has flown into the restaurant and whirls chaotically around the light. Then a little grey cat softly comes in and catches it with her paws and gently in her mouth, takes the insect out of the house, into the rainy night.

Last night I dreamt I saw Bridget moving towards me in a field of wheat and she was singing and crying at the same time. 'Ireland,' she said to me as she passed (or was it our land?), singing and crying in the ripe green corn.

There are two mothers: the mother of the corn and the mother of the sky. The sky mother sits amongst the stars and hers is the clearest sight of all. She looks down upon us on this sad earth and, from her eyes of vision, she weeps her crystal tears.

GALAPAGOS

~~~

They are proud of two things in Ecuador: of the oil that gushes from the jungle floor, and the tourism on the islands of the Galapagos. They are proud, these Ecuadorian men in suits, of the revenue these things bring.

I was talking to a good-looking boy in a suit one day at the *posada* where Mark and I once lived. Perhaps I should call him pretty. I used to like pretty boys until I recognized their cruelty. He was about twenty-six and had been working as a guide in the Galapagos since he was sixteen. A suitable case for burn-out, I would say.

'Have you had a holiday recently?' asked Mark.

I could see he was not impressed by the flashy confidence or the prettiness.

'The tourism is increasing on the islands,' he said proudly, 'with more boats.'

'Have you had a holiday recently?'

The boy-in-a-suit said he had been travelling around America visiting the houses of the rich tourists for whom he had been a guide ('I have hundreds of letters every week,' he said). Some of the people knew movie directors. He told us this story of how he had gone to a barbecue at a very smart address in California and had worn a blazer ('I like to dress up,' he said). But everyone else there had worn jeans. I imagined him then walking about the lawn with a plate in his hand, feeling very awkward and out of place.

'I have been to lots of places,' he said.

But he didn't look too happy about it.

And it was with something like desperation in his eyes that he told us too of some articles he was writing for the newspaper in Quito about the development in the Galapagos.

'I think everyone should just leave the animals alone,' I said, suddenly very irritated.

'I thought the numbers of visitors were restricted,' said Mark. (In 1991 the number of visitors tripled in spite of the correlative rise in the air fares – and tourists have to pay twice the amount for admission than Ecuadorian residents.)

'Anyone who has the money can go,' said the guide. 'Anyway, you can't make laws like that. You can't just stop someone at the airport because they are the one over the restriction, can you?' And before we had time to argue, he added, 'Lots of old people visit the islands when there is nothing else to see in the world.'

'See Galapagos and die,' I remarked drily.

'Besides,' he said, 'there is lots of room on Santa Clara for more people. We are expecting at least forty thousand more.'

'If everyone goes to the Galapagos, young, middle-aged or half in the grave,' I said, 'all the animals will leave.'

Jane told me last week that the iguanas are already beginning to know fear and do not stand as quietly as once they did when the camera-clickers weaved a path through their ancient stillness.

'Look, it's just lizards and rocks – there is plenty of space.'

'No, there isn't.'

'Have you been to the Galapagos?' he asked.

'No,' I replied, 'but I can guess what the people eat there.'

He looked at me with troubled eyes. He was pretty but he was no fool.

'What will the animals eat then, when the nets are everywhere, when there's no fish?'

'They are investigating a marine park,' he said. 'We are looking at America and how they run game parks.'

'As soon as you enclose something wild, you kill it,' I said. 'I know this because I come from Europe where every magical place in nature from the Alps to the Mediterranean has been turned into a theme park for tourists, where every city market has been turned into a nice safe, clean film set for shoppers. You will destroy the Galapagos too.'

'But we want to preserve it.'

'You want to make money. No one makes a game reserve without thinking of the revenue. And when the bottom line is the dollar something dies, something that was once alive, because greed always destroys.'

'You should leave it alone,' snarled Mark suddenly across the breakfast table. 'You should let the animals and the sea be. They did not invite you to come. They do not want you and your boredom anymore than the tribes in the Amazon want so-called eco-tourists gawping at them, or the Kogui in Colombia want gringo trailers tramping across their sacred Lost City. You should just let everything live in peace without interference. It's just an ego-trip to go to these places. Everyone should stay at home and look for these things within them. If they want to see animals, let them watch documentaries.'

'But everyone has a right to see the world.'

'Not if they don't bring it anything,' I said. 'The earth is not a peep show.'

'But what's the point of the islands if nobody visits them?'

I was getting angry. The boy in the suit was getting confused. Mark was getting another cup of coffee.

'Sometimes it's necessary to have empty quarters,' I explained, more softly, 'like the mountains in Bolivia, like the deserts in Africa, like the oceans. It's not always necessary to go somewhere to know it, to see it with your own eyes in order to believe it. I think we should give back the Galapagos to the lizards and the rocks.'

'Why?' he asked. 'What for?'

'Where will your dreaming go?' I asked him. 'And where will God live tomorrow?'

But he was not listening, the pretty boy who liked to dress up, whilst silently in the forest fields of Ecuador, the black oil bubbled chaotically up, as if from a severed artery.

NOSTALGIA

~~~

Colombia

An old friend came to see me, an old close friend, in this country of unpredictable taxis and beggars on the street with missing limbs.

'I can understand it,' you said that day my face grew dark and angry over lunch of fish and rice on the Caribbean island where the storm raged hot and heavy and the children danced in mud and pouring rain, smiling. Always smiling. 'I can understand the cautiousness of the tourists,' you said. The tourists who do not give back.

What are we giving back?

Yes, an old friend came to see me, annoyed by the sellers of oysters and coral, those insistent sellers. 'I am on holiday,' you said. 'This is my relaxation,' you said. You work hard all year. It is your right, is it not? And the sign on your door said, *Not to Disturb*. But you were disturbed.

Cold you said I had become, in that hot town by the unruffled sea. You were looking at me, but were you looking at yourself?

We went to the house of the Indians of the mountain. You bought a handmade bag. 'I want to see my Indians,' you said. But you did not hear me when I said these people do not want us on their land, and the message that they bring, the one that made you sad for them, was not for them alone, but for us all: 'The mother is bleeding. If the warm seas rise and the snows upon the mountain melt away, there will be no more hope. The world will die. There is still time. A little.'

So what meaning does our sadness have when we cling so tightly to our separateness?

Aggressive you said I had become, not the same and loving person I once was. Alone you said I would end up, with my hard words and my direct approach. But I cannot serve a comfortable complicity or live with others in false sentiment. You came to see an old friend and you found me. In the cold mountain town, by the hot calm sea. I felt you full of old years and fear of disharmony, and upset by the beggars, the sellers, the cracked-skinned cripples and kids shouting, 'Hey you, gringo, money!'

You saw the change but you did not see me.

INNER HAIR

~~~

Dear Mark . . . I just have to write this. It's got nothing to do with kings or gods or Marko or a bus trip we took once in the furthest Andes. No, this does not even entail San Pedro and his shiny keys. But it is about something so intrinsic to our trip that I feel I must share it with the universe. I would not be truthful if I did not honour and celebrate the creativity of our third travelling companion, without whom this book would never have been written: I am referring of course to your hair.

Never in the course of my life, including the time I was beauty editor of Tatler *magazine, have I been so intimate with a haircut. I feel my inner growing process has coursed along the same lines as your now very long, wavy locks. I did get a sign in the London Underground before we left ('How can I control my life,' said the advertisement, 'when I can't even control my hair'). It was for 7UP so I thought it was something to do with chakras. Nothing permanent. Nothing of such major and cosmic proportions.*

But, as you like to say, if you don't take notice of the wisps, you will just have to listen to the highlights.

Then in Spain you told me: maybe growing your hair was part of freeing yourself up. I agreed (after all, wasn't I growing mine too?). I connected with the symbolic gesture: I knew the biblical, political and historical impact of hair (Samson, the Cavaliers, hippies and punks . . . hey, remember I was a fashion writer for years) although I could somehow never fit your styling into that paradigm. And then I read Iron John *and got the psychological concept of Wild Hair. The duende of the ponytail! Yes! It was definitely time to let your hair down. My bigger self recognized the importance of Bigger Hair. It was a shamanic statement.*

I know God has not got a crewcut.

But I have to say my smaller self could never cope with the fallout. I mean, I know men are afraid of losing their hair (hair is power) and your dad is bald, but never in the whole history of hair has there been quite so much fear about letting go of a few follicles. So let me now write this affirmation out in print:

YOUR HAIR IS NOT FALLING OUT.

OK?

I have lived in the moment, every moment, fully, in the present, yes, I have Just Been with your hair. I am aware of hair. OK, I took away your time but I gave back to your hair: I have bought it gelatine and gels, elastic bands and Alice bands, and eccentric and expensive conditioners with papaya seeds and savila. I have trimmed it with my paper scissors (God, I have taken responsibility!) I have photographed it in every light (yes, it has got red and gold in it). I have witnessed it swept over your face as you leapt out of the mineral spring, like a Masai warrior mask: swept up in profile like a Mayan priest (your hair has starred in past lives) or shining like a lion's mane in the sun. Your astrological rising sign is Leo, your node is in Leo. It is where you are going.

Your path is your hair.

And it has been valuable, even though it was not always comfortable.

In fact, it was a pain in the arse sometimes, watching you comb your hair, very very slowly, whilst I have wanted the shower or to go to breakfast. But as you say: who said growth was easy.

So what?

'It's just stuff!' you yelled at me.

'It's just your hair!' I yelled at you. And it's all right for you, you haven't got split ends.

Jung says neurosis is a substitute for legitimate suffering. This may be true. But in the case of your Higher Hair, it has been much more fun than suffering. After all, where would our angst have gone if it had not been directed upwards. It might have all gone inwards. And you cannot be too serious in this world. I, more than anyone, know the true value of superficiality.

So as I sit here with my own hair (now bobbed) gone mahogany red, thanks to a chemical system, and yours gone into another dimension in beads ('It is the time of beads,' you will say in three days' time when I will spend three hours unplaiting it, 'when I finally realize that when there is falling out there is also re-growth'), I salute you, O Hair, you who are about to die under English scissors.

Thank you, as our shampoo and set girl Blanche would say, for being on the planet.

One from the heart,

Charlotte X

LAST DAYS IN SANTA FÉ DE BOGOTÁ
~~~

'I shall miss the light of the Andes and the lorries that rush past with the names of eagles and deer on them,' I said, mostly to myself, as I stood on the vertical street with the mountains rising above me and the golden spires and roofs of the modern city spread below me.

I feel suspended between two worlds.

Mark and I are living in the Candelaría district, the cobbled old town of Bogotá. We are staying in a dark beamed hotel with bright courtyards and tiled roofs and a café under a skylight where poets and painters meet and a smiling waiter called Sebastian brings you a magical green soup made of corn and chicken and avocado and capers called *ajiaco*.

'How is it at the Candelaría?' asked a writer who gave me a lift back last night. 'I have a group of musicians staying there. I hired them for my sister's birthday.'

'O they are next door to us,' I replied, trying to appear as if five bodyguards, two armoured cars and a motorcade was my normal transport home. 'I heard them practising today, they're marvellous.'

'They are from the coast,' he said proudly. 'Come for lunch tomorrow and bring your friend.'

Mark and I go for lunch in apartments all over the city, served by maids in blue uniforms, where there are oil paintings above the beds and kidnapping lurks unexpectedly in the conversation. At Edgar's we read our coffee cups and he tells me the heart is a golden cup and how our friend the sculptress must uncover herself: Liliana is waiting for Liliana, he says.

But I am not waiting in Santa Fé de Bogotá. I am leaving.

In the mornings that are bright blue I work in one of the shuttered dining rooms off the café. Among the heavy sideboards and mottled portraits of unknown patriarchs, I write an article about Mexico where our journey first began and I write letters to my friends Amy and Jo in North America and Andrew in Provence.

'How can I live in those small gardens and those neat towns,' I write. 'Now I have all this wild complicated continent inside me? Where will the volcanoes and forests and jaguars live? How can I face those cold manners after this city has opened its doors to me? Will I be able to sit back in those polite concert halls and drawing rooms, will I smell old roses and brown apples and still be satisfied? Or will it mean nothing at all?'

Although I have long since realized that return has nothing to do with your homeland but a return to your true self, I do not want to go back to England.

Jane arrives from the coast (her hair shining like a new-minted coin) to say goodbye. We read cards sitting on our high beds loaded with quilts against the mountain chill and we take double-exposure photographs at night, so that we appear in the windows, standing behind ourselves in the room. Like ghosts.

It is our last week in South America.

In the afternoons that are sharp as lemons, we go to the sauna under a big hotel. I shall miss the South American bathing scene too: all these Turkish baths scented with eucalyptus branches, and those mineral baths in the mountains where you can lie like a Japanese snow monkey, embraced by the hot water while the fresh earthy air fills your head, and a river rushes by and hummingbirds dart among the trees of white lantern flowers. I shall miss the peace.

Except today's was not a peaceful experience. The women's changing room was filled with noisy men, a businessman grabbed my thigh in the jacuzzi ('You speak good Spanish,' he said whiskily.

'How many times a night do you like sex?') and in the steam room there was a heavily charged atmosphere in which I was definitely out of my league. 'God, everywhere I go I am followed,' grumbled Mark at me when I fled finally into the sauna. 'Everywhere I go there are men making me feel horrible,' I thought as I escaped and made my way to the lobby. If they want to be naked and intimate with their own sex they should make it a single-sex sauna. Which is worse, to be harassed by a straight man or ignored and resented by a gay man? Fuck the lot of them, I growl to myself as I sit on a big red sofa that sails in a sea of cream marble and smoochy piano music. I feel like I did in a dream last week when all these men turned into machines and I turned into a jaguar and roared at them and woke everyone up.

I'll never get it right: I'm either invisible to men, or a nuisance, or just a gringa in Doc Martens. Where do I fit in? I sure as hell will not go to the extremes of these women-waiting-to-be-noticed-on-the-other-sofas-by-suited-men in high heels and major Latino lipstick.

'It's impossible being a universal woman!' I tell Mark tearfully, when he appears beatifically from behind a pillar.

He gives me a hug. 'You shouldn't go where you do not belong. Come on, we're going to be late for Edgar.'

'But I was invited!' I say following him.

'This is about attention, isn't it, on some level?'

'No, it's about separation. I hate ghettoes. Anyway, you felt like this when all those feminists blanked you at Kena's birthday party in Santiago.'

'Look, Charlie, either you change a situation or you leave. It's as simple as that. It's not about being protected by rules or invitations or shoulds or women's rights or men's clubs. I was invited too remember. But I left.'

'So did I.'

'Yes, but I didn't take it so personally.'

A man reels out of the shadows waving a paper cup. He whines and complains at us. Some days I give and some days I don't but

I never feel like giving anything to anyone who cringes at my feet. It makes me feel violent.

'It's a message,' I say gloomily.

'It's a man who wants money,' Mark says. 'Don't be so complicated all the time.'

'I thought you said that every time you reacted to someone in the street or you lost your temper at the telephone exchange or a taxi driver overcharged you, it was a mirror.'

'Did I?'

'As soon as I get the hang of something, you say something completely different.'

'Well, you shouldn't look for approval all the time.'

'I don't.'

'Yes you do, or it wouldn't matter so much that you get it right. Ten out of ten. Jolly good. Well done.' He turns towards me and laughs. 'You see, I told you it was about attention.'

'You are the most infuriating man I have ever met!' I say and punch him in the arm. 'And you can stop taking the mickey out of my bloody accent. Taxi!'

'Yes, well, you'd better make good use of it,' he says and climbs into the yellow cab, 'because one day I won't be here.'

I shut up then because a cold wind has blown over my heart. I don't like thinking of the day when my *compañero* won't be at my side any more.

'Come,' says Edgar, 'the moon is exquisite,' and he leads us to his secret study. We sit and watch the giant moon in the platinum clouds and listen to the drumming of Navajo Indians. Edgar is an architect and charming host in his flat downstairs but here amongst the alchemical books and gold talismans that hang from the ceiling, he is someone else. He shows me his shaman's wand hewn out of Amazonian wood (which I am not allowed to touch because I am a woman) and a logo he is designing for the conference of Indians throughout the Americas that will take place in the autumn. It is of a gold heart made with the curl of a snake, the wing of a condor and the roar of the jaguar. And then he shows me his painting of a jaguar coat.

'In this coat,' he says, 'is contained all the knowledge of God. No one is the same.'

'It's like a map,' I say.

'Come and see the sunrise tomorrow,' he says, 'and we will eat a fruit that is filled with little stars.'

But we do not go.

'You are going to be given the Ace of Pentacles,' I declare dramatically, 'some wisdom that is only revealed to you.'

We are reading cards in Mark's room. He has been given some peyote by a French musician who was staying here with his family. I am trying to cover up my jealousy by playing Mrs Know-it-All High Priestess.

'I see you singing,' says Jane matter-of-factly.

'It's *very* spiritual.'

'I just see you singing.'

We sit in the courtyard in the late sunshine in squeaky rose-coloured rocking chairs. Jane is painting bats and jaguars and jester suns from the Gold Museum. I am reading a book about the Quabbalah which is completely beyond me. Mark is waiting for something momentous. It's taking its time.

'We destroy a lot in our desire for a convenient life,' he says suddenly.

The musicians who were staying next door wave goodbye, carrying the writer's gifts of precious china wrapped up for the long bus journey home to the coast.

'It's a drain.'

'What?'

'The Ace of Pentacles.'

'The Ace of Pentacles is a *drain*?'

'And I can see a dragon in the sky.'

'So can I,' says Jane, looking up into the evening clouds.

'Look, I'm the one who's supposed to be having visions.'

'I'm sorry, Mark,' says Jane, 'but that cloud definitely looks like a dragon to me.'

'O yes,' I say, 'there's the fire coming out of his mouth.'

'Well, so much for peyote. I'm going to see if there's anyone interesting in the café.'

'So much for higher chakras,' I laugh and go to buy some wine from a grocery store round the corner called Siberia. All the men stand up, talking and drinking beer at the counter, on their way home from work. It is a purple dusk outside.

'What's that?' asks Mark on my return.

'It's wine, Mr Judgemental.'

'Give me some.'

'I'm not sure it's shamanic to mix your drugs.'

'Stop being controlling and give me some wine.'

'It's in the room,' says Jane.

He holds out his hand and smiles at me.

'Look,' I say, 'I've told you a hundred times before, I have no planets in the sixth house. I am not your servant.'

'Go on, Charlie dear. You said you'd look after me today.'

So I do. I mean I fetch the wine, because I think it's OK to serve your friend a glass of wine just so long as you know you are a queen and not a servant. And it is given with grace and not in expectation of love-in-return.

In the café with the pink tablecloths, four women are singing for the opening of an exhibition. Sebastian brings round trays of little glasses filled with hot aguardiente and lemon and sugar. The women ask the audience to sing for them: so a shy black boxer sings a sweet song about a flower that he composed himself, and a young man in a suit sings a song by Lorca, and a big breathless woman sings a song by Pablo Neruda and Mark sings 'Alfonsina Y El Mar', and I join him for 'Moon River'.

One more time for the road.

Everyone cheers and congratulates us. It is a very joyful evening.

'When you come back,' says the owner of the hotel, 'I will arrange a concert for you and launch your career.'

'Are you coming back?' asks Jane. 'I thought you were going to Provence.'

'I don't know where I am going,' I say happily. 'But I think you were right about the singing.'

'I'll miss you,' she says and looks at me with her cornflower eyes.

'I'll miss you too,' I say and kiss her.

I will miss you, goldenhair, for your wit and your warmth and your abundant energy, and mostly because you were the first woman ever to celebrate me as a woman and not some peculiar androgyne. You made me feel like a queen and I will love you for ever for that.

But I do not feel sad saying goodbye.

I have taken my last line of cocaine. I didn't have to but I thought, well, hell, this is Colombia. We are dancing at an office party of Fernando's.

'It's so easy to be with you two,' he laughs. 'It's so easy!' Fernando is teaching me how to salsa. He is warm and slinky like a little snake but I don't feel happy with this kind of dancing, that is all ironic and flirty and self-conscious. I prefer dancing with Mark who dances wildly and dangerously, so that the sweat runs down his face.

I used to spend a lot of my time like this at office parties in London, sitting on the toilet and chopping up the contents of a small white envelope with my Visa card. Cocaine made me feel brighter and buzzier and more brilliant. But tonight even with reckless amounts of pure Colombian I do not feel anything except a brain full of tinsel and very cold feet. Outside everyone is talking as fast as possible and I am singing as loudly as possible (quick quick, before the time runs out!). How can I sing like this and not give a fuck?

Because I don't give a fuck for anything. I've drawn a thin

white line around myself like a corpse. Don't cross this border, it says.

A mouth talks to me of the Pacific coast. You must go there, it says (before your time runs out). In the morning along the white beaches thousands of crabs emerge out of the blue blue sea. You walk out and they part like a scarlet wave. The eyes were shining at me as the mouth insisted I must go to the place that it had discovered with all those crabs and the owner of the mouth was shaking all over, with the excitement and urgency of it all. But I don't think this was from the cosmic force of Nature.

I walk through a red sea, all creatures part from me. No one may enter my zone, not even you, small numbed heart who chirps inside of me like a cicada. Not even you. So be quiet.

In Calle 82, the young crowd swell in their holy indifference and I feel that black hole yawn inside of me: more rum, more cigarettes, more of that white stuff! 'I miss cigarettes,' a man said to me at lunch today, 'because the smoke always created a protection around me.' But I do not miss cocaine. And I do not miss those parties, all that shine and talk, and this old hunger.

The neon is pink and green and in the salsa club where we are supposed to meet our friends the dance floor is jammed: the couples move hardly at all, while their eyes dart in every other direction but at the person to whom they cling so closely.

In the corner there is a painting of a man holding up a dying woman while a wild cat chews his leg. Perhaps she is dead already, or perhaps he had killed her. Anyway the man is indifferent to them both. And we have lost everybody.

It *was* so easy to be with you that night but it was so hard, so difficult to get close, beyond that dance that pretends intimacy but is so full of clever barriers.

We get a cab back to the hotel. It roars down the dark windy highway that snakes above the city in the pine-scented hills. The taxi driver says he has started a transport firm. He wants to know how we pronounce the name in English. He spells it out for us: E-A-G-L-E.

We can't recognize it.

'*Aguila*,' he finally says in desperation. '*El pájaro*.'

'O the bird!' we say.

'Is that a message?' I whisper to Mark. He looks at me with his dark eyes but says nothing as the lights of Bogotá spread below us like broken jewels on a wet black coat.

Whence do we come? Where shall we live? Whither do we go? Shall we all meet again like this?

Fernando is going west to Cali, Jane is going north to Guatemala and I for the last time go walking through the streets of middletown.

Down by the feral markets I walk without thinking, in amongst the stalls and carts and the plastic sheets on pavements selling everything for something: breadfruit, bananas, matchboxes, pens, combs with beads, combs with feathers, plastic bowls, plastic toys, glasses, peaches, roasted corn, (a crowd of scarlet-coated school-children stream over a bridge), religious pictures, medicinal herbs, maps of the city, saucepans, baby rabbits, (a man wipes his bum with newspaper on a roundabout, his testicles hang purple in the cold air), earrings, watches, plums, dried fish, counterfeit sun-glasses, salsa tapes, *empanadas*, (a young black boy without shoes throws up a broomhandle down by the square, catches and twirls it, mimicking the drum-major in the changing of the guard), blood-pressure checks, weight checks, shampoo, rollers, vast pale brassieres, crystals and coins, (a group of Otavalan Indians dance round a maypole in front of the Palace of Justice – still under re-construction), and, at the crossroads of the Séptima, where the black-suited emerald sellers pause with their briefcases, I stop in this flow of buy-and-go because I see a pair of antlers bobbing towards me over the heads of the dealers in precious gems.

A deer is galloping through the city.

* * *

When I return to England I will not stay. After six weeks I will leave to make my way back to Bogotá, via the cities and deserts of North America. I shall have with me even less than I had before: no music, no books, no silver spoon, no family album.

'You scare me because when I do not see your needs I think I should have none,' my friend Amy will say when I arrive in Boston.

'I have a gypsy soul,' I will reply. 'I do not dream of a white picket fence like you. Nor do I imagine anyone can tell me where I am going. I do not need what you need.'

I will wake in a snowy New England morning in the arms of a man who says he loves the winter sunlight on my body but when I look into his eyes, I will see the delight of one who has caught a wild thing and longs to domesticate it and hold it for ever to his breast.

I will not be able to stay behind safe walls (in this warm kitchen, in this embrace), though this leaving saddens me. 'You fear loneliness,' Mark once said to me, 'because you are a social animal. But it is far lonelier to stay with what you know because you are never your true self. Loneliness is living in a world where you are not sacred.'

When I was a child a bird flew into my room and it circled around and around. Its noise frightened me. 'O please be free!' I cried out in distress, and shut my eyes. When I opened them, it had gone.

But it had left a feather at my feet.

I am the wolf who runs in the mountains. I cannot stay in the valley, I cannot live there. Not for you, not for me. Because when I went west to find myself I was not who I imagined I was all those years in England. I was someone quite different.

I was never the child in the gardens playing in that pretty dress (O Mother, how carefully you sculpted my hair!). I ran wild through another country. O Father, I was never that girl you taught to argue so cleverly in the vicissitudes of your mind. I told myself stories in an alien tongue. O beloved, I was never your invisible nursemaid, I never rescued you from that darkening green where you were lost. I was the lover who swam in your rough seas, who covered you in salty kisses. I was the friend who loved the hidden soul in you.

I was born a shadowdancer in a city of mirrors. I lived a circus life. I learned from my cradle to find love by reflecting back what everyone wished to see. But now I am myself I cannot be surprised if you flee from me, or I from you. Because I cannot be what you hope to find, standing there.

'You are the cat who walks by herself and all places are the same to you,' my mother will quote to me, half in annoyance, half in admiration. Yes, I will say, I am the wolf who runs in the mountains.

'You make me want to run away,' my friend Jo will say in New York.

'Just keep moving,' sang Mark.

> Man of no lands
> Land of no man
> No man's land
> Nomad.'

'I feel I am dancing on the edge of the world,' Amy will say.

'Jump,' I will tell her. 'Just let go.'

'The whole book is about letting go,' said Mark, 'like a snake shedding skins.'

REMINDER

In the end we are all
we are all
Mum and Dad
the Sky makes love to the Mountain
and the River pours
down to the Valley
in the end we are all
in the end we are all
in the Rain stands the Tree
the Sun
lights the Bird's wing
the Wind
carries its song

In the end we are all
we are all
Son and Daughter
the Sky dances
the Mountain sings
the River carries the boat
to another place
in the end we are all
in the end we are all
in the Earth stands the Tree
and the Stone shelters Life

in the end we are all
we are All
who will live by the sword

but not by machine
by the word but not by decree
in the end we are all
in the end we are all
we do not just
cut down the Tree
the Sky does not just
fuck the Mountain
the Wind does not just
rob the Bird of its Song

in the end we are all
we are all
Mum and Dad
Son and Daughter
in the Earth and the Rain
stands the Tree

Ecuador, December 1991

Rory MacLean

Stalin's Nose

Across the Face of Europe

'A minor masterpiece of comic surrealism.'   *The Times*

'The best book I've read for a very long time.'   John Wells

'Crazy, charming, a delight.'   John Le Carré

Winston the pig fell into Aunt Zita's life when he dropped on to her husband's head and killed him dead. It was a distressing end to a distinguished life of spying. After the funeral Zita, a faded Austrian aristocrat and a vivacious eccentric, refused to remain at home. Instead, together with Winston, she hijacked her nephew Rory and set out in a rattling Trabant puffing and wheezing across the continent on one last ride . . .

'The farce with which Rory MacLean often clothes his narrative is a metaphor for the much blacker and indeed surreal comedy of the Communist years. As an allegory it is powerful and frequently moving. As a tale it is tremendous . . . It is also a thing of beauty.'   Jan Morris

'With the unlikely cast of a Tamworth pig, a coffin, two elderly aunts and a battered Trabant, Rory MacLean creates a fantastic tableau that embraces the horrors, betrayals and ironies of modern East European history. *Stalin's Nose* is a dark, sardonic and brilliant book which grows in stature with every page – the most extraordinary debut in travel writing since Bruce Chatwin's *In Patagonia*.'   William Dalrymple

'The wittiest, most surreal travel writing of recent years.'   Frank Delaney

'At once eccentric, amusing and chilling . . . A Gogolesque tour in a Trabant.'   *Economist*

📖 *flamingo*

M. F. K. Fisher

Long Ago in France

'As beautiful a travel book as you can hope to read.'

Quentin Crewe

In 1929, Mary Frances Kennedy Fisher, young, innocent and newly married, arrived in Burgundy, and discovered a profusion of tastes, pastimes and sensuous pleasure in Dijon, France's gastronomic capital. Picaresque, mouth-watering and crowded with unforgettable characters, *Long Ago in France* is indeed a feast of a book, a delightful journey back to a voluptuous, genteel world, now vanished for ever.

'*Long Ago in France* is a Burgundian feast, robust but exquisitely delicate, as fresh as the ingredients bought in this morning's market. Laughter spills over the table. The background music, naturally, is Josephine Baker singing *J'ai deux amours*. The whole thing is absolutely delicious.' *Observer*

'The enveloping glow of a young American couple in love, living on the cheap in 1920s France, is reminiscent of Hemingway – as are the lush discoveries of French wine and food . . . Marvellously evocative.' *Sunday Times*

'M. F. K. Fisher is a poet of the appetites.' John Updike

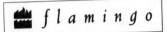 flamingo

Hunter S. Thomas

Fear and Loathing in Las Vegas

A Savage Journey to the Heart of the American Dream

'We were somewhere around Barstow on the edge of the desert when the drugs began to take hold . . . And suddenly there was a terrible roar all around us and the sky was full of what looked like huge bats, all swooping and screeching and diving around the car, which was going about a hundred miles an hour with the top down to Las Vegas . . .'

So begins *Fear and Loathing in Las Vegas*, the now legendary quest by ace Gonzo journalist Hunter S. Thompson into the heart of the American Dream. As knights of old on hazardous quest for the Holy Grail buckled on armour of supernatural power, so Hunter Thompson entered Las Vegas armed with a veritable arsenal of 'heinous chemicals'. His perilous, drug-enhanced confrontations with casino operators, bartenders, police officers and other representatives of the Silent Majority have a hallucinatory humour and nightmare terror rarely seen on the printed page. This is the true story of a man who passed through hell – and lived to tell the tale.

'*Fear and Loathing in Las Vegas* is a scorching epochal sensation. There are only two adjectives writers care about any more . . . 'brilliant' and 'outrageous' . . . and Hunter Thompson has a freehold on both of them'   Tom Wolfe

'What goes on in these pages makes Lenny Bruce seem angelic . . . the whole book boils down to a mad, corrosive prose poetry that picks up where Norman Mailer's *An American Dream* left off and explores what Tom Wolfe left out'   *New York Times*

ISBN 0 586 08132 1

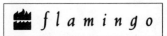 *flamingo*

William Dalrymple

In Xanadu

A Quest

'A classic.'   *Sunday Express*

'William Dalrymple's *In Xanadu* carries us breakneck from a pre-
dawn glimmer in the Holy Sepulchre right across Asia to a bleak
wind in Kubla Khan's palace . . . it is learned and comic, and a
most gifted first book touched by the spirits of Kinglake, Robert
Byron and E. Waugh.'
            Patrick Leigh Fermor, 'Books of the Year', *Spectator*

'*In Xanadu* is, without doubt, one of the best travel books
produced in the last 20 years. It is witty and intelligent, brilliantly
observed, deftly constructed and extremely entertaining . . .
Dalrymple's gift for transforming ordinary, humdrum experience
into something extraordinary and timeless suggests that he will go
from strength to strength.'
                        Alexander Maitland, *Scotland on Sunday*

'The new Theroux.'   *Today*

'Exuberant.'   Colin Thubron

'Dalrymple writes beautifully, is amazingly erudite, brave and
honest, and can be extremely funny.'
                              Quentin Crewe, *Sunday Telegraph*

'The delightful, and funny, surprise mystery tour of the year.'
                                 Sir Alec Guinness, *Sunday Times*

'Erudite, adventurous and amusing . . . reminded me of Evelyn
Waugh.'   Piers Paul Read

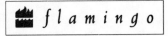 *flamingo*

Nick Danziger

Danziger's Travels

Beyond Forbidden Frontiers

'A marvellous account of a truly epic journey . . . Puts him in the forefront of modern travel writers.'
Mail on Sunday

Nick Danziger's graphic account of his hair-raising adventures during an eighteen-month journey 'beyond forbidden frontiers' in Asia makes a vivid and unforgettable impact. Travelling in disguise as an itinerant Muslim, his journey on foot and using traditional means of local transport cost him £1,000 in all – exactly one-third of the Winston Churchill travel fellowship he received in London.

After walking and hitch-hiking through southern Turkey and the ayatollahs' Iran, he entred Afghanistan illegally in the wake of a convoy of Chinese weapons and spent two months dodging Russian helicopter gunships with rebel guerrillas. He was the first foreigner to cross from Pakistan into the closed western province of China since the revolution of 1949.

Living and travelling with local people and pitting his wits against officialdom, Danziger broke barriers and crossed boundaries of all kinds. Written with engaging humour and a great zest for life, *Danziger's Travels* is an exceptional travel book in every way, handsomely illustrated with the author's own outstanding photographs and drawings.

'Danziger is the stuff of which legends are made . . . His remarkable story contains some of the most exciting travel writing I have ever read.'
William Dalrymple, *Literary Review*

'Even the most travel-crazy person I know looks unadventurous alongside Nick Danziger.'
Midweek

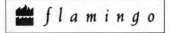

flamingo

Flamingo is a quality imprint publishing both fiction and non-fiction. Below are some recent titles.

Fiction
- [ ] No Other Life *Brian Moore* £5.99
- [ ] The Kitchen God's Wife *Amy Tan* £4.99
- [ ] A Thousand Acres *Jane Smiley* £5.99
- [ ] Spidertown *Abraham Rodriguez* £5.99
- [ ] Tess *Emma Tennant* £5.99
- [ ] Pepper *Tristan Hawkins* £5.99
- [ ] Dreaming in Cuban *Cristina Garcia* £5.99
- [ ] Happenstance *Carol Shields* £5.99
- [ ] Blood Sugar *Suzannah Dunn* £5.99
- [ ] Postcards *E. Annie Proulx* £5.99

Non-fiction
- [ ] The Gates of Paradise *Alberto Manguel* £9.99
- [ ] Sentimental Journeys *Joan Didion* £5.99
- [ ] Epstein *Stephen Gardiner* £8.99
- [ ] Love, Love and Love *Sandra Bernhard* £5.99
- [ ] City of Djinns *William Dalrymple* £5.99
- [ ] Dame Edna Everage *John Lahr* £5.99
- [ ] Tolstoy's Diaries *R. F. Christian* £7.99
- [ ] Wild Swans *Jung Chang* £7.99

You can buy Flamingo paperbacks at your local bookshop or newsagent. Or you can order them from HarperCollins Mail Order, Dept. 8, HarperCollins*Publishers*, Westerhill Road, Bishopbriggs, Glasgow G64 2QT. Please enclose a cheque or postal order, to the order of the cover price plus add £1.00 for the first and 25p for additional books ordered within the UK.

NAME (Block letters)_____

ADDRESS_____

_____

_____